T0220942

Artificial Intelligence
for Renewable Energy Systems

Scrivener Publishing
100 Cummings Center, Suite 541J
Beverly, MA 01915-6106

Artificial Intelligence and Soft Computing for Industrial Transformation

Series Editor: Dr. S. Balamurugan (sbnbala@gmail.com)

Scope: Artificial Intelligence and Soft Computing Techniques play an impeccable role in industrial transformation. The topics to be covered in this book series include Artificial Intelligence, Machine Learning, Deep Learning, Neural Networks, Fuzzy Logic, Genetic Algorithms, Particle Swarm Optimization, Evolutionary Algorithms, Nature Inspired Algorithms, Simulated Annealing, Metaheuristics, Cuckoo Search, Firefly Optimization, Bio-inspired Algorithms, Ant Colony Optimization, Heuristic Search Techniques, Reinforcement Learning, Inductive Learning, Statistical Learning, Supervised and Unsupervised Learning, Association Learning and Clustering, Reasoning, Support Vector Machine, Differential Evolution Algorithms, Expert Systems, Neuro Fuzzy Hybrid Systems, Genetic Neuro Hybrid Systems, Genetic Fuzzy Hybrid Systems and other Hybridized Soft Computing Techniques and their applications for Industrial Transformation. The book series is aimed to provide comprehensive handbooks and reference books for the benefit of scientists, research scholars, students and industry professional working towards next generation industrial transformation.

Publishers at Scrivener
Martin Scrivener (martin@scrivenerpublishing.com)
Phillip Carmical (pcarmical@scrivenerpublishing.com)

Artificial Intelligence for Renewable Energy Systems

Edited by

Ajay Kumar Vyas
S. Balamurugan
Kamal Kant Hiran
and
Harsh S. Dhiman

Scrivener
Publishing

WILEY

This edition first published 2022 by John Wiley & Sons, Inc., 111 River Street, Hoboken, NJ 07030, USA and Scrivener Publishing LLC, 100 Cummings Center, Suite 541J, Beverly, MA 01915, USA
© 2022 Scrivener Publishing LLC
For more information about Scrivener publications please visit www.scrivenerpublishing.com.

Wiley Global Headquarters
111 River Street, Hoboken, NJ 07030, USA

For details of our global editorial offices, customer services, and more information about Wiley products visit us at www.wiley.com.

Limit of Liability/Disclaimer of Warranty
While the publisher and authors have used their best efforts in preparing this work, they make no representations or warranties with respect to the accuracy or completeness of the contents of this work and specifically disclaim all warranties, including without limitation any implied warranties of merchantability or fitness for a particular purpose. No warranty may be created or extended by sales representatives, written sales materials, or promotional statements for this work. The fact that an organization, website, or product is referred to in this work as a citation and/or potential source of further information does not mean that the publisher and authors endorse the information or services the organization, website, or product may provide or recommendations it may make. This work is sold with the understanding that the publisher is not engaged in rendering professional services. The advice and strategies contained herein may not be suitable for your situation. You should consult with a specialist where appropriate. Neither the publisher nor authors shall be liable for any loss of profit or any other commercial damages, including but not limited to special, incidental, consequential, or other damages. Further, readers should be aware that websites listed in this work may have changed or disappeared between when this work was written and when it is read.

Library of Congress Cataloging-in-Publication Data

ISBN 978-1-119-76169-3

Cover image: Pixabay.Com
Cover design by Russell Richardson

MIX
Paper from
responsible sources
FSC® C013604

Contents

Preface

Renewable energy systems, including solar, wind, biodiesel, hybrid energy and other relevant types, have numerous advantages compared to their conventional counterparts. These advantages are facilitated by the application of machine learning and deep learning techniques for renewable energy system modeling, forecasting, and optimization for efficient system design. Due to the importance of renewable energy in today's world, this book was designed to enhance the reader's knowledge based on current developments in the field. For instance, the extraction and selection of machine learning algorithms for renewable energy systems, forecasting of wind and solar radiation are featured in the book. Also highlighted are intelligent data, renewable energy informatics systems based on supervisory control and data acquisition (SCADA); and intelligent condition monitoring of solar and wind energy systems. Moreover, an AI-based system for real-time decision-making for renewable energy systems is presented; and also demonstrated is the prediction of energy consumption in green buildings using machine learning. The authors also provide both experimental and real datasets with great potential in the renewable energy sector, which apply machine learning (ML) and deep learning (DL) algorithms that will be helpful for economic and environmental forecasting of the renewable energy business. A brief synopsis of each of the eleven information-intensive chapters on the application of AI for renewable energy and relevant areas follows.

- Chapter 1 discusses a six-phase synchronous machine selected as a potential option to a generator in the grid-connected mode for a wind power generation system. An exhaustive dynamic analysis was conducted under various working conditions. Moreover, the generator was further investigated under steady-state conditions with the inclusion of a small disturbance (i.e., small signal stability) through the linearized model using the dq0 approach. A linearized model was used to determine the absolute stability using eigenvalue criteria, wherein the effect of parametric variation is presented, related to both the stator and rotor side.

- Chapter 2 deals with the utilization of AI in solar energy
  models such as multilayer perceptron (MLP), fuzzy ART
  (adaptive resonance theory), Bayesian Regularization (BR),
  and shark smell optimization (SSO) algorithm, and feed-
  forward and back-propagation is employed. For wind
  energy, models like ensemble Kalman filter (EnKF), wavelet neural network (WNN), LM, nonlinear autoregressive
  exogenous (NARX) artificial neural networks (ANN), and
  MLP are used. For geothermal energy, models such as artificial bee cloning (ABC) algorithm and MLP feed-forward
  algorithm are used to forecast it. All these models have been
  reviewed comprehensively concerning their structures and
  methodologies during implementation.
- Chapter 3 describes the use of AI in wireless technologies,
  which has been an impetus for researchers to delve into the
  study of wireless-based IoT systems. Their unique features
  are reliable monitoring services, increased network lifetime and minimized energy consumption rate. Moreover, a
  complete solution is possible due to issues like the congestion and overload of network scenarios. In this chapter, the
  design of an energy-efficient hybrid hierarchical clustering
  algorithm for wireless sensor devices in the IoT is presented.
  It is explored by two phases, namely, cluster head selection
  using the AI approach and shortest route pathfinding using
  AI-based energy-aware routing protocol.
- Chapter 4 discusses the role that AI has played in the significant growth of renewable energy and sustainable development, and how the deployment of AI has greatly helped to
  achieve its goals. Biogas is the source of renewable energy,
  which is generated from the anaerobic digestion of biomass,
  cow dung, wastewater sludge, kitchen waste, etc. Anaerobic
  digestion is a nonlinear biological process where biomass
  is digested to generate biogas and slurry in the absence of
  oxygen. Artificial intelligence models have been developed
  for predicting the yield and energy content of the produced
  biogas. This chapter presents a comprehensive review of AI
  techniques for modeling the biogas production process.
- Chapter 5 throws light on the integration of a solar photovoltaic (PV) array with the first-order RC circuit implemented
  utilizing MATLAB (Simulink Library). For experimentation, the open-circuit voltage (Voc) and short-circuit current

(Isc) of the solar panel were considered as 36.3 volts and 7.84 amperes. The continuous fluctuating irradiance from 110–580 W/m2 led to the variation of the output voltage of the solar PV arrays. Also, the variations of battery charging current, the voltage across battery and battery SOC due to variations in irradiance are examined in detail. The proposed methodology of this study explains the authentic time modeling of SoC utilizing the second-, third-, fourth-, and fifth-order of a polynomial regression technique.

- Chapter 6 reviews all of the deep learning models used for wind speed/power forecasting. The forecasting of wind power includes planning of economic dispatch, estimation of candidate sites for wind farms, and scheduling the operation and maintenance of wind farms. It also describes the challenges for wind forecasting models in terms of their accuracy, robust nature and ability to handle huge volumes of data at a much lower computational cost.

- Chapter 7 describes the forecasting of wind energy, including short-, medium- and long-term forecasting. Forecasting involves the extraction of single or multiple features from the time series data for more accurate prediction. The different wind speed and power forecasting model includes a physical model, statistical model, computational model and hybrid model. Pre-processing the raw data, feature extraction and prediction are the steps involved in forecasting the wind speed and wind energy. Included among the different wind speed and power forecasting models are a physical model, statistical model, computational model and hybrid model.

- Chapter 8 describes the forecasting of short-term wind speed by incorporating an adaptive ensemble of deep neural networks and then compares it to machine learning algorithms like gated recurrent unit (GRU), long short-term memory (LSTM) neural network and bidirectional long short-term memory (Bi-LSTM) neural network. In this chapter, various parameters like the mean absolute error (MAE) and root mean square error (RMSE) are computed. Also, the mean square error (MSE) is computed for the given algorithms and the performance of the Bi-LSTM is compared for MSE, RMSE and MAE.

- Chapter 9 gives an overview of various attack scenarios associated with advanced metering infrastructure (AMI), with a major focus on data falsification attacks. In data falsification attacks, attackers aim to inject malicious codes or false data to tamper with legitimate data. A detailed analysis of the various available detection schemes to effectively detect such attacks is also presented in this chapter.

- Chapter 10 describes how to forecast the actual amount of electricity consumed with respect to the energy demand in G20 countries, wherein recurrent neural networks, linear regression, support vector regression and Bayesian ridge regression have been used for forecasting, while the sliding window approach has been used for the generation of the dataset. Predictions of electricity consumption up until 2025 are also included.

- Chapter 11 is a detailed discussion of the ways and means available for India to harness biodiesel energy. It also delves into the major issues inhibiting India in the realm of biofuels in general. The objective of this chapter is to highlight the measures taken to achieve the 40% renewable energy target under the Paris Agreement. To this end, a novel model is proposed that can be utilized for optimizing the use of information communication technology (ICT) in the extraction, marketing and management of biodiesel energy. The use of green and clean fuel is not a luxury anymore, but rather will make India more self-reliant in a real sense, paving the way for a sustainable "Make-In-India".

The editors would like to thank the contributing authors for their innovative submissions that has led to a successful culmination of this book under the series titled "Artificial Intelligence and Soft Computing for Industrial Transformation". We believe the content of this book has significant potential to serve the industry-grade real-time problems and has potential to serve the society at large.

Ajay Kumar Vyas
S. Balamurugan
Kamal Kant Hiran
Harsh S. Dhiman
December 2021

Analysis of Six-Phase Grid Connected Synchronous Generator in Wind Power Generation

Arif Iqbal[1]* and Girish Kumar Singh[2]

*[1]Department of Electrical Engineering,
Rajkiya Engineering College Ambedkar Nagar, Akbarpur, India*
*[2]Department of Electrical Engineering,
Indian Institute of Technology Roorkee, Roorkee, India*

Abstract

Owing to meet the incremental need of energy with exhaustion of fossil fuel in few upcoming years, renewable power generation has emerged as a potential and permanent solution in present scenario. In this regard, research has diverted toward exploration and development of various new techniques of renewable power generation for last few decades, and various systems have been adopted in both isolated and grid connected modes. Among various available options (solar, wind, biomass, tidal, etc.), the wind power generation system has a major market share due to its pollution-free operation together with its economic viability and mature technology. Presently, wind power generation system is increasing exponentially, particularly in on-shore sites of India and European subcontinents. Wind power generation system works on a successful operation and coordination of various parts, where an electric generator is an important component. Hence, the selection of suitable electrical machine (as generator) is of paramount importance for reliable operation of complete wind power generation system. Conventionally, three-phase electrical machine is employed. But, in last two decades, the multiphase (more than three-phase) machine is replacing the conventional one. This is because of various inherent potential advantageous features present in multiphase machines, when compared with its three-phase equivalent. This includes the elimination of lower order space, resulting in lower torque pulsation, enhanced power handling capability in the same frame (approximately 175%), and higher

*Corresponding author: arif.iqbal.in@gmail.com

Ajay Kumar Vyas, S. Balamurugan, Kamal Kant Hiran and Harsh S. Dhiman (eds.) *Artificial Intelligence for Renewable Energy Systems*, (1–36) © 2022 Scrivener Publishing LLC

degree of freedom with improved reliability. Hence, multiphase machines have to be explored and investigated in various operational aspects for power generation. In this chapter, a six-phase synchronous machine is selected as a potential option as generator in grid connected mode for wind power generation system. An exhaustive dynamic analysis has been presented during various working conditions. Moreover, generator has been further investigated under steady state with the inclusion of small disturbance (i.e., small signal stability) through linearized model using $dq0$ approach. Linearized model was used to determine the absolute stability using eigenvalue criteria wherein, the effect of parametric variation is presented, related with both stator and rotor side. It was noted that the stability of generator operation can be enhanced with increased values of stator resistance. On rotor side, with higher value of leakage reactance of field winding circuit and/ or by increased resistance of damper winding along q axis.

Keywords: Wind power generation, six-phase synchronous generator, small-signal stability, dynamic analysis

1.1   Introduction

The development of human civilization resulted in a tremendous demand of electrical power with a fear of fossil fuel exhaustion within a few years. This has diverted the researcher's attention to explore and develop the renewable resources for power generation as a potential and permanent solution in present scenario. Motivation toward the development of different types of renewable power generation (like solar, wind, biomass, and tidal) is also due to the presence of various attractive advantages, particularly pollution-free operation, free availability with economic viability, and advanced technology [1, 2]. Among the various developed options, wind power generation has been adopted worldwide and exhibits a major market share in the field of renewable resources. Presently, wind power generation system is increasing exponentially, particularly in on-shore sites of India and European subcontinents. According to report updated on Global Wind Energy Council (GWEC) [3], power extraction is drastically increased by 52 GW and 60 GW by 2017 and 2020, respectively, and expected to reach a total of 840 GW by 2022.

Wind power generation system works on a successful operation and coordination of various parts, where an electric generator is an important component. Hence, the selection of suitable electrical machine (as generator) is of paramount importance for reliable operation of wind power generation system. Conventionally, three-phase electrical machine (mostly synchronous machine) is employed. But, in last two decades, the multiphase (more than three-phase) machine is replacing the conventional one. This is because of the presence of various potential advantages when compared with its three-phase equivalent. This includes the elimination of lower order space harmonics, resulting in lower torque pulsation, higher power handling capability in the same frame (approximately 175%), and higher degree of freedom with improved reliability [4]. This signifies the technical and economic suitability of using multiphase machine when compared with its three-phase equivalent. Hence, an enhanced use of multiphase drives have been reported in different high power applications, not limited to ship propulsion, electric traction, more-electric aircraft, thermal and nuclear power plant, and battery and hybrid electric vehicles. Research in this field is tremendously going on, particularly from electric power generation point of view. Available literatures are showing a general feasibility of multiphase system [4, 5]. On generation side, the concept of multiphase (more than three-phase) machine was initially originated in late 1920s when larger power generation got hampered due to the limitations in circuit breaker interrupting capability. To overcome this situation, attention of scientists was diverted to the machine having double windings embedded in its stator [6]. It was after this time that research continued in the field of multiphase machine with steady, but in slower way. Utilization of multiphase synchronous generator was used in 1980 [7] for power generation in electric railway coaches. A few mathematical analysis of alternator with two three-phase winding was carried out by using orthogonal transformation for the elimination of time-dependent coefficient from system differential equations [8]. Six-phase synchronous generator in conjugation with three- to six-phase conversion transformer was analyzed for harmonic content [9]. In six-phase synchronous machine, mutual coupling effect between two sets of balanced three-phase stator winding is considered in [10], and under steady-state ac-dc stator connection [11] has been also presented and analyzed by using average-value modeling with line commutated converter [12]. A detailed mathematical modeling of six-phase synchronous generator using Park's variable has been carried out in [13] under different working conditions at stand-alone mode, where an enhanced power handling capability by 173% was achieved when compared with its three-phase equivalent. A detailed experimental investigation of six-phase synchronous generator in stand-alone mode was carried out for renewable power generation in conjugation with hydropower plant [14]. Considering the suitability in generating mode, this chapter presents a mathematical modeling of grid connected six-phase synchronous generator applicable for wind power generating system, followed by the dynamic response under load variation.

Being an integral component in wind power generation, an operational stability of six-phase synchronous generator under steady state (i.e., small signal stability) is also of prime importance. Although, the small-signal stability analysis of three-phase synchronous machine is available in few available literature [15] using root locus [16] and Nyquist criteria [17]. But, for multiphase (i.e., six-phase) synchronous machine, a very limited literature is available for small-signal stability analysis. An introductory analysis of synchronous machine was reported in [18] followed by the determination of stability limits under parametric variation and different working conditions [19] when compared with its three-phase counterpart [20]. With the aim to access the suitability and applicability in wind power generating system, this chapter is dedicated to present a small-signal stability analysis of grid connected six-phase synchronous generator showing a comparison with its three-phase equivalent. For this purpose, a linearized version of six-phase synchronous generator model has been derived and used to evaluate the system eigenvalue. Eigenvalue criteria are used for small signal stability analysis under different machine parametric variation. A comparative analysis, from stability view point, is also presented using Park's ($dq0$) variable for both grid connected three- and six-phase synchronous generator.

1.2   Analytical Modeling of Six-Phase Synchronous Machine

To design a six-phase machine, it is a common strategy to split the stator winding into two through phase belt splitting namely, *abc* and *xyz* having the angular displacement of $\alpha = 30°$, to have asymmetrical winding [4, 18, 19]. Rotor of the machine remains same having the field winding *fr* and damper windings k_d and k_q along *d-q* axes, respectively. While going onward for the mathematical modeling, some of the important simplifying assumptions are considered [21, 22]:

- Both the three-phase stator windings (*abc* and *xyz*) are symmetrical balanced having a perfectly sinusoidal distribution in the air-gap.
- Flux and mmfs are sinusoidal with no space harmonics.
- Saturation and hysteresis effects are ignored.
- No skin effect, i.e., winding resistance, is not dependent on frequency.

Although, voltage and electromagnetic torque can be mathematically expressed in terms machine variables, which results in non-linear differential equations [22]. The non-linearity is due to the time varying inductance term. For simplicity, with constant inductance terms, concept of reference frame theory is used, and equations are preferably written in rotor reference frame using Park's equation. Mathematically, voltages and flux linkage per second of a six-phase synchronous machine using Park's variables are as follows [21–23]:

1.2.1   Voltage Equation

$$v_{q1} = r_1 i_{q1} + \frac{\omega_r}{\omega_b} \psi_{d1} + \frac{p}{\omega_b} \psi_{q1} \tag{1.1}$$

$$v_{d1} = r_1 i_{d1} - \frac{\omega_r}{\omega_b} \psi_{q1} + \frac{p}{\omega_b} \psi_{d1} \tag{1.2}$$

$$v_{q2} = r_2 i_{q2} + \frac{\omega_r}{\omega_b} \psi_{d2} + \frac{p}{\omega_b} \psi_{q2} \tag{1.3}$$

$$v_{d2} = r_2 i_{d2} - \frac{\omega_r}{\omega_b} \psi_{q2} + \frac{p}{\omega_b} \psi_{d2} \tag{1.4}$$

$$v_{Kq} = r_{Kq} i_{Kq} + \frac{p}{\omega_b} \psi_{Kq} \tag{1.5}$$

$$v_{Kd} = r_{Kd} i_{Kd} + \frac{p}{\omega_b} \psi_{Kd} \tag{1.6}$$

$$v_{fr} = \frac{x_{md}}{r_{fr}} \left(r_{fr} i_{fr} + \frac{p}{\omega_b} \psi_{fr} \right) \tag{1.7}$$

where p shows the differentiation function w.r.t. time.

1.2.2   Equations of Flux Linkage Per Second

$$\psi_{q1} = x_{l1} i_{q1} + x_{lm}(i_{q1} + i_{q2}) - x_{ldq} i_{d2} + \psi_{mq} \tag{1.8}$$

$$\psi_{d1} = x_{l1} i_{d1} + x_{lm}(i_{d1} + i_{d2}) + x_{ldq} i_{q2} + \psi_{md} \tag{1.9}$$

$$\Psi_{q2} = x_{l2}i_{q2} + x_{lm}(i_{q1} + i_{q2}) + x_{ldq}i_{d1} + \Psi_{mq} \tag{1.10}$$

$$\Psi_{d2} = x_{l2}i_{d2} + x_{lm}(i_{d1} + i_{d2}) - x_{ldq}i_{q1} + \Psi_{md} \tag{1.11}$$

$$\Psi_{Kq} = x_{lKq}i_{Kq} + \Psi_{mq} \tag{1.12}$$

$$\Psi_{Kd} = x_{lKd}i_{Kq} + \Psi_{md} \tag{1.13}$$

$$\Psi_{fr} = x_{lfr}i_{fr} + \Psi_{md} \tag{1.14}$$

where

$$\Psi_{mq} = x_{mq}(i_{q1} + i_{q2} + i_{Kq}) \tag{1.15}$$

$$\Psi_{md} = x_{md}(i_{d1} + i_{d2} + i_{Kd} + i_{fr}) \tag{1.16}$$

The parameters of rotor circuit are referred to the stator winding set *abc*. These voltage and flux linkage equations suggest the equivalent circuit, as shown in Figure 1.1, wherein L_{lm} and L_{ldq} represent leakage inductance of common mutual and cross mutual coupling between *d* and *q*-axis of stator circuit, respectively:

$$x_{lm} = x_{lax}\cos(\alpha) + x_{lay}\cos(\alpha + 2\pi/3) + x_{laz}\cos(\alpha - 2\pi/3) \tag{1.17}$$

$$x_{ldq} = x_{lax}\sin(\alpha) + x_{lay}\sin(\alpha + 2\pi/3) + x_{laz}\sin(\alpha - 2\pi/3) \tag{1.18}$$

where x_{lax}, x_{lay}, and x_{laz} indicate leakage reactance between phase *a* (of winding set *abc*) with each phase of other winding set *xyz*.

Phenomenon of mutual coupling is due to the sharing of same slot by stator winding conductor of different phase. This is signified by the term of common mutual leakage reactance (x_{lm}). Value of x_{lm} is dependent on displacement angle (α) and winding pitch, resulting in the variation in harmonic coupling of windings. By neglecting x_{lm}, some variation is noted in the voltage harmonic distortion [13] with no change in transient effect. A detailed procedure for the determination of slot reactance is available [24] together with the standard method to evaluate the machine parameters [25, 26].

Detailed mathematical simulation of six-phase synchronous machine is based on determination of voltage and torque equations in integral form with flux linkage per second and speed as state variable, winding currents

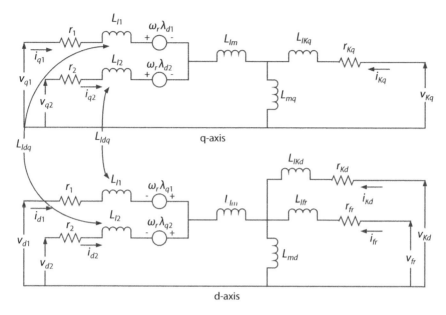

Figure 1.1 Equivalent circuit representation of a six-phase synchronous machine.

as output, connected grid voltage and prime mover torque as input variables. The voltage equations (1.1) to (1.7) together with the flux linkages equations (1.8) to (1.14) are firstly solved for the currents, which are then substituted in the voltage equations. Integral forms of mathematical equations are as follows:

$$\psi_{q1} = \frac{\omega_b}{p}\{v_{q1} + \frac{\omega_r}{\omega_b}\psi_{d1} - \frac{r_1}{X_b}[(x_{l2}+x_{lm})\psi_{q1}$$

$$-x_{lm}\psi_{q2} - x_{l2}\psi_{mq} + x_{ldq}(\psi_{d2}-\psi_{md})]\}$$

(1.19)

$$\psi_{d1} = \frac{\omega_b}{p}\{v_{d1} + \frac{\omega_r}{\omega_b}\psi_{q1} - \frac{r_1}{X_b}[(x_{l2}+x_{lm})\psi_{d1}$$

$$-x_{lm}\psi_{d2} - x_{l2}\psi_{md} - x_{ldq}(\psi_{q2}-\psi_{mq})]\}$$

(1.20)

$$\psi_{q2} = \frac{\omega_b}{p}\{v_{q2} - \frac{\omega_r}{\omega_b}\psi_{d2} - \frac{r_1}{X_b}[(x_{l1}+x_{lm})\psi_{q2}$$

$$-x_{lm}\psi_{q1} - x_{l1}\psi_{mq} - x_{ldq}(\psi_{d1}-\psi_{md})]\}$$

(1.21)

$$\psi_{d2} = \frac{\omega_b}{p}\{v_{d2} + \frac{\omega_r}{\omega_b}\psi_{q2} + \frac{r_1}{X_b}[(x_{l1} + x_{lm})\psi_{d2}$$
$$- x_{lm}\psi_{d1} - x_{l1}\psi_{md} + x_{ldq}(\psi_{q2} - \psi_{mq})]\}$$

(1.22)

$$\psi_{Kq} = \{v_{kq} - \frac{r_{Kq}}{x_{lkq}}[\psi_{Kq} - \psi_{mq}]\}$$

(1.23)

$$\psi_{Kd} = \{v_{kd} - \frac{r_{Kd}}{x_{lKd}}[\psi_{Kd} - \psi_{md}]\}$$

(1.24)

$$\psi_{fr} = \{\frac{v_{fr}x_{md}}{r_{fr}} - \frac{r_{fr}}{x_{lfr}}[\psi_{fr} - \psi_{md}]\}$$

(1.25)

Current in terms of flux is written as follows:

$$i_{q1} = \frac{1}{x_b}[(x_{l2} + x_{lm})\psi_{q1} - x_{lm}\psi_{q2} - x_{l2}\psi_{mq} + x_{ldq}(\psi_{d2} - \psi_{md})]$$

(1.26)

$$i_{d1} = \frac{1}{x_b}[(x_{l2} + x_{lm})\psi_{d1} - x_{lm}\psi_{d2} - x_{l2}\psi_{md} - x_{ldq}(\psi_{q2} - \psi_{mq})]$$

(1.27)

$$i_{q2} = \frac{1}{x_b}[(x_{l1} + x_{lm})\psi_{q2} - x_{lm}\psi_{q1} - x_{l1}\psi_{mq} - x_{ldq}(\psi_{d1} - \psi_{md})]$$

(1.28)

$$i_{d1} = \frac{1}{x_b}[(x_{l1} + x_{lm})\psi_{d2} - x_{lm}\psi_{d2} - x_{l1}\psi_{md} - x_{ldq}(\psi_{q1} - \psi_{mq})]$$

(1.29)

$$i_{Kq} = \frac{1}{x_{lKq}}[\psi_{Kq} - \psi_{mq}]$$

(1.30)

$$i_{Kd} = \frac{1}{x_{lKd}}[\psi_{Kd} - \psi_{md}]$$

(1.31)

$$i_{fr} = \frac{1}{x_{lfr}}[\psi_{fr} - \psi_{md}]$$

(1.32)

ψ_{mq} and ψ_{md} are defined using state variables as follows:

$$\psi_{mq} = x_{aq}\left[\frac{x_{l2}\psi_{q1} + x_{l1}\psi_{q2} + x_{ldq}(\psi_{d2} - \psi_{d1})}{x_b} + \frac{\psi_{Kq}}{x_{lKq}}\right] \quad (1.33)$$

$$\psi_{md} = x_{ad}\left[\frac{x_{l2}\psi_{d1} + x_{l1}\psi_{d2} + x_{ldq}(\psi_{q1} - \psi_{q2})}{x_b} + \frac{\psi_{Kd}}{x_{lKd}} + \frac{\psi_{fr}}{x_{lfr}}\right] \quad (1.34)$$

where

$$x_{aq} = \left[\frac{1}{x_{mq}} + \frac{1}{x_{lKq}} + \frac{x_{l1} + x_{l2}}{x_b}\right]^{1} \quad (1.35)$$

$$x_{ad} = \left[\frac{1}{x_{md}} + \frac{1}{x_{lKd}} + \frac{1}{x_{lfr}} + \frac{x_{l1} + x_{l2}}{x_b}\right]^{-1} \quad (1.36)$$

$$x_b = x_{l1}x_{l2} + (x_{l1} + x_{l2})x_{lm} - x_{ldq}^2 \quad (1.37)$$

Developed electromagnetic torque (T_e) and rotor dynamic equations for the machine can be expressed as follows:

$$T_e = T_{e1} + T_{e2} \quad (1.38)$$

where

$$T_{e1} = k(i_{q1}\psi_{d1} - i_{d1}\psi_{q1}) \quad (1.39)$$

the developed torque associated with the first winding set *abc*, and

$$T_{e2} = k(i_{q2}\psi_{d2} - i_{d2}\psi_{q2}); k = \frac{3}{2}\frac{P}{2}\frac{1}{\omega_b} \quad (1.40)$$

the developed torque associated with the second winding set *xyz*.

$$\frac{\omega_r}{\omega_b} = \frac{1}{p}\left[\frac{1}{\omega_b}\frac{P}{2}\frac{1}{J}(T_e - T_l)\right] \quad (1.41)$$

$$\delta = \frac{\omega_b}{p}\left(\frac{\omega_r - \omega_e}{\omega_b}\right) \tag{1.42}$$

where T_e is overall developed electromagnetic torque and T_l is the prime mover torque. In the mathematical modeling, both motoring and generating mode is possible. In this chapter, generating mode is considered, where mechanical input torque T_l is fed from prime mover to generate the electrical output power, resulting the flow of current from machine to connected utility grid.

Input voltages v_{abcs} and v_{xyzs} in stationary frame coordinate are transformed directly to v_{dq0s}^r and $v_{dq0s}^{r-\alpha}$ in rotor reference frame by using the transformation matrix [20, 22] K_s^r and $K_s^{r-\alpha}$, associated with each winding sets abc and xyz, respectively. The voltages applied to the damper windings are not shown, because voltages are zero due to short-circuited windings.

1.3   Linearization of Machine Equations for Stability Analysis

In above section, current and flux linkage per second are both related to each other [Equation (1.26) to (1.32)], one variable vector (current or flux linkage per second) can be taken as state variable. The choice of state variable is generally determined by the application [15]. Here, current is selected as state variable (i.e., independent variable). Hence, the voltage-current relation of machine in matrix form is expressed as follows:

$$[v] = [z][i] \tag{1.43}$$

where

$[v] = [v_{q1}, v_{d1}, v_{q2}, v_{d2}, v_{Kq}, v_{fr}, v_{Kd}]^T$
$[i] = [i_{q1}, i_{d1}, i_{q2}, i_{d2}, i_{Kq}, i_{fr}, i_{Kd}]^T$
$[z]$ is the impedance matrix defined in the Appendix.

Using the concept of Taylor series expansion, the linearization of machine equations (1.40), (1.41), (1.42), and (1.43) results in a set of equations, which are expressed in matrix form:

$$\begin{bmatrix} \Delta v_{1qds} \\ \Delta v_{2qds} \\ \Delta v_{rr} \end{bmatrix} = \begin{bmatrix} w_1 & x_1 & y_1 \\ x_2 & w_2 & y_2 \\ q_1 & q_2 & s \end{bmatrix} \begin{bmatrix} \Delta i_{1qds} \\ \Delta i_{2qds} \\ \Delta i_{rr} \end{bmatrix} \tag{1.44}$$

where matrix elements are explained in the Appendix.

Grid voltage with constant magnitude and frequency is presented in synchronous reference frame. Hence, it is advantageous to relate the variables in synchronously rotating reference frame (i.e., and F_{ds}^e) to rotor reference frame (i.e., F_{qs}^r and F_{ds}^r) and is given by Equation (1.45).

$$\begin{bmatrix} F_{kqs}^r \\ F_{kds}^r \end{bmatrix} = \begin{bmatrix} \cos\delta_k & -\sin\delta_k \\ \sin\delta_k & \cos\delta_k \end{bmatrix} \begin{bmatrix} F_{kqs}^e \\ F_{kds}^e \end{bmatrix} \tag{1.45}$$

where $k = \begin{cases} 1, \text{for winding set } abc \\ 2, \text{for winding set } xyz \end{cases}$

$\delta_1 = \delta_0$ (rotor angle)

$\delta_1 = \delta_0 - \alpha - \beta$

whereas β shows the phase difference between the terminal voltage of phases a and x. Numerically, the numerical value of both α and β is 30° electrical.

The linearized version of above of nonlinear differential equation (1.45) with suitable approximation ($cos\Delta\delta_k = 1$ and $sin\Delta\delta_k = \Delta\delta_k$) results in

$$\Delta F_{kdqs}^r = T_k\Delta F_{kdqs}^e + F^r\Delta\delta \tag{1.46}$$

Inverse transformation of above equation yields

$$\Delta F_{kdqs}^e = (T_k)^{-1}\Delta F_{kdqs}^r + F^e\Delta\delta \tag{1.47}$$

where F^r and F^e represent the d-q performances indices under steady state.

$$T_k = \begin{bmatrix} \cos\delta_k & -\sin\delta_k \\ \sin\delta_k & \cos\delta_k \end{bmatrix} \tag{1.48}$$

$$(T_k)^{-1} = \begin{bmatrix} \cos\delta_k & \sin\delta_k \\ -\sin\delta_k & \cos\delta_k \end{bmatrix} \tag{1.49}$$

Substituting Equations (1.46) and (1.47) into Equation (1.44) results in

$$\begin{bmatrix} T_1\Delta v_{1dqs}^e \\ T_2\Delta v_{2dqs}^e \\ \Delta v_{rr} \end{bmatrix} = \begin{bmatrix} w_1 & x_1 & y_1 \\ w_2 & w_2 & y_2 \\ q_1 & q_2 & s \end{bmatrix} \begin{bmatrix} T_1\Delta i_{1dqs}^e \\ T_2\Delta i_{2dqs}^e \\ \Delta i_{rr} \end{bmatrix} \tag{1.50}$$

and is rearranged as

$$
\begin{bmatrix}
\Delta v_{1dqs}^e \\
\Delta v_{2dqs}^e \\
\Delta v_{rr}
\end{bmatrix}
=
\begin{bmatrix}
(T_1)^{-1} w_1 T_1 & (T_1)^{-1} x_1 T_2 & (T_1)^{-1} y_1 \\
(T_2)^{-1} x_2 T_1 & (T_2)^{-1} w_2 T_2 & (T_2)^{-1} y_2 \\
q_1 T_1 & q_2 T_2 & s
\end{bmatrix}
\begin{bmatrix}
\Delta I_{1dqs}^e \\
\Delta I_{2dqs}^e \\
\Delta I_{rr}
\end{bmatrix}
\tag{1.51}
$$

Simplified version of above equation can be written as

$$
Epx = Fx + v \tag{1.52}
$$

where $(x)^T = [(\Delta i_{1qds}^e)^T \ (\Delta i_{2qds}^e)^T \ (\Delta i_{rr})^T]$

$$
= \left[\Delta i_{q1}^e, \Delta i_{d1}^e, \Delta i_{q2}^e, \Delta i_{d2}^e, \Delta i_{Kq}, \Delta i_{fr}, \Delta i_{Kd}, \frac{\Delta \omega r}{\omega_b}, \Delta \delta \right]
$$

$$
(v)^T = [(\Delta v_{1qds}^e)^T \ (\Delta v_{2qds}^e)^T \ (\Delta v_{rr})^T]
$$

$$
= \left[\Delta v_{q1}^e, \Delta v_{d1}^e, \Delta v_{q2}^e, \Delta v_{d2}^e, \Delta v_{Kq}, \Delta v_{fr}, \Delta v_{Kd} \Delta T, 0 \right]
$$

In above expressions, the additional subscript "0" ($i_{d10}, i_{d20}, i_{fr0}, i_{q10}, i_{q20}$) represent the value during steady state. Rewriting Equation (1.52) in fundamental form

$$
px = Ax + Bv \tag{1.53}
$$

where
$A = (E)^{-1} F$
$B = (E)^{-1}$

In above linearized model of machine, the effect of mutual coupling between stator winding sets *abc* and *xyz* is considered (by using mutual leakage reactance, x_{lm} and x_{ldq}). Results are presented in consideration of the asymmetrical six-phase synchronous machine ($\alpha = 30°$ electrical) in comparison with its three-phase equivalent.

1.4   Dynamic Performance Results

Dynamic analysis of any electrical system is of prime importance to understand its operating characteristic under different conditions changing suddenly.

Therefore, the mathematical model developed in previous section has been effectively used to analyze the behavior of grid connected six-phase synchronous generator under sudden change in active load. For this purpose, a set of differential equations that describe the synchronous machine operation were simulated in MATLAB/Simulink environment. Simulation has been carried out for a machine of 3.2 kW, 6 poles, whose parameters are mentioned in the Appendix.

Computer traces in Figures 1.2 and 1.3 are showing the dynamic behavior of six-phase synchronous generator due to a step change in output active power from 0% to 50% of rated/base value at time $t = 5$ s and further increase in output power by 50% (i.e., at full load) at time $t = 15$ s. It is assumed that the terminal voltage and frequency is constant irrespective of the change in load torque. Input phase voltage was maintained constant at 240 V, 50 Hz, operating at 0.85 power factor (lagging). Initially, generator is operating at no load condition at synchronous speed. At time $t = 5$ s, a step increase in output power, and hence, increase in prime mover applied torque T_l is considered. This resulted in the increase in rotor speed immediately, following the step increase in prime mover torque as shown in Figure 1.2a, where the load angle δ increases in Figure 1.2c. The rotor speed continues to increase till the accelerating torque on the rotor vanishes. It can be noted from Figure 1.2b that the speed increases to approximately 105 rad/sec at the time when T_e equal to T_l. At this time, accelerating torque is zero and the rotor is running above synchronous speed; hence,

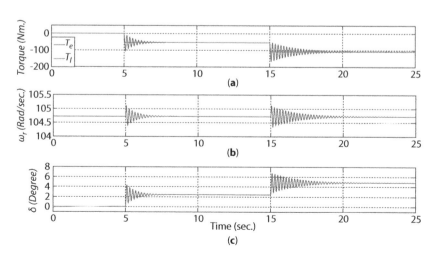

Figure 1.2 Dynamic response of motor following the change in load torque showing (a) motor torque T_e, (b) rotor speed $ω_r$, and (c) load angle, *delta*.

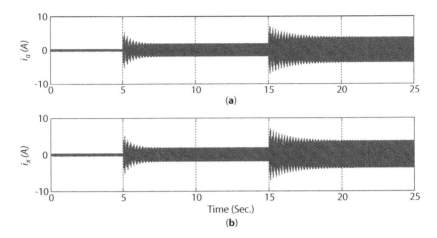

Figure 1.3 Dynamic response of motor following the change in load torque showing stator currents (a) i_a and (b) i_x.

load angle δ, and thus motor torque T_e will keep on decreasing. Decrease in torque T_e results in decrease in output power of the machine that causes the rotor to decelerate toward synchronous speed. Hence, due to rotor inertia, it will continue to decelerate below synchronous speed, and consequently, load angle δ begins to increase, with increase in generated torque T_e. In this way, damped oscillation of machine continues and settles to a new-steady state value.

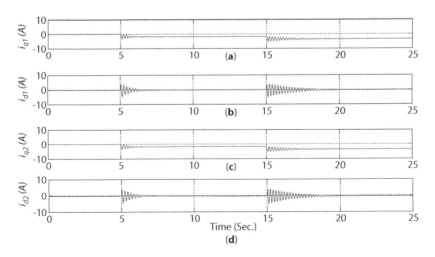

Figure 1.4 d-q component of stator winding currents (a) I_{q1}, (b) I_{d1}, (c) I_{q2}, and (d) I_{d2}.

Due to the increase in generator prime mover input torque, increase in stator phase current can be noted in Figure 1.3, which is required to meet the increased output. The increase in stator current is associated with the increase in active output power of the generator, while maintaining its operation at constant power factor (i.e., constant reactive power). Hence, the change in q-axis component of stator current (active component of current changes from 1.8 A at 50% output power to 3.6 A at rated output, approximately) is depicted in Figure 1.4, with no change in its d-axis component of stator current (reactive component of current), of both the winding sets abc and xyz.

1.5   Stability Analysis Results

For small signal stability analysis, eigenvalue is calculated from system characteristic equation:

$$\det(A - \lambda I) = 0 \qquad (1.54)$$

where unknown root λ is calculated (i.e., eigenvalue) with A and I as system matrix and identity matrix, respectively. For a system to be stable, all the real and/or real component of eigenvalues must be negative [15, 18–20].

State equation (1.53) and equation 8.3-45 of reference [15] are using nine and seven state variables, respectively. Hence, nine and seven eigenvalues will be obtained for six and three-phase generator, respectively. In six-phase generator, out of nine evaluated eigenvalues, three eigenvalues are complex conjugate pairs and the remaining are real. Evaluated eigenvalue of six-phase and three-phase generator is given in Tables 1.1 and 1.2, respectively. Eigenvalue was evaluated by considering the same flux level in both three- and six-phase machine. This was ensured by considering

Table 1.1 Eigenvalues of six-phase synchronous generator.

Nomenclature	Eigenvalues
Stator eigenvalue I	$-107.8 \pm j104.7$
Stator eigenvalue II	$-19.2 \pm j110.3$
Rotor eigenvalue	$-5.1 \pm j38.2$
Real eigenvalue	$-9136.3, -703.5, -21.0$

Table 1.2 Eigenvalues of three-phase synchronous generator.

Nomenclature	Eigenvalues
Stator eigenvalue	$-38.3 \pm j103.2$
Rotor eigenvalue	$-27.9 \pm j50.4$
Real eigenvalue	$-8719.7, -503.3, -10.7$

the stator voltage of three-phase machine as twice of six-phase machine [27]. Hence, value of the terminal voltage for three-phase and six-phase machine was taken as 240 and 120 V, respectively. Results are given for both machine considering the same load at 50% of rated value, at power factor 0.85 (lagging). It is worthwhile to mention here that it is a difficult to establish a correlation of eigenvalue with machine parameter [15]. It has been considered by changing a machine parameter, keeping other at nominal value and noting the variation in eigenvalue [18].

In Equation (1.53), derivative component (i.e., with its elements with subscript p) is indicated by coefficient matrix E, with remaining terms (i.e., subscript k) of linearized machine equations are shown by the coefficient matrix F. Matrices E and F elements are defined in the Appendix.

1.5.1   Parametric Variation of Stator

During the analysis, it was assumed that the two sets of stator winding, say, abc and xyz, are identical. Hence, value of resistance and winding leakage inductance will be same (i.e., $r_s = r_1 = r_2$ and $x_{ls} = x_{l1} = x_{l2}$). It may be noted that in figures of the following sections, dark and dash line indicate the real and imaginary component of eigenvalue, respectively.

With increase in stator resistance, generator operation tends toward stability from both stator and rotor side due to higher magnitude of negative real component of eigenvalue, as shown in Figure 1.5a for three-phase generator and Figures 1.6a and b for six-phase generator. Real eigenvalue I and II was found to be decreased as shown in Figures 1.5b and c for three-phase generator, and in Figures 1.6c and d for six-phase generator. But a slight increase in real eigenvalue III of three-phase generator with no change was noted in six-phase generator as shown in Figures 1.5d and 1.6e, respectively.

With the increase in stator leakage reactance, a trend of eigenvalue variation was found to be reversed. On stator side, real component of eigenvalue was increased by 31.5% (shown in Figure 1.7a) for three-phase generator,

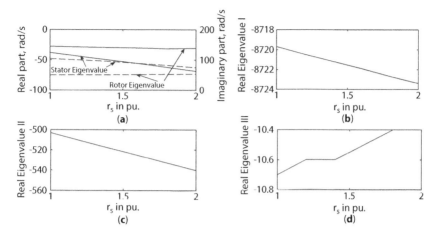

Figure 1.5 Variation in eigenvalue of three-phase synchronous machine with stator resistance change (a) stator and rotor eigenvalue, (b) real eigenvalue I, (c) real eigenvalue II, (d) real eigenvalue III.

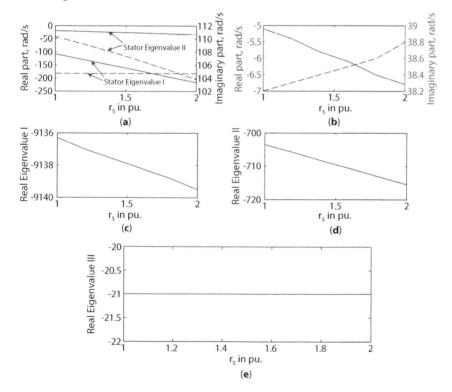

Figure 1.6 Variation in eigenvalue of six-phase synchronous machine with stator resistance change (a) stator eigenvalue I and II, (b) rotor eigenvalue, (c) real eigenvalue I, (d) real eigenvalue II, (e) real eigenvalue III.

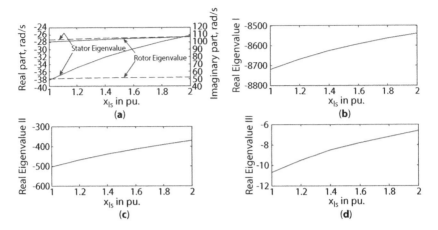

Figure 1.7 Variation in eigenvalue of three-phase synchronous machine with stator leakage reactance change (a) stator and rotor eigenvalue, (b) real eigenvalue I, (c) real eigenvalue II, (d) real eigenvalue III.

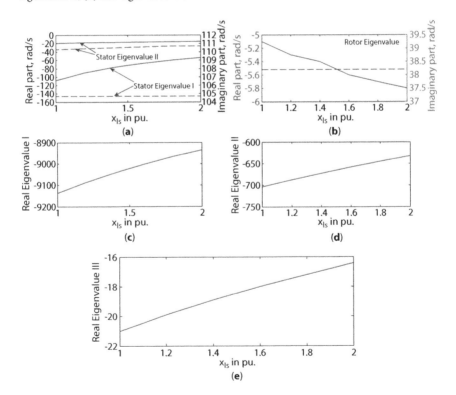

Figure 1.8 Variation in eigenvalue of six-phase synchronous machine with stator leakage reactance change (a) stator eigenvalue I and II, (b) rotor eigenvalue, (c) real eigenvalue I, (d) real eigenvalue II, (e) real eigenvalue III.

and by 50% and 19.8% in stator eigenvalue I and II for six-phase generator, as shown in Figure 1.8a. However, a slight increase in real component of rotor eigenvalue for three-phase generator was noted, shifting the operation toward instability. But, in six-phase generator, increased magnitude of real component of rotor eigenvalue (shown in Figure 1.8b), signifying the tendency of stable operation. The remaining three eigenvalues remain negative with small variation as shown in Figures 1.7b–d and Figures 1.8c–e for three- and six-phase generator, respectively. It may be noted that the magnitude (with negative sign) real eigenvalues of six-phase generator remain higher (in magnitude); and hence, is more stable when compared with three-phase generator.

1.5.2 Parametric Variation of Field Circuit

In this section, the effect of variation in field circuit parameter (resistance r_{fr} and leakage reactance x_{lfr}) is presented for both three- and six-phase generator. With the increase in field circuit resistance, variation in real component of stator eigenvalue was not observed in case of three-phase generator, as shown in Figure 1.9a. But, stator eigenvalue I was increased by 50%, showing the tendency of instability as shown in Figure 1.10b. But on rotor side, operation tends toward stability as shown in Figure 1.10b. A small increase in the value of real component of rotor eigenvalue was noted in three-phase generator, as shown in Figure 1.9a. Real eigenvalue I and III

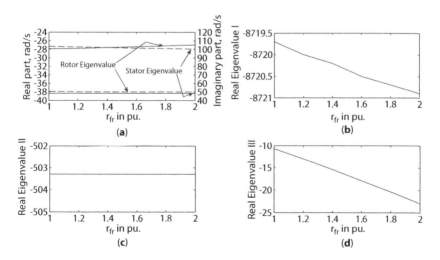

Figure 1.9 Variation in eigenvalue of three-phase synchronous machine with field circuit resistance change (a) stator and rotor eigenvalue, (b) real eigenvalue I, (c) real eigenvalue II, (d) real eigenvalue III.

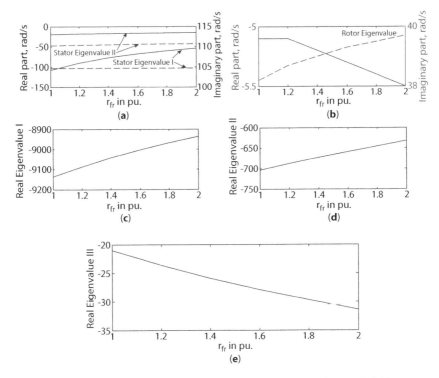

Figure 1.10 Variation in eigenvalue of six-phase synchronous machine with field circuit resistance change (a) stator eigenvalue I and II, (b) rotor eigenvalue, (c) real eigenvalue I (d) real eigenvalue II, (e) real eigenvalue III.

is decreased for three-phase generator as shown in Figures 1.9b and d, respectively, with no variation in real eigenvalue II as shown Figure 1.9c. On the other hand, trend of variation in real component of eigenvalue was found to be different for six-phase generator. All the real eigenvalue I, II, and III was found to be decreasing (in magnitude with negative sign) as shown in Figures 1.10c, d, and e, respectively. It may be noted here that the larger variation was in the smallest real eigenvalue III with no or smaller change in other real eigenvalues. This is because, on rotor, field circuit has largest time constant giving rise to smallest eigenvalue III [15, 18].

With the increase in field leakage reactance x_{lfr}, magnitude of real component of stator eigenvalue was decreased for both three- and six-phase generator, as shown in Figures 1.11a and 1.12a, respectively. But, a small variation in real component of rotor eigenvalue was noted for both three- and six-phase generator, as shown in Figures 1.11a and 1.12b, respectively. A small linear or no change was noted in eigenvalue I and II for both three- and six-phase generator, as shown in Figures 1.11b and c

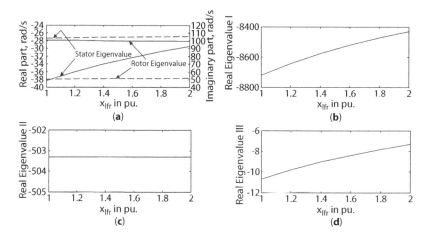

Figure 1.11 Variation in eigenvalue of three-phase synchronous machine with field circuit leakage reactance change (a) stator and rotor eigenvalue, (b) real eigenvalue I, (c) real eigenvalue II, (d) real eigenvalue III.

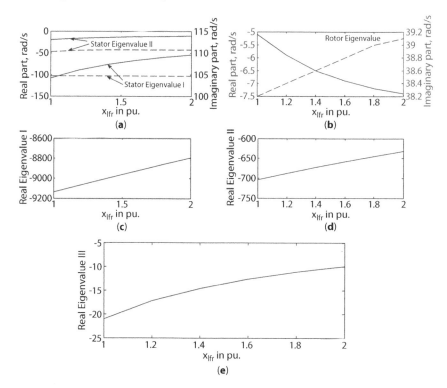

Figure 1.12 Variation in eigenvalue of six-phase synchronous machine with field circuit leakage reactance change (a) stator eigenvalue I and II, (b) rotor eigenvalue, (c) real eigenvalue I, (d) real eigenvalue II, (e) real eigenvalue III.

and Figures 1.12c and d, respectively. But, a larger variation in real eigenvalue III was noted for both three- and six-phase generator, as shown in Figures 1.11d and 1.12e, respectively.

1.5.3   Parametric Variation of Damper Winding, K_d

In this section, parameter variation of damper winding along d-axis K_d (i.e., resistance r_{Kd} and leakage reactance x_{lKd}) is considered in the evaluation of generator eigenvalues. With the increase in resistance r_{Kd}, both the stator and rotor eigenvalues were found to be unchanged for three-phase generator, as shown in Figure 1.13a. However, some change was found in stator eigenvalue I and rotor eigenvalue for six-phase generator, as shown in Figures 1.14a and b, respectively. A pronounced increase in the magnitude of real eigenvalue I was found for both three- and six-phase generator, as shown in Figures 1.13b and 1.14c, respectively. But no change in eigenvalue II and III was found for three-phase generator with small variation for six-phase generator, as shown in Figures 1.13c and d and Figures 1.14d and e, respectively.

With the increased value of leakage reactance x_{lKd}, a major variation was only noted on real eigenvalue I for both three- and six-phase generator as shown in Figures 1.15b and 1.16c, respectively. A slight variation in real eigenvalue III was noted for both three- and six-phase generator as shown in Figures 1.15d and 1.16e, respectively. On stator side, a small variation in real component of eigenvalue was noted (with decrease in real

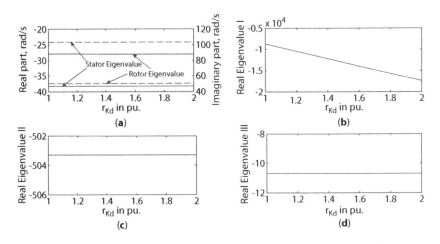

Figure 1.13 Variation in eigenvalue of three-phase synchronous machine with damper resistance change along d-axis (a) stator and rotor eigenvalue, (b) real eigenvalue I, (c) real eigenvalue II, (d) real eigenvalue III.

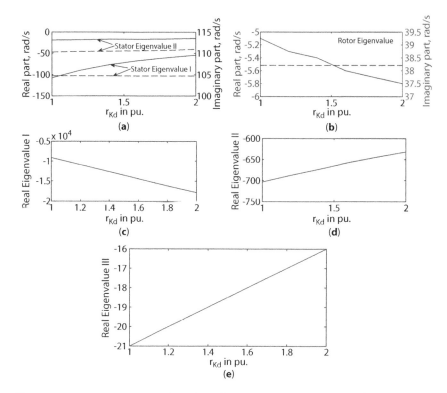

Figure 1.14 Variation in eigenvalue of six-phase synchronous machine with damper resistance change along d-axis (a) stator eigenvalue I and II, (b) rotor eigenvalue, (c) real eigenvalue I, (d) real eigenvalue II (e) real eigenvalue III.

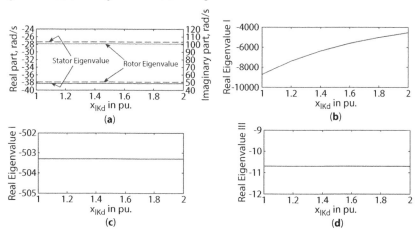

Figure 1.15 Variation in eigenvalue of three-phase synchronous machine with damper leakage reactance change along d-axis (a) stator and rotor eigenvalue, (b) real eigenvalue I, (c) real eigenvalue II, (d) real eigenvalue III.

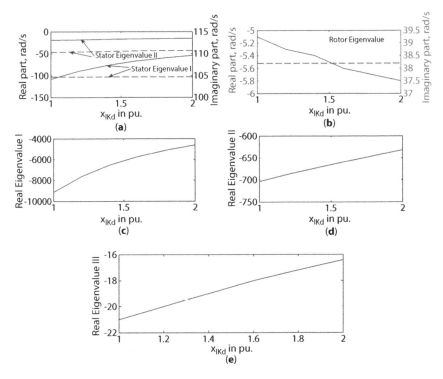

Figure 1.16 Variation in eigenvalue of six-phase synchronous machine with damper leakage reactance change along d-axis (a) stator eigenvalue I and II, (b) rotor eigenvalue (c) real eigenvalue I, (d) real eigenvalue II, (e) real eigenvalue III.

component of stator eigenvalue I for six-phase generator) both three- and six-phase generator as shown in Figures 1.15a and 1.16a, respectively. Real component of rotor eigenvalue was noted to have no/small variation for both three- and six-phase generator as shown in Figures 1.15a and 1.16b, respectively.

1.5.4   Parametric Variation of Damper Winding, K_q

With the increase in damper winding resistance r_{Kq}, small variation was noted on real component of stator eigenvalue in three-phase generator. But in six-phase generator, it was increased by 50% in stator eigenvalue I (and slight increase in stator eigenvalue II), as shown in Figures 1.17a and 1.18a, respectively. On rotor side, real part of eigenvalue was increased by 46.2% and 49% for both three- and six-phase generator, as shown in Figures 1.17a and 1.18b, respectively. A major effect was found on real eigenvalue II which was decreased by 112% and 82.2% for three-phase and six-phase generator

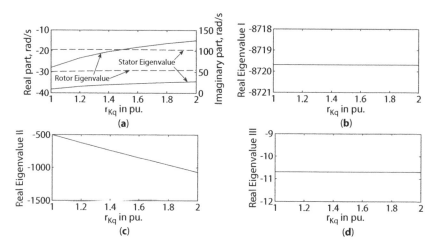

Figure 1.17 Variation in eigenvalue of three-phase synchronous machine with damper resistance change along q-axis (a) stator and rotor eigenvalue, (b) real eigenvalue I, (c) real eigenvalue II, (d) real eigenvalue III.

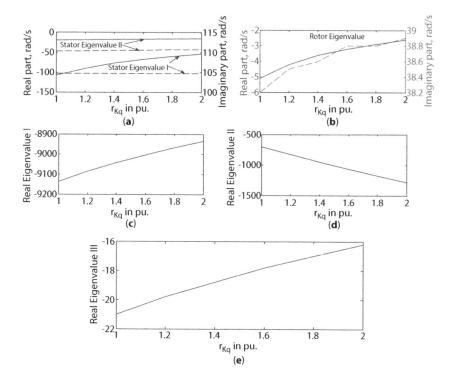

Figure 1.18 Variation in eigenvalue of six-phase synchronous machine with damper resistance change along q-axis (a) stator eigenvalue I and II, (b) rotor eigenvalue, (c) real eigenvalue I, (d) real eigenvalue II, (e) real eigenvalue III.

as shown in Figures 1.17c and 1.18d, respectively. In three-phase generator, no change was noted in eigenvalue I and III as shown in Figures 1.17b
and d, respectively. But in case of six-phase generator, slight variation was
found in real eigenvalue I and III, as shown in Figures 1.18c and e, respectively. During the analysis, it was noted that the effect of variation in the
value of reactance x_{lKq} was only found in real eigenvalue II, with no variation on other eigenvalues, hence not shown. Value of real eigenvalue II was
increased by 45.7% and 48.2% for three- and six-phase generator as shown
in Figures 1.19a and b, respectively.

1.5.5   Magnetizing Reactance Variation Along q-axis

With the increase in magnetizing reactance x_{mq} along q-axis, real part
of stator eigenvalue of three- and six-phase generator was decreased by
34.4% and 68.8% (with no variation in stator eigenvalue I), as shown in
Figures 1.20a and 1.21a, respectively. A major effect was noted from rotor
side. Value of real part of rotor eigenvalue is increasing linearly for both
three-phase and six-phase generator. It may be noted that the generator
operation becomes unstable at higher value of x_{mq} due to positive value of
real part of rotor eigenvalue, as shown in Figure 1.21b. Hence, six-phase
generator is more sensitive toward the variation of magnetizing reactance
x_{mq}. Also, a linear increase in the value of real eigenvalue II was noted for
both three- and six-phase generator as shown in Figures 1.20c and 1.21d,
respectively. But in three-phase generator, a higher decrease in real eigenvalue III was found in comparison with six-phase generator as shown in
Figures 1.20d and 1.21e, respectively. No variation in real eigenvalue I was

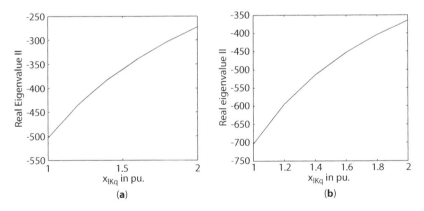

Figure 1.19 Variation in eigenvalue II with damper leakage reactance change along q-axis
in (a) three-phase and (b) six-phase generator.

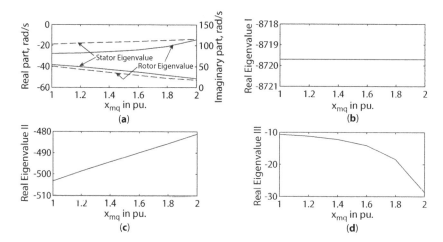

Figure 1.20 Variation in eigenvalue of three-phase synchronous machine with magnetizing reactance change along q-axis (a) stator and rotor eigenvalue, (b) real eigenvalue I, (c) real eigenvalue II, (d) real eigenvalue III.

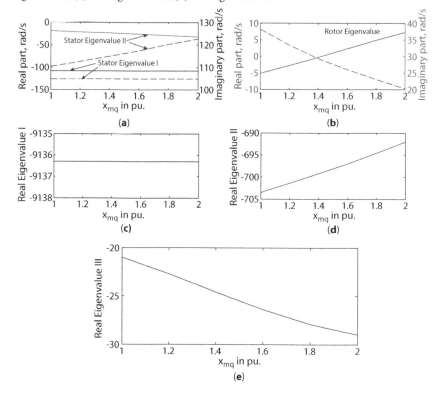

Figure 1.21 Variation in eigenvalue of six-phase synchronous machine with magnetizing reactance change along q-axis (a) stator eigenvalue I and II, (b) rotor eigenvalue, (c) real eigenvalue I, (d) real eigenvalue II, (e) real eigenvalue III.

found for both three- and six-phase generator, as shown in Figures 1.20b and 1.21c, respectively.

Both three- and six-phase generator evaluated eigenvalues were found to unchanged with the variation in magnetizing reactance x_{md} along d-axis. Hence, it is not presented.

1.5.6   Variation in Load

Considering the constant grid voltage at 240 V (rms value per phase), eigenvalue of both three- and six-phase generator is plotted in Figure 1.18 for increase in load from 0.25 to 1.0 pu. From stator side, real component of stator eigenvalue decreases (increase in magnitude with negative sign) for both three- and six-phase generator, as shown in Figure 1.22a. (No variation was noted in stator eigenvalue I, hence not shown). Decrease in the value of real part of stator eigenvalue was higher (70.8%) than its three-phase counterpart (47.9%). Hence, tendency toward stability of six-phase generator is higher than three-phase generator. On rotor side, increase (i.e., decrease in magnitude with negative sign) in real component was noted to be same (20.7%) for both three- and six-phase generator as shown in Figure 1.22b. Hence, under load variation, rotor behavior will be the same for both three- and six-phase generator. On real eigenvalue II, a slight increase in the value for three-phase (by 4.5%) and six-phase generator (by 1.5%) was noted, as shown in Figure 1.22c. Also, a very small decrease in real eigenvalue III for six-phase (by 3.2%) was noted with 17.1% variation in three-phase generator as shown in Figure 1.22d. Hence, both rotor and damper winding behavior will be approximately the same for both

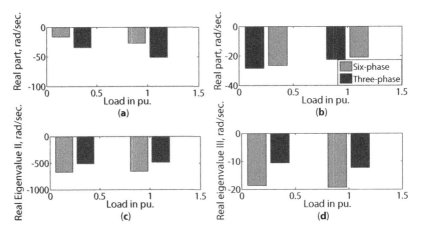

Figure 1.22 Change in real/real component of generator eigenvalue due to load variation. (a) stator eigenvalue, (b) rotor eigenvalue, (c) real eigenvalue II, (d) real eigenvalue III.

three- and six-phase generator. Since, variation in real eigenvalue I was not noted, and hence not shown.

1.6   Conclusions

This chapter deals with a detailed analysis of six-phase synchronous generator, applicable for wind power generation system. This includes the mathematical modeling of grid connected six-phase synchronous generator and its dynamic performance under load variation. Initially, machine was operated at no-load followed by the step increase in output power (i.e., active power increased at time $t = 5$ and 15 s from no-load to 50% of rated, to rated value). Hence, increase in active component (i.e., q-axis component) of current was noted to be increased with no change in reactive component (i.e., d-axis component) current, associated with both the three-phase stator winding. This has resulted in an overall increase in current of both stator winding sets. On the basis of performance results, it may be inferred that a stable operation is achieved with a step change in output power for a grid connected six-phase synchronous generator.

Furthermore, a detailed small signal stability analysis was presented for grid connected six-phase synchronous generator with its three-phase counterpart. For this purpose, a linearized mathematical model was developed using Park's variables, where eigenvalue criteria were used to access the stability under small disturbance. A larger effect was found with the change in stator resistance on both six-phase and three-phase generator. Six-phase generator was found to be more stable due to larger magnitude of negative component of both stator and rotor eigenvalues. Variation of stator leakage reactance also affects the machine stability. It was found that from rotor side, six-phase generator operation is tending toward stability, while three-phase generator is approaching toward instability. Hence, machine operation will remain more stable under stator leakage reactance variation in comparison with three-phase generator. On the field side, major effect was noted in smallest real eigenvalue III, where under variation in resistance r_{fr} and leakage reactance x_{lfr}, wherein six-phase generator remains stable with respect to its three-phase counterpart. From damper side also, operation of six-phase generator was found to have higher stability when compared with its three-phase equivalent.

Hence, stability of generator operation can be enhanced with increased values of stator resistance and, on rotor side, with higher leakage reactance value of field winding circuit or/and by increased damper winding resistance along q axis.

References

1. Singh, G.K., Self-excited induction generator research—a survey. *Electr. Power Syst. Res.*, 69, 2, 107–114, 2004.
2. Chinmaya, K.A. and Singh, G.K., Performance evaluation of multiphase induction generator in stand-alone and grid connected wind energy conversion system. *IET Renewable Power Gener.*, 12, 7, 823–83, 2018.
3. https://gwec.net/global-figures/wind-energy-global-status
4. Singh, G.K., Multi-phase induction machine drive research survey. *Electr. Power Syst. Res.*, 61, 2, 139–147, 2002.
5. Levi, E., Multiphase electric machines for variable speed applications. *IEEE Trans. Ind. Electron.*, 55, 5, 1893–909, 2008.
6. Alger, P.L., Freiburghouse, E.H., Chase, D.D., Double windings for turbine alternators. *AIEE Tans.*, 49, 1, 226–244, 1930.
7. Kataoka, T. and Watanebe, E.H., Steady-state characteristic of a current-source inverter/double-wound synchronous machine system for AC power supply. *IEEE Trans. Ind. Appl.*, 16, 2, 262–270, 1980.
8. Fuchs, E.F. and Rosenberg, L.T., Analysis of an alternator with two displaced stator windings. *IEEE Trans. Power Appar. Syst.*, 93, 6, 1776–1786, 1973.
9. Hanna, R.A. and Macdonald, D.C., The six-phase generator and transformer into a three-phase power system. *IEEE Trans. Power Appar. Syst.*, 102, 8, 2600–2607, 1983.
10. Schiferl, R.F. and Ong, C.M., Six-phase synchronous machine with ac and dc stator connections, Part I: equivalent circuit representation and steady-state analysis. *IEEE Trans. Power Appar. Syst.*, 102, 8, 2685–2693, 1983.
11. Schiferl, R.F. and Ong, C.M., Six-phase synchronous machine with ac and dc stator connections, Part II: harmonic studies and a proposed uninterruptible power supply schemes. *IEEE Trans. Power Appar. Syst.*, 102, 8, 2694–701, 1983.
12. Sudhoff, S.D. and Wasynczuk, O., Analysis and average value modeling of line commutated converter-synchronous machine systems. *IEEE Trans. Energy Convers.*, 8, 1, 92–99, 1993.
13. Singh, G.K., Modeling and analysis of six-phase synchronous generator for stand-alone renewable energy generation. *Energy*, 36, 9, 5621–5631, 2011.
14. Singh, G.K., A six-phase synchronous generator for stand-alone renewable energy generation: experimental analysis. *Energy*, 36, 3, 1768–1775, 2011.
15. Krause, P.C., Wasynczuk, O., Sudhoff, S.D., *Analysis of electrical machinery and drive Systems*, IEEE Press, A John Wiley & Sons, Inc. Publication, Piscataway, New Jersey, 2004.
16. Stapleton, C.A., Root-locus study of synchronous-machine regulation. *IEE Proc.*, 111, 4, 761–768, 1964.
17. Lipo, T.A. and Krause, P.C., Stability analysis for variable frequency operation of synchronous machines. *IEEE Trans. Power Appar. Syst.*, 87, 1, 227–234, 1968.

18. Iqbal, A., Singh, G.K., Pant, V., Stability analysis of an asymmetrical six-phase synchronous motor. *Turk. J. Elec. Eng. Comp. Sci.*, 24, 3, 1674–1692, 2016.

19. Iqbal, A. and Singh, G.K., Eigenvalue analysis of six-phase synchronous motor for small signal stability. *EPE J.*, 28, 2, 49–62, 2018.

20. Singh, G.K. and Iqbal, A., Small Signal Stability of Three-phase and Six-phase Synchronous Motors: A Comparative Analysis. *Chin. J. Electr. Eng.*, 6, 1, 22–40, 2020.

21. Singh, G.K. and Iqbal, A., Modeling and analysis of six-phase synchronous motor under fault condition. *Chin. J. Electr. Eng.*, 3, 2, 62–75, 2017.

22. Iqbal, A., Singh, G.K., Pant, V., Steady-state modeling and analysis of six-phase synchronous motor. *Syst. Sci. Control Eng.*, 2, 1, 236–249, 2014.

23. Iqbal, A., Singh, G.K., Pant, V., Vector control of asymmetrical six-phase synchronous motor. *Cogent Eng.*, 3, 1134040, 1–10, 2016.

24. Alger, P.L., *Induction machines*, New York, Gorden and Breach, 1970.

25. Aghamohammadi, M.R. and Pourgholi, M., Experience with SSSFR test for synchronous generator model identification using Hook-Jeeves optimization method. *Int. J. Syst. Appl. Eng. Dev.*, 2, 3, 122–127, 2008.

26. Jones, C.V., *The unified theory of electric machine*, Butterworths, London, 1967.

27. Bojoi, R., Lazzari, M., Profumo, F., Tenconi, A., Digital field-oriented control of dual three-phase induction motor drives. *IEEE Trans. Ind. Appl.*, 39, 3, 752–760, 2003.

Appendix

Parameter of 3.2 kW, 6 poles, 50 Hz, 36 slots, six-phase synchronous machine.

$X_{mq} = 3.9112\ \Omega$	$X_{l1} = X_{l2} = 0.1758\ \Omega$	$R_1 = 0.210\ \Omega$
$X_{md} = 6.1732\ \Omega$	$X_{ldq} = 0$	$R_2 = 0.210\ \Omega$
$X_{lKq} = 0.66097\ \Omega$	$X_{lm} = 0.001652\ \Omega$	$R_{Kq} = 2.535\ \Omega$
$X_{lKd} = 1.550\ \Omega$	$R_{fr} = 0.056\ \Omega$	$R_{Kd} = 140.0\ \Omega$
$X_{lfr} = 0.2402\ \Omega$		

Symbols   Meaning

vd_1, vq_1	d-q voltage of abc winding set
v_{d2}, v_{q2}	d-q voltage of xyz winding set
i_{d1}, i_{q1}	d-q current of abc winding set
i_{d2}, i_{q2}	d-q current of xyz winding set
v_{fr}	Voltage of field circuit excitation
i_{fr}	Field circuit excitation current
v_{Kd}, v_{Kq}	Damper circuit voltage along d-q axes
i_{Kd}, i_{Kq}	Damper circuit current along d-q axes
r_1, r_2	Per phase resistance of stator windings abc and xyz, respectively
x_{l1}, x_{l2}	Per phase leakage reactance of stator windings abc and xyz, respectively
x_{lKd}, x_{lKq}	Damper circuit leakage reactance along d-q axes
x_{lfr}	Leakage reactance of field winding
x_{md}, x_{mq}	Magnetising inductance along d-q axes
x_{lm}	Common mutual leakage reactance between abc and xyz stator windings
x_{ldq}	Cross mutual coupling reactance between stator windings along d-q axes
ψ_{d1}, ψ_{q1}	Flux linkage per second of stator winding abc along d-q axes
ψ_{d2}, ψ_{q2}	Flux linkage per second of stator winding xyz along d-q axes
ψ_{md}, ψ_{mq}	Magnetising flux linkage per second along d-q axes
T_e, T_l	Developed electromagnetic torque and prime mover torque, respectively
$\omega_b, \omega_r\grave{}$	Base speed and rotor speed, respectively
J	Moment of inertiaof rotor assembly
P	Number of poles
δ	Rotor angle

$$
z = \begin{bmatrix}
r_1 + \dfrac{p}{\omega_b}(x_{l1}+x_{lm}+x_{mq}) & x_{l1}+x_{lm}+x_{md} & \dfrac{p}{\omega_b}(x_{lm}+x_{mq})+x_{ldq} & -\dfrac{p}{\omega_b}x_{ldq}+(x_{lm}+x_{md}) & \dfrac{p}{\omega_b}x_{mq} & x_{md} & x_{md} \\[2mm]
-(x_{l1}+x_{lm}+x_{mq}) & r_1+\dfrac{p}{\omega_b}(x_{l1}+x_{lm}+x_{md}) & \dfrac{p}{\omega_b}x_{ldq}-(x_{lm}+x_{mq}) & \dfrac{p}{\omega_b}(x_{lm}+x_{md})+x_{ldq} & -x_{mq} & \dfrac{p}{\omega_b}x_{md} & \dfrac{p}{\omega_b}x_{md} \\[2mm]
\dfrac{p}{\omega_b}(x_{lm}+x_{mq})-x_{ldq} & \dfrac{p}{\omega_b}x_{ldq}+(x_{lm}+x_{md}) & r_2+\dfrac{p}{\omega_b}(x_{l2}+x_{lm}+x_{mq}) & x_{l2}+x_{md}+x_{lm} & \dfrac{p}{\omega_b}x_{mq} & x_{md} & x_{md} \\[2mm]
-\dfrac{p}{\omega_b}x_{ldq}-(x_{lm}+x_{mq}) & \dfrac{p}{\omega_b}(x_{lm}+x_{md})-x_{ldq} & -(x_{l1}+x_{lm}+x_{mq}) & r_2+\dfrac{p}{\omega_b}(x_{l2}+x_{lm}+x_{md}) & -x_{mq} & \dfrac{p}{\omega_b}x_{md} & \dfrac{p}{\omega_b}x_{md} \\[2mm]
\dfrac{p}{\omega_b}x_{mq} & 0 & \dfrac{p}{\omega_b}x_{mq} & 0 & r_{Kq}+\dfrac{p}{\omega_b}(x_{lKq}+x_{mq}) & 0 & 0 \\[2mm]
0 & \dfrac{p}{\omega_b}\dfrac{x_{md}^2}{r_{fr}} & 0 & \dfrac{p}{\omega_b}\dfrac{x_{md}^2}{r_{fr}} & 0 & \dfrac{x_{md}}{r_{fr}}\left\{r_{fr}+\dfrac{p}{\omega_b}(x_{lfr}+x_{md})\right\} & \dfrac{p}{\omega_b}\dfrac{x_{md}^2}{r_{fr}} \\[2mm]
0 & \dfrac{p}{\omega_b}x_{md} & 0 & \dfrac{p}{\omega_b}x_{md} & 0 & \dfrac{p}{\omega_b}x_{md} & r_{Kd}+\dfrac{p}{\omega_b}(x_{lKd}+x_{md})
\end{bmatrix}
$$

$$
E = \begin{bmatrix}
(T_1)^{-1}w_{1p}T_1 & (T_1)^{-1}x_{1p}T_2 & (T_1)^{-1}y_{1p} \\[2mm]
(T_2)^{-1}x_{2p}T_1 & (T_2)^{-1}w_{2p}T_2 & (T_2)^{-1}y_{2p} \\[2mm]
q_{1p}T_1 & q_{2p}T_2 & S_p
\end{bmatrix}
$$

$$
F = -\begin{bmatrix}
(T_1)^{-1}w_{1k}T_1 & (T_1)^{-1}x_{1k}T_2 & (T_1)^{-1}y_{1k} \\[2mm]
(T_2)^{-1}x_{2k}T_1 & (T_2)^{-1}w_{2k}T_2 & (T_2)^{-1}y_{2k} \\[2mm]
q_{1k}T_1 & q_{2k}T_2 & S_k
\end{bmatrix}
$$

$$
y_{1p} = \left(\dfrac{1}{\omega_b}\right)\begin{bmatrix}
x_{mq} & 0 & 0 & 0 & -(x_{l1}+x_{lm}+x_{mq})i_{d10}-(x_{mq}+x_{lm})i_{d20} \\[2mm]
0 & x_{md} & x_{md} & 0 & (x_{l1}+x_{lm}+x_{md})i_{q10}+(x_{md}+x_{lm})i_{q20}
\end{bmatrix}
$$

$$
y_{2p} = \left(\dfrac{1}{\omega_b}\right)\begin{bmatrix}
x_{mq} & 0 & 0 & 0 & -(x_{l2}+x_{lm}+x_{mq})i_{d20}-(x_{mq}+x_{lm})i_{d10} \\[2mm]
0 & x_{md} & x_{md} & 0 & (x_{l2}+x_{lm}+x_{md})i_{q20}+(x_{md}+x_{lm})i_{q10}
\end{bmatrix}
$$

$$
sp = \left(\dfrac{1}{\omega_b}\right)\begin{bmatrix}
(x_{lKq}+x_{mq}) & 0 & 0 & 0 & -(x_{mq}i_{d10}+x_{mq}i_{d20}) \\[2mm]
0 & \dfrac{x_{md}(x_{lfr}+x_{md})}{r_{fr}}\dfrac{x_{md}^2}{r_{fr}} & 0 & 0 & \dfrac{x_{md}^2}{r_{fr}}(i_{q10}+i_{q20}) \\[2mm]
0 & x_{md} & (x_{lKd}+x_{md}) & 0 & x_{md}(i_{q10}+i_{q20}) \\[2mm]
0 & 0 & 0 & -\dfrac{2J\omega_b^2}{P} & 0 \\[2mm]
0 & 0 & 0 & 0 & -\omega_b
\end{bmatrix}
$$

$$w_{1k} = \begin{bmatrix} r_1 & (x_{l1} + x_{lm} + x_{md}) \\ -(x_{l1} + x_{lm} + x_{mq}) & r_1 \end{bmatrix}; w_{2k} = \begin{bmatrix} r_2 & (x_{l2} + x_{lm} + x_{md}) \\ -(x_{l2} + x_{lm} + x_{mq}) & r_2 \end{bmatrix}$$

$$x_{1k} = \begin{bmatrix} x_{ldq} & (x_{lm} + x_{md}) \\ -(x_{lm} + x_{mq}) & x_{ldq} \end{bmatrix}$$

$$x_{2k} = \begin{bmatrix} x_{ldq} & (x_{lm} + x_{md}) \\ -(x_{lm} + x_{mq}) & x_{ldq} \end{bmatrix}$$

$$w_{1p} = \left(\frac{1}{\omega_b}\right) \begin{bmatrix} (x_{l1} + x_{lm} + x_{mq}) & 0 \\ 0 & (x_{l1} + x_{lm} + x_{md}) \end{bmatrix}$$

$$w_{2p} = \left(\frac{1}{\omega_b}\right) \begin{bmatrix} (x_{l2} + x_{lm} + x_{mq}) & 0 \\ 0 & (x_{l2} + x_{lm} + x_{md}) \end{bmatrix}$$

$$x_{1p} = \left(\frac{1}{\omega_b}\right) \begin{bmatrix} (x_{mq} + x_{lm}) & -x_{ldq} \\ x_{ldq} & (x_{md} + x_{lm}) \end{bmatrix}$$

$$x_{2p} = \left(\frac{1}{\omega_b}\right) \begin{bmatrix} (x_{mq} + x_{lm}) & -x_{ldq} \\ -x_{ldq} & (x_{md} + x_{lm}) \end{bmatrix}$$

$$q_{1p} = q_{2p} = \left(\frac{1}{\omega_b}\right) \begin{bmatrix} x_{mq} & 0 \\ 0 & x_{md}^2 \\ 0 & x_{md}^{r_{fr}} \\ 0 & 0 \\ 0 & 0 \end{bmatrix}$$

$$q_{1k} = q_{2k} = \begin{bmatrix} 0 & 0 \\ 0 & 0 \\ 0 & 0 \\ (x_{md}(i_{d10} + i_{d20} + i_{fr0}) - x_{mq}(i_{d10} + i_{d20})) f_{qs} & (x_{md}(i_{q10} + i_{q20}) - x_{mq}(i_{q10} + i_{q20})) f_{qs} \end{bmatrix}$$

$$Y_{1k} = \begin{bmatrix} 0 \; x_{md} \; x_{md}(x_{l1}i_{d10} + x_{md}(i_{d10} + i_{d20} + i_{fr0})) & (-r_1 i_{d10} + (x_{l1} + x_{bn} + x_{md})i_{q10} - x_{ldq}i_{d20} + (x_{md} + x_{lm})i_{q20} + v_{d10}) \\ -x_{mq} \; 0 \; 0 \; -(x_{l1}i_{q10} + x_{mq}(i_{q10} + i_{q20})) & (-r_1 i_{q10} + (x_{l1} + x_{bn} + x_{mq})i_{q10} - (x_{mq} + x_{lm})i_{d20} + v_{q10}) \end{bmatrix}$$

$$Y_{2k} = \begin{bmatrix} 0 & x_{md} & x_{md}(x_{l2}i_{d20} + x_{md}(i_{d10} + i_{d20} + i_{fr0})) & (-r_2 i_{d20} + (x_{l2} + x_{lm} + x_{md})i_{q20} + x_{ldq}i_{d10} + (x_{md} + x_{lm})i_{q10} + v_{d20}) \\ -x_{mq} & 0 & 0 & -(x_{l2}i_{q20} + X_{mq}(i_{q10} + i_{q20})) & (-r_2 i_{q20} + (x_{l2} + x_{lm} + x_{mq})i_{d20} + (x_{mq} + x_{lm})i_{d10} - v_{q20}) \end{bmatrix}$$

$$s_k = \begin{bmatrix} r_{Kq} & 0 & 0 & 0 & 0 \\ 0 & rfr\left(\dfrac{x_{md}}{r_{fr}}\right) & 0 & 0 & 0 \\ 0 & 0 & r_{Kd} & 0 & 0 \\ -x_{mq}(i_{d10} + i_{d20})f_{qs} & x_{md}(i_{q10} + i_{q20})f_{qs} & x_{md}(i_{q10} + i_{q20})f_{qs} & 0 & f_{qs}s_{45} \\ 0 & 0 & 0 & \omega_b & 0 \end{bmatrix} \quad \text{where,}$$

$$s_{45} = -i_{d10}\left(x_{md}(i_{d10} + i_{d20} + i_{fr0}) \quad x_{mq}(i_{d10} + i_{d20})\right) + i_{q10}\left(x_{md}(i_{d10} + i_{d20})\right.$$
$$\left. - x_{mq}(i_{q10} + i_{q20})\right)$$

$$- (x_{md}(i_{d10} + i_{d20} + i_{fr0}) - x_{mq}(i_{d10} + i_{d20}))$$

$$+ i_{q20}\left(x_{md}(i_{q10} + i_{q20}) - x_{mq}(i_{q10} + i_{q20})\right)$$

$$f_{qs} = 3P/4\omega_b$$

Artificial Intelligence as a Tool for Conservation and Efficient Utilization of Renewable Resource

Vinay N.[1], Ajay Sudhir Bale[1]*, Subhashish Tiwari[2] and Baby Chithra R.[3]

[1]Dept. of ECE, School of Engineering and Technology, CMR University, Bengaluru, India
[2]Dept. of ECE, Vignan's Foundation for Science, Technology & Research (Deemed to be University), Guntur, India
[3]Dept. of ECE, New Horizon College of Engineering, Bengaluru, India

Abstract

Energy is the most significant factor in the development of a society and country. As a basic requirement, it is important to provide safe, inexpensive, uninterrupted, secure, and diversified energy supplies. At present, the major source of energy is produced from renewable and fossil resources. As the level of fossil resources is decreasing day by day, the application of renewable resources is increasing. This work describes the efficient utilization of renewable resources like water, solar, wind, and geothermal using various Artificial Intelligence (AI) techniques. The models like Back-Propagation, Multilayer Perceptron (MLP), Whale Optimization Algorithm (WOA), Radial Basis Function Neural Network (RBFN), Bayesian Regularization (BR), Levenberg-Marquardt (LM) algorithm, and Gradient Descent with momentum and adaptation learning rate back-propagation algorithm (GDX) are used in the forecasting of water resources. For solar energy, models such as MLP, Fuzzy ART (Adaptive Resonance Theory), RB, and Shark Smell Optimization (SSO) algorithm and Feed-Forward Back-Propagation are employed. For wind energy, models like Ensemble Kalman Filter (EnKF), Wavelet Neural Network (WNN), LM, Nonlinear Autoregressive Exogenous (NARX) ANN, and MLP are used. For geothermal energy, models such as Artificial Bee Colony (ABC) algorithm and MLP Feed-Forward algorithm are used to forecast it. All these models have been reviewed comprehensively with respect to their

*Corresponding author: ajaysudhirbale@gmail.com

Ajay Kumar Vyas, S. Balamurugan, Kamal Kant Hiran and Harsh S. Dhiman (eds.) Artificial Intelligence for Renewable Energy Systems, (37–78) © 2022 Scrivener Publishing LLC

structures and methodologies during implementation. We are hopeful that this review article provides future directions in AI.

Keywords: Artificial Intelligence, renewable resource, efficiency, optimization, prediction

2.1   Introduction

Renewable energy resources [1–3] include solar [4], biomass, hydro, geo-thermal, and wind. They have a major role in the production of electricity, since 14% of world's electricity demand is met by them [5]. As the demand for renewable resources is increasing gradually, the balance of these resources is changing, which means that the available/produced quantity does not equal the required quantity in the appropriate place and time. For example, there is scarcity of water [6] in some places where its demand is high and plenty of water is available at places where its demand is low [7–9], leading to the wastage of the resource. Similarly, solar energy is underutilized [10, 11] in areas of high insolation and longer hours of availability. Biomass [12, 13] derived from organic material is not utilized efficiently at its place of availability. The same holds in the case of wind and geothermal resources. The implication is that there is underutilization or wastage of renewable energy. Hence, emerging technologies should concentrate on saving, and at the same time efficiently utilize these resources. Artificial Intelligence (AI) is an emerging technology that can support the balanced use of renewable resources both in production and further utilization [14, 15].

AI can help the industrial and commercial sectors in proper utilization of water by building efficient water systems that involve seeking new sources of water and by managing the existing water reserves and systems in a sustained manner [16].

Some parts of the world make use of wind [15] and solar power as their energy source due to it being environmentally friendly. The energy produced from this source is not efficient enough, but with proper analysis and planning, this resource can supplement many energy sources. AI techniques can be used for predicting better usage of available energy and how this energy can be preserved for future. Similarly, AI can be used in the geothermal sector, such as in the optimization of well-placed geothermal reservoirs.

Recent research and experience have proved that biomass [17] is the most sustainable and abundant renewable resource which can act as a replacement for crude oil-based products. Artificial Neural Network (ANN) is suitable for prediction, modeling, and optimization of several processes related to this.

This work discusses various renewable energy resources and the application of AI techniques for efficient utilization of them.

2.2 AI in Water Energy

2.2.1 Prediction of Groundwater Level

The research [18] aimed to forecast groundwater levels based on precipitation and temperature, on different timings. It uses the multiple layer-based perception model, genetic programming, and the Radial Basis Function Neural Network (RBFN) which is the Whale Optimization Algorithm (WOA) model. The MLP model is designed and tested with the multiple inputs with the delay of 3, 6, and 9 months to obtain the best results.

Ground level water is part of most significant resources of water supply. But, in recent years, it has dropped due to inappropriate mining and soil depletion, resulting in shortage of water in present and also in future [18, 19]. In recent years the usage of soft computing groundwater forecast models such as ANN has seen a rapid growth in groundwater forecasting [20, 21], for preparing itself structurally for the prediction [22]. Using factors such as bias, weights interconnected, volume of hidden layers, and neurons, ANN model demands that its structure parameters should exhibit precise determination [23]. Among ANN model, the WOA-based model is the most powerful ones because of its various characteristics to pair with other algorithms. Further, optimization algorithms can be used to resolve issues with wide number of variables for the decisions. So, it is widely used in numerous fields like addressing the optimal control issues [24], improving the power infrastructure [25] and engines in vehicles [26].

WOA [27] has been proposed based on the hunt humpback whale activity that enhances the neural network by recognizing the effective input data using the correlation method with the numerous time delays, undergoing the normalization and training stage on that data, which later controls the stop criteria simulations depending on the error threshold. If the stop criteria are appropriate, then it executes the test stage and demonstrates the production results. If the stop criteria are not appropriate, then it undergoes different steps to pick parameters for neural network perception. The parameters also include kernel distance, neuron content width, and quantity of weights as the variables of decision and whale's primary position to get the production results. The genetic programming prediction which is the approach based on the three-formula structure that includes the mathematical formulations like addition and multiplication, with the terminals of constant numbers and problem variables. This model is used for predicting the variables value. The genetic programming model is one among the most significant hydrological variables prediction model.

Yazd is Iranian province which is struggling from aridity and drought, due to its exotic climatic conditions. The Yazd-Ardakan desert area [27] is one of the Yazd region's biggest water reservoirs having 1,085 depth wells with the water discharge rate of 260,182 m³/year, 255 semi-depth wells with a discharge rate of 19,764 m³/year, 827 ducts with a discharge rate of 104,124 m³/year. At the present, the rate of exploitation in Yazd-Ardakan desert is 515.5 million m³ with 132 million m³ balanced ground water, that is dropping drastically which is resulting in the change of aquifers width level in different regions. Anticipating aquifer level plays a major role. The data for various weather conditions in different time intervals were collected for the period between 2000 and 2012 in the Yazd-Ardakan desert area. These data were fed as an input to the modeling process at different stages using genetic, whale, and firefly algorithm for predicting the water level, in which the WOA was completely successful.

The WOA [28] model's results obtained were successful in the prediction of ground water level. The foresight executed will enable planners prepare better for the development of water management in areas of high quality [27]. Basically, the forecasting analytics are valuable instruments for showing the dropping groundwater during times of drought. Integrating the pre-processed data with the soft computing-based model will decide the groundwater duration and value of ground water level.

As drought conditions are harder to define in terms of time and in space, they are associated to water shortage precipitation, river flows, soil humidity, or a composite of all three [29, 30]. Drought is not an immediate occurrence but a slow response of hydrological cycle elements to scarcity of rain which makes it important to minimize its effect along the effective decision-making systems. Agricultural water management is becoming drastically high in case of limited water availability caused by drought, since the agriculture uses maximum quantity of water when compared to all other sectors. If the agriculture sector incorporates the efficient method of using the water, then most amount of water can be saved for other sectors. For this, the knowledge about the relationship of crop yield with the usage of water gains an important role [31–33]. The nations with long-term drought strategies are better equipped to cope with droughts than the nations with small term strategies [34–37]. So, it is necessary to have effective management system incorporated with prediction and smart alert [33, 34].

In the region of Ethiopia, the occurrence of the drought is highly normal, specifically in the regions of the Awash River Basin [35, 36], so far, no advance warning system has been introduced there. So, the long-term model was developed to forecast the stream flow for the irrigation in Middle Awash Agricultural Development Enterprise (MAADE) [37, 38] in the regions of Awash River Basin of Ethiopia. The design has been used to suggest effective management plans for agricultural water. It is implemented during the phases of drought-induced water deficit to reduce the effect of water scarcity. Strategies proposed were entirely focused on surface-based irrigation, where water from the river is supplied directly to the stream canal diversion. This method can be used by the water managers for the effective planning of water management which is based on the water supply forecasting [37].

The Awash River stream flow forecasting model was developed using with a three-layer back-propagation network. Statistics on weekly time series (1987–2001) was used to implement a long-term stream flow prediction model based on the historical data at the MelkaSedi stream gauge station [37]. The model developed was improved using the 10.5 years data and was verified with evidence from the next 3.5 years (1997–1999/2000). So, whenever the water falls below the predefined threshold level in the river that will be reported by the time series predicted for stream flow and thus the effective water management strategy can be adopted in the MAADE irrigation scheme [37].

So, depending on the predictions, different assessments were taken. The assessments were based on various scenarios of MAADE's agricultural growth strategies such as current planting trends, shifting the year for planting, modified crop varieties, and decreased area of cultivation [39]. Potential options for agricultural production in the system with suitable methods for the control of agricultural water is determined on the basis of residual surviving stream through the river after the water requirement scheme was met [39]. Thus, the implemented water conservation techniques were successful.

In most of the coastal areas ground water is unfit for drinking due to the over-exploitation. So, tracking of groundwater level is extremely significant in this area, which depends on the logical resources that are available and the hydro-geological aspects. The continuous tracking of ground water level is at the most priority in order to manage the groundwater resources in the coastal zone.

The visualization of hydrological variables and the analysis of physical process mainly undergo the important resources like physical and conceptual models [40, 41]. These models contain a massive quantity of advanced, high quality data, measurement systems using systematic methods of optimization, and a thorough knowledge of the relevant physical process [42]. A one-dimensional, conceptual approach of the flowing water would be used to estimate the yearly groundwater with weather-based variables [43]. The modeling of shallow water tables is done through the open-loop with self-exciting threshold autoregressive and using stochastic differential equations [44, 45]. In most of the water table fluctuation modeling, ANN-based models are used. Groundwater level prediction using ANN is framed by continuous monitoring of the individual well and the climatic changes [46, 47].

Kakinada is the Eastern Godavari Headquarters in Andhra Pradesh, located to the east cost of India. It has a tropical weather conditions and often impacted by cyclonic storms and dispersion in Bay of Bengal [48]. The area of this region was taken to study, that is parallel to the cost. The data pertaining to temperature, rainfall, and evaporation were collected and the water level data on monthly basis were collected from the open wells (data from 1995 to 2004). The largest amount of rainfall in this area comes from southwest monsoon between July and October [48]. The groundwater levels in this region are dropping, and this may be due to groundwater demand rises and low rainfall.

The different ANN algorithms were performed for the data obtained to forecast the levels of ground water at one-month lead for a coastal urban aquifer in Kakinada, Andhra Pradesh, India [48]. The algorithms where taken forwarded by the RBFN [49], Bayesian Regularization (BR) [50], and Levenberg-Marquardt (LM). Among these, the LM [51] showed the effective results in individual wells. The ANN platform is only good for making short-term yet numerical predictions modeling fits long-term forecasts. Thus, ANN dependent architectures were a superior option for groundwater prediction where Hydrological Parameter Information is limited. The architecture of RBFN [50] is shown in Figure 2.1.

The models of groundwater emulation have evolved as a significant tool for water resource analysts and developers, to maximize and protect groundwater exploitation. Physically dependent numerical models have been used primarily in groundwater systems modeling and research. If the data is insufficient, then the physically dependent models will not give the effective results. So, empirical models are used in order to produce better outcomes by taking less time and data. The technology of ANN is regarded as universal approximators and is capable of defining a relationship from defined pattern [53]. The ANN has the capacity to learn and generalize from the limited data available that allows them to solve the large-scale

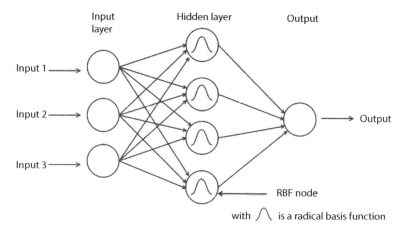

Input layer   Hidden layer   Output

Input 1

Input 2   Output

Input 3

RBF node

with /\ is a radical basis function

Figure 2.1 Radial basis neural network architecture. Reprint with copyright permission from [50].

problems with much complexity [54] which includes the problems of water management [55].

'The study was made on forecasting the level of groundwater in the group of wells on weekly basis. The study was based on the Mahanadi Delta of Odisha region in India. The River Kathajodi and its branch Surua flow in this region [56]. The river island is with a total 35 km^2 surface area, occupation of the inhabitants as agriculture, where paddy is the main croup of cultivation in monsoon season and other vegetables in the post monsoon season [56]. The research area includes around 100 tube wells by government as a primary source of groundwater. Along with these tube wells, there are also some dug wells in this area which becomes dry during summer seasons, thus creating water scarcity in this region.

The data was collected on weekly basis, related to the level of groundwater between February 2004 and June 2007. The weather data are acquired from nearby weather stations [56]. The feed-forward neural network (FNN) is designed, keeping the obtained data as the base used effectively for modeling and predicting variable water sources [57] simultaneously. GDX [58] is used to predict level of groundwater in a broad number of wells. Simulation results shows relatively good ground water level prediction, while accuracy of prediction is found to decline with growth in lead time. This resulted in a week advance groundwater prediction [56] as well as helping in effective groundwater utilization and planning.

Water systems use estimated modeling of long-range demand of water to build their systems and prepare potential plans for water needs [59].

As water distribution systems overloads, water services must modify the implementation and control of their current water distribution schemes. They also need to advance the identification and forecasting of water requirements to prevent expensive plans overdesign using the prediction models through the effective AI techniques [60]. The daily water demand will be very high per day, so the average rainfall and air temperature is considered for building the AI-based neural network models which can be termed as ANN. An ANN is a fully integrated network with several basic processing operations blocks which are highly used in water-based modeling [61, 62]. The widely employed ANN in engineering disciplines is a back-propagation-based [63] ANN model due to repeated training [63, 64] to minimize error.

The Kentucky American Water Co. (KAWC), the biggest water distribution company provides daily water to Lexington, KY, and nearby areas requests Lexington data for 11-year duration [65]. The data collected were used for regression models that are forecasted based on the weekly water demand [65] (Figure 2.2). The back-propagation model is developed from the data with the two-rule–based expert system models, characterized by three notable patterns that are historical water data request, rainfall, and the peak air temperature per day.

In this research, eight model structures were built to daily water forecasting, the first four models were developed using the conventional modeling with time and regression series and other four for modern AI

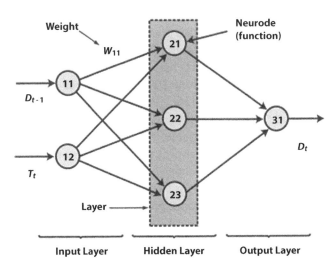

Figure 2.2 Back-propagation architecture. Reprint with copyright permission from [65].

methods [65]. Water consumption usage, peak humidity on the daily bases from total rainfall data of Lexington (1982–1992) are used to develop and test the models. The research shows that the comparatively recent team of advanced ANN techniques provides a better system for short-term water management prediction than other modern approaches [65].

Ground level water is growing as important resource of the nature and integral part of the reliable water supply in all the regions around the world [66], as it can be supplied quite cost-effectively, quickly, and conveniently to deprived communities compared to surface water [67]. But due to increased population, rise in water contamination, and biodiversity, the ground water has got the negative effect which leads to imbalance in the supply of water and other water habitats [68, 69]. Thus, the groundwater planning gained its importance [70] for existing and future decades using physical and ANN models. The most supportive system for this planning is ANN models [71] because the physical models are costly and require more labors and data intensive [72], whereas ANN does not specifically require the characteristic of the surveillance system which makes them cost-effective and able to learn from the past data that have been collected. The ANN models were developed with the collection of input variables, established for the prediction of ground level water in a single or few well. The triangle algorithms are mainly employed in implementing groundwater level prediction ANN, notably BR, LM, and GDX algorithm. The back-propagation algorithm has worked efficiently in many applications, but even that has some limitations, these algorithms are developed to overcome those limitations. The LM algorithm (LMA) will limit the sum of square error and increases the process than back-propagation [73]. Increased hidden layer neurons leads to over fitting issues, resulting in less performance in prediction of both big and small networks. This can be overcome by BR algorithm [74, 75]. The algorithm's output is really sensible to the right setting on the pace of learning. To overcome this issue, the GDX algorithm is used which is the combination of adaptive learning rate with momentum training.

The Bayalish Mouza in the basin of Kathajodi river of Orissa state, India, is the region selected for research [76]. It is the river island of 35 km^2 in area, enclosed by river Kathajodi and Surua with the humified topical weather conditions and an average rainfall of 1,535 mm per year. Ground-based water is the primary agricultural source of this region; there are 69 tube wells that are significant groundwater drainage sites [76]. The level of ground water drastically responds to the level of rainfall, change in the stage of the river that strongly reflects the relation to surface-based water body [77]. The water is sufficient during the monsoon season, but there is scarcity

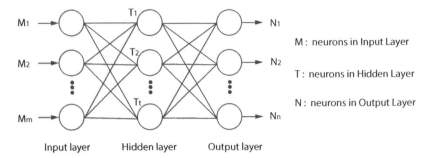

Figure 2.3 Feed-forward neural network architecture. Reprint with copyright permission from [80].

in the summer season. Weakly data related to ground water level in this region are collected at 18 sites between February 2004 and June 2007. The collected data is used to train the three ANN algorithms with feed-forward architecture, namely, BR [78, 79], LM [73], and GDX algorithm. The generic representation of feed-forward architecture [80] is depicted in Figure 2.3.

The weekly statistics related to the rainfall, evaporation, channel's stage, rate of water pumped, and also data related to the level of ground water in the past week are feed to the ANN as input, to form 40 and 18 input-output nodes, respectively [76]. The results of the three ANN algorithms, *viz.*, GDX, LM, and BR algorithm, were tested through visual awareness and statically salient indicators. All the three model's outcomes were quite similar, but the BR algorithm performance was highly effective [76]. Thus, all the models that were developed can be recommended to forecast the ground level water on weekly basis over the research area, eve for the high lead time wells [76].

2.2.2   Rainfall Modeling

The correlation between rainfall and runoff is one among the most challenging hydrological processes to be understood because of changing watershed parameters. In the modern decades, the ANN are mostly involved in the modeling of rainfall-runoff, as practically any feature can be approximated to an arbitrary level of precision by ANN [81]. Despite a multitude of studies are carried out on rainfall-runoff modeling using ANNs, there are still some concerns that need to be discussed even while using ANN for rainfall-runoff modeling network optimal structure, selection of transfer function or form of network, and development algorithm choice [82]. The RBFN and MLP models are efficient models for the rainfall-runoff modeling, as the specifications for RBFN are calculated from input space directly [83], they use the transfer functions of sigmoid type [84] and could be prepared within a small amount of time. MLP can generate precise forecasting data, but training a suitable MLP [85] can take a very long time and range of parameters need to be generated by the neural network.

The study was made on the Malaprabha river basin, which is a tributary to the right of the river Krishna, India, lies 15 ° 000 to 16 ° 120 North and 74 ° 140 to 76 ° 050 East. It has a drainage area of 515 km² stretching up to Khanapur [86]. The catchment weather is usually dry; the average rainfall in the region is 770 mm per year. The detail study was made on this region based on the data from 1987 to 1991. The ANN was developed with the MLP and RBFNconfigurations for rainfall-runoff model. The data from the first 2 years were employed for network training and the balanced data are employed for validation process [86] where the RBFN show much higher efficiency than the MLP during the validation process. Thus, RBFN appears to be better in rainfall-runoff analysis than MLP.

It is clear from the findings that the efficiency of forecast model depends on the type of network selected [86]. The minimal number of neurons in the MLP hidden layers is resolved after a prolonged repetitive process which yielded in less errors, while large repressors can be placed in the RBFN nodes using the orthogonal least squares (OLS) algorithm [83, 87]. The impact of the study reveals that the generalization characteristics of RBFN nodes in rainfall-runoff modeling are corporately limited with MLP [86].

2.3   AI in Solar Energy

2.3.1   Solar Power Forecasting

Solar radiation is a key parameter in the study of solar energy. But there are no proper modes measuring the solar radiation. So, at present, the solar radiation is measured using the different climatic parameters that are obtained from satellite and weather station data. Thus, the ANN [88] finds its significance in the prediction of solar radiation, using the data related to the meteorological and climatological. The types of ANN mainly employed are MLP [89] and back-propagation learning algorithm in the prediction of solar radiation [90]. Feed-forward, back-propagation algorithm [91], and adaptive model are used in hourly solar irradiance forecasting [92].

The ANN [93–98] fed with the input will first make the non-linear mapping to represent them in the form of biases and weighs. The basic ANN model will have the input layer that is inputted with the collected data, and then, output layer that sends the final data to the computer and multiple hidden layers. In multilayer neural network [95, 96], weights and transfer or activation function plays an important role. The net feed to active function is weights and input vectors scalar product. The activation function is fed to input and then to the output accordingly [95]. The formation of the ANN is followed by collecting the input data, selecting the architecture, learning algorithms, and the training-test set [97, 98].

The data related to 67 cities in India is collected from the Centre for Wind Energy and Technology (CWET), India, and Atmospheric Science Data Centre (ASDC) at NASA Langley Research Centre [99] that contains the 19 input variables for the period of 12 months [95]. Eight complete months are reserved for training, whereas the remaining months are for testing. Similar designs are pursued for other 67 cities. The MLP with three-layer structure is designed using the feed-forward back-propagation [95, 96]. The normalization method was used to set data and network. The minimum square error and regression values have been achieved. Thus, solar radiation in remote areas has less solar measurement sources.

The solar irradiance is beneficial in the study of balanced energy, atmosphere, thermal effect on buildings, and organization of power plants that operate on renewable source, agricultural, and also assessment of environmental behavior [100–103]. This leads to the growth of applications that are based on solar energy giving rise to increased requirement of accurate and prediction modeling of solar irradiance. This helps in monitoring and optimization of solar energy system operations. The computation models developed solar data forecasting are depending on the model accuracy and inputted data [104]. The ANN models forecasting solar irradiance in hourly basis are developed depending on the irradiance data represented in time series [101]. The solar irradiance ANNs developed were modeled using the three approaches that are based on the meteorological parameters [103–109], past observed data [110–113], and the combination of both the meteorological and past observed data [114–117]. Majority of these models forecast an hour ahead, with the major requirement of input is requirement of large meteorological parameters, and in some cases, the parameters are unavailable [102]. To overcome this issue, MLP network was introduced which can forecast one day in advance for the solar irradiance prediction.

The MLP was developed and tested using the data that was collected from the Italian city Trieste, as an application of forecasting the energy that was produced by Grid Connected Photovoltaic Plants (GCPV) established on the roof of Trieste municipality [118]. The data about the air temperature and solar irradiance was collected from the region from July 1st 2008 to May 23rd 2009 and from November 23rd 2009 to January 24th 2010 for developing MLP. The data collected was divided into training, validation, and test set. The parameters for architecture and training were selected [118]. The model was trained employing K-fold (K =10) for each training set. The developed model was then evaluated employing validation set for individual K-ford (K = 10). The process was repeated for different architectures and selected the suitable efficient architecture, tested it finally with the test set. The selection of the architecture depends on the activation function and neuron count in the hidden layer. The cross-validation is the technique used for predicting the efficiency of the model over the unseen data as feature yet [106].

A 24-hour ahead predicting MLP network was developed for solar irradiance forecasting. After many modeling, it was found that the best model for solar irradiation forecasting in Trieste was with the three neurons (TðtÞ; GðtÞ, t); one input layer, 11 and 17 neurons; two hidden layers and 24 neurons; and output layer [118]. That result ranges between 98% and 95% correlation coefficients for sunny days and cloudy days, respectively. A review of the power generated by a GCPV plant of 20 kWp and the one predicted using the established MLP-predictor demonstrated the effective forecasting for 4 sunny days (56 hours) [118]. Thus, the method implemented gave good insights in the planning of sustainable renewable systems operation.

The photovoltaic (PV) power systems with large-scale grid recently established around the world due to the evolution of PV technology [119]. The power that is generated by the PV systems heavily reliant on the change in the solar irradiance with the other factors of environment, the unpredictable change in the PV system results may drastically rise the service expenses of the electricity system [117]. So, the major responsibility of the grid operator is to identify the change in the power generated by the PV system and to plan the power of spinning reserve and for grid operations controlling. So, the operator for the transmission system adding online forecasting of power for the PV systems plays a major development of support system for energy trading, independent power production and energy services to deliver energy from different functions like trading of energy, assessment of security, and financial phrasing [119].

There are many researches going on to build the online forecasting model for PV power production. The most recent one is to have the two-stage approach. At first stage, solar irradiance is forecasted in various time scales based on ANNs, fuzzy logic (FL), hybrid systems [120, 121], and Auto Regressive (AR); the past data and meteorological data are employed in building the regression models. The models developed in the recent years are mostly based on the recurrent neural network [122, 123] that uses past historical data [118], hybrid models that is developed by integration of ANNs and wavelet analysis [119], multistage ANN [124], integration of ANN and library of Markov transition matrices [125], two-dimensional model approach [126], combination of special designed training algorithm and a diagonal recurrent wavelet neural network (DRWNN) [127]. At the second stage, the forecasted data that represents the temperature and irradiance are sourced to simulation based commercial PV software's like HOMER [128, 129], TRNSYS [130, 131], and PVFORM [132, 133]. The outcome of these is the simulated forecast data related to the AC power that is outputted from the PV system per hour. There are also some other models to forecast, that are produced using the weather data [134]. All these modules drastically increased their limitation as the solar PV systems increase from small scale to larger scale.

The recent research for forecasting the hourly data types for the present day and the next day using Fuzzy ART (Adaptive Resonance Theory), that showcases the energy from PV was built to interact the Distributed Intelligent Energy Management System (DIEMS) [135]. This model can forecast the power output only up to level seven, that makes it less accurate [119]. To overcome this limitation, the 24-hour ahead generated power is forecasted using a RBFN [119]. This RBFN will forecast the PV systems output power directly from the meteorological services and its past data. The numerical weather prediction (NWP) input variables are classified using the self-organized map (SOM) that increases the accuracy of forecasting [136]. The values that are predicted and the PV devices operating data are compared to verify the efficiency of the approach [119].

The radial basis function network model was applied on the PV system located in the Renewable Energy Research Centre (RERC), Huazhong University of Science and Technology (HUST) [119]. It can produce the highest power of 18 kW. The data related to the amount of power delivered to the grid in hourly basis (from December 19th 2006 to December 25th 2006) by PV system that is represented by supervisory control and data acquisition (SCADA) systems was collected along with the other climatically data like speed and direction of the wind, humidity, temperature, and pressure of the air, cloud, solar irradiance, and sunshine [119]. The radial basis function network model was developed from the data collected, resulting in the model output as the 24-hour ahead output power of the system. After many simulations, the excellent results were obtained from modeling having input layer and output layer with 6 and 24 neurons, respectively. These are having 11, 15, and 15 hidden nodes in the hidden neuron and 0.4, 0.3, and 0.1 spread values in three models (sunny, cloudy, and rainy), respectively [119]. The efficient results obtained from the proposed model shows its significance in using it for PV power systems output power forecasting, thus enabling effective planning of operation involved in PV system [119].

Solar had gained its attention due to its non-carbon generation property, and named as source of green energy. In recent years, the advancement of PV generation has led in the growth of capability of installation from 34% to 82% over history, for the Economic Co-operation and Development Organization [137]. But due to the change in the energy sources, it is difficult to determine the power that is outputted from the PV. So, the uncontrolled, non-deterministic output behavior of the PV plant leads in degradation of system by lowering the efficiency [138]. So, the best solution for this condition is to have a good prediction method for the output power of the large-scale PV system connected to grid that leads to the efficient operation of the system.

The prediction in PV system using neural network [139, 140] includes the neural network with the combination of fuzzy rules for solar irradiation forecasting [141]; integration of neural network and wavelet transform for hour ahead PV output power prediction [142], recurrent WNN for solar irradiation prediction [143], firefly algorithm, and fuzzy adaptive resonance theory mapping network with wavelet transform is used for prediction of power in solar [144]. Although there are several methods, each method has their own limitations, which affects the accuracy of the prediction of solar generation. This increases the demand for efficient prediction model. So, the new module that is the advanced version of the Shark Smell Optimization (SSO) algorithm [145] was introduced, called the metaheuristic optimization algorithm that will optimize the PV forecasting's free parameters, and therefore improving the search ability for both local and global.

The triple stage forecasting model based on neural network with the hydride framework for training with the combination of LM metaheuristic algorithm was developed for PV output prediction which overcomes the limitation of under and over fitting [146]. The prediction model was fed with the temperature, solar radiation and past 24-hour data related to the PV generation as input [142]. The feature selection model [147] with two cascaded filters has been employed for filtering the irrelevant inputs.

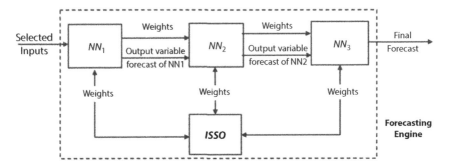

Figure 2.4 Cascaded systems of neural networks (ISSO). Reprint with copyright permission from [146].

The three neural networks with multilayer perceptron (MLP) architecture are trained to derive the mapping function for selected input and output vectors, that makes all three neural networks to use each of their weights by the another one. After learning, the neural network 1 will send its weight to neural network 2; the neural network 2 will learn better with more accuracy (for prediction) and send its weights to neural network 3; similarly, the neural network 3 will become more accurate in its efficiency of prediction. So, by increasing the number of neural networks in cascaded structure as shown in Figure 2.4, the efficiency of the model can be increased, that makes models accuracy negligible with respect to last neural network in the cascaded system [146].

The three neural networks are first trained using LMA, even though LMA is quick learning and efficient, it has the problem of local minima trapping leads to objective function's (OF) gradient as zero. So, after training with LMA, the resulting weights are fed to metaheuristic optimization algorithm. Based on the criterion of early stopping, each neural network's LMA state is terminated, in order to eliminate the issues of overfitting [148, 149]. The resulting neural network weights will be fed to improved SSO (ISSO) algorithm; the ISSO's has error of the neural network training, and thus, the local minimum problems of LMA are solved by ISSO [146].

The model is developed with the combination of two networks; one is the neural network. The other one is ISSO which was further applied on 15KW PV system that is situated in Ashland, Oregon of USA [150]. The efficacy of the metaheuristic algorithm proposed is assessed by correlation with six other algorithms, where the proposed model gave the most efficient results. This model can be used for the photo power forecasting in PV systems [146].

2.4   AI in Wind Energy

2.4.1   Wind Monitoring

A BPN was developed for checking the performance of a turbine rear bearing by means of SCADA [119] data. The collected information and analogy can be applied for similar turbines. The ANN was implemented for one component and would have been tested in abnormal conditions as well. An unambiguous turbine without gear box was monitored [151]. The technology has come across a gradual transition from fixed speed to variable speed. Pitch controlled has also become feasible to be analyzed in the place of stall controlled. Drive trains with gear boxes are being replaced by with/without gear box. Such transition was made possible with the help of power electronics. Detention of power has proven to be improved with grid and the mechanical stress was also reduced [152].

The convergent steepest descent algorithm has dual parts that include step size and direction of descent. LMA [52] that has Newton's method and steepest descent algorithm was handed down, which has the advantage of optimizing in a smaller number of steps with better accuracy. Condition Monitoring System (CMS) using ANN can be well explained by Figure 2.5. The imitation of the normal functioning parameters from the monitored data is realized by the ANN and simultaneous application of the detected anomaly. The ANN of single input with 20 neurons and one hidden layer was employed as a regular model. The Nonlinear Autoregressive Exogenous (NARX) ANN that has exogenous inputs was used in which Mahalanobis distance was used as a prediction technique in the anomaly detection. Thus, a turbine can be continuously monitored by which disastrous failure can be evaded 26 hours in advance [153].

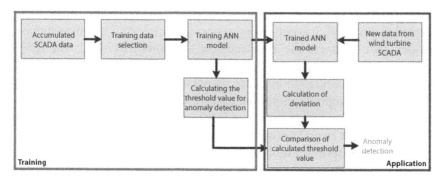

Figure 2.5 ANN-based condition monitoring method using SCADA data. Reprint with copyright permission from [153].

Genetic algorithm associated with multilayer autoregressive neural network, FL, and a SIMAP conquered a maintenance calendar based on the technical and financial standards [154]. Only the important aspects of interest would be presented to the operator in a succinct fashion out of large volume of SCADA data to make the fault detection easier [155].

Feed-forward ANN multiple hidden layers were tested for condition monitoring and NARX ANN accomplished the best performance monitoring [156].

2.4.2   Wind Forecasting

The dependency on non-renewable sources has to be reduced. The growing population and existing technologies consume lot of power from non-renewable sources which will soon result in extinction of non-renewable sources. Our need for electricity can be fulfilled only by renewable energy sources. Power systems can assimilate wind power in large scale by forecasting the speed of wind. Perfectness in the wind speed prediction is significant. The united technique of emplacement of electric power and wind patterns can improve the prediction of speed of wind [157]. MLP training algorithm can be used in the prediction of wind speed. The researchers' responsiveness toward MLP has increased due to its accomplishments of deep learning. The spatial weights can be added to the input and output weights of MLP, which is well suitable for environmental variables [158].

The 24-hour wind direction, air pressure, and wind speed statistics are collected in hourly basis from March to December. The data was fed to the algorithm for training and the output was resulting the successful prediction of the feature 24-hour wind speed in hourly basis and the wind speed for the next consecutive hours [159].

To forecast the wind speed, feed-forward and feedback ANNs are widely used [160]. Power generation using wind energy is improved in the United States [159]. It is obligatory to have a precise wind speed prediction models that enhances the assortment of locations [161, 162]. The ANN model using the mean squared error criterion for enhancement was tested in Savannah, Georgia. To estimate the wind speed, the ANN model was inputted with longitude, elevation, day, latitude, and min/max of temperature. The results are 95.2% accurate for the feed-forward and 93.2% accurate for feedback neural networks [163].

One of the important tools that can be used in the estimation of linear system parameters is Kalman filter. It necessitates the noise to be Gaussian white noise [164]. In order to spread over this recursive tool for non-linear applications, it needs proper modifications. The Ensemble Kalman Filter

(EnKF) is a method to predict wind speed. EnKF linearizes the mean and covariance in the non-linear predictions. Better results are proven to be achieved when EnKF is combined with ANN. Superlative estimation of wind speed by modifying the outputs of ANN using EnKF was one of the preeminent correction structures with better accuracy [165].

The physical, statistical and combined approaches of wind speed forecasting are analyzed and combined method was accepted as a better methodology for the estimation of wind energy. A type-2 fuzzifier was developed to transfigure the nonlinear approach into linear and applied to the MLP which can deal only with linear parameters. The vagueness in the inputs is deliberated by type-2 fuzzifier. The Particle Swarm Optimization (PSO) resolved the ambiguities of the measured parameters from SCADA. Thus, the computational cost has been condensed in the MLP which has only single layer [166]. In WNN, Mexican hat and Morlet wavelets are hidden layer activation functions. WNN is more advantageous over normal Feedforward networks in such a way that it provides greater simplification due to its adaptive wavelet shapes in conformity to the training statistics [167].

The momentary wind speed was predicted using ANN and the results are altered for the extrapolation of long-term applications with the additive advantages and properties of Markov chains [168]. More accurate prediction of wind power has been achieved by an ANN with LM optimization approach by considering the physical parameters like wind power, pressure, direction, and speed of wind at Jodhpur, Rajasthan in India [169].

A four-layer Recurrent MLP (RMLP) was employed in the prediction of wind power. The network was accomplished with Extended Kalman Filter for training back-propagation through time algorithm. The extremely dynamic altering wind power can be predicted using the combination of RMLP and Extended Kalman Filter [170].

2.5 AI in Geothermal Energy

The main sources of energy are renewable resources that include biomass, solar, wind energy and hydraulic energy [171, 172]. The basic issue in the renewable resources is that the energy from them is not baseload power generation. To make them baseload providers, the fixed amount of energy should be generated from the power stations, with the proper prediction mechanism [173]. Biomass and geothermal are invulnerable to peripheral weather conditions, so they can be used as basic sources of energy [174, 175].

Geothermal as heat energy is transmitted to ground level through hot water and steam. It is created based on the different heat generated inside the crust, atmospheric temperature and also due to the presence of various salts, gases, and minerals [176]. Therefore, the geothermal resources are more related to the temperature. In general, the resources with heavy temperature are employed in production of electricity. The resources with less and medium temperature are employed as direct fields [177]. In the recent research, resources with less temperature are also employed in applications with heat pumps. From 2010 to 2015, globally geothermal power and electricity generation raised 17% and 10%, respectively [174]. The countries like Philippines, USA, Mexico, New Zealand, and Indonesia occupy the top five places in the world in geothermal power and electricity production [177]. The Turkey's Energy Atlas states that it produces 921.5 MW of total installed power from 32 of geothermal power plants situated there, that contributed 1.2% to the total produced in 2016 [178]. The geothermal power production aims to meet the growing demands of USA that makes the major requirement of feasibility and optimum design configuration for geothermal power plant.

Increase in demand leads in increase of energy cost. So, the analysis of energy to identify the energy losses is necessary. Thus, the exergy diagnosis possesses the important role [179, 180]. The conventional exergy analysis cannot determine the proper dependency and independency between the systems components [177], that effects systems component's improvement. The recent research has focused on the development and use of advanced exergy analysis models for geothermal power plants [181–183].

The advanced exergy analysis models include ROSENB [184] optimization algorithm, organic ranking cycle (ORC) optimization [185], regenerative ORC optimization, Kalina cycle optimization, and thermal efficiency optimization using ANN and artificial bee colony (ABC) [186–188], supercritical ORC optimization with ANN [189], non-dominated sorting genetic algorithm-II (NSGA-II) for Rankina cycle [190], and PSO [191, 192].

The ABC model [174, 193–196] was developed to optimize the geothermal power plant's exergy efficiency. The model is assessed by comparing the results of developed model with conventional and advanced analysis methods [174]. By this, geothermal power plant with efficient exergy is designed. The developed model was implemented in geothermal field of Büyük Menderes basin continental rift belt in Turkey [174]. The model was used to optimize and analyze the performance of the binary geothermal power plant with respect to thermodynamical properties. The study suggests that there is a close match in exergy efficiency between advanced and ABC model. It can be concluded that advanced model analysis provides an arbitrary value, whereas ABC model provides a constraint limits that includes minimum and maximum ranges, which is no longer arbitrary [174].

In the recent world, the scarcity of renewable resources is increasing day by day that includes the geothermal energy. The geothermal energy is low temperature resource that generates more than 10% of power, through the geothermal power plants [197]. In the cold regions like Iceland, the 85% heat required is sourced by geothermal energy [198]. The less temperature thermodynamic cycle that is used as the working fluids in organic fluids is called ORC [199–202]. The advanced part of the ORC is Kalina power generation cycle [203–206], that uses ammonia with water as the working fluid, generate power from the unwanted heat [179, 207]. The rate of change in temperature in heat source with respect to working fluid that leads to exergy losses are relatively less in Kalina cycle [208, 209]. The properties of water, ammonia, and their mixture with respect to thermodynamics play a major role in the Kalina cycle [210–212]. The power produced by the kalian cycle through waste heat recovery is greater than the ORC [201]. There are many implementations of Kalina systems like solar Kalina cycle [186], Kalina power system [213], Kalina cycle with waste heat (low-temperature), and LNG cold energy as heat source and heat sink, respectively [214], and Kalina geothermal cycle used in a power plant [215–219]. The continuous monitoring of exergy and energy also plays a major role in the thermodynamic cycles, as the exergy study helps to assess the dropped pressure and heat that is transferred in thermodynamic system [218].

In the recent years, the optimization algorithms are mostly using in the applications of energy systems [219–222]. Using evolutionary algorithms, Kalina and ORC cycles have been commonly optimized to determine the best configuration for thermodynamic cycles [222]. The ABC algorithm [223, 224] is one among the advanced algorithm that helps to achieve the desired thermal and exercise efficiency of the Kalina geothermal cycle. It has advantages in multi-dimensional, multi-objective function, and multi-model issues compared with other popular optimizations techniques [219]. The ABC algorithm [220] as shown in Figure 2.6 has three mains components, namely, food source, employed bees, and the unemployed bees. The unemployed bees are of two types. They are scouts and onlookers [223–226].

The study was carried out on thermodynamic power plant–based geothermal Kalina cycle located in the Husavic power plant, Iceland. The analysis related to thermodynamic is done through the MATLAB. The thermodynamic characteristics of ammonia-water mixtures were measured using the EES software [227]. The ABC algorithm is developed for identifying the optimal exergy and thermal values. Ultimately, the data related

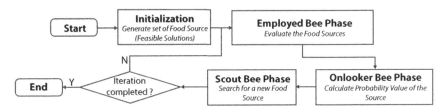

Figure 2.6 Procedure for Artificial Bee Colony (ABC) algorithm. Reprint with permission from [220].

to impact of temperature in separator inlet, mass function of ammonia, and working fluid's flow rate are analyzed [219]. The ABC algorithm has resulted in the behavior of achieving the thermal optimum efficiency. The algorithm may not obtain the appropriate random solution at the initial levels, to find the perfect thermal efficiency [219], but it can in 37 foraging cycles and the optimum thermal efficiency converges gradually. The final optimum thermal efficiency resulted in 20.36% [219].

The geothermal resources utilized for generating the electricity are extracted by boreholes which are deeply drilled in the thermal regions within the geothermal fields [228, 229]. Drilling of this borehole is a complicated task and it affects the initial rock formation around the borehole [230]. After borehole creation, thermal regeneration is assessed by examining shut-in measurements in time and build-up bottom-hole temperature (BHT) [231]. During the process of borehole drilling at various shut in times, the build-up BHT is calculated [232]. The build-up BHT utilizes the sophisticated logging equipment that makes it more costly [233, 234]. In the assessment of geothermal system, critical part is to analyze static formation temperature (SFTs) using the build-up BHT [235, 236].

The analysis of SFS data at early drilling time gives the opportunity to consider the temperature during the creation of virgin, months before the precision calculation [237]. This development helps for the planning, discovery, production and exploitation. The data related to the SFTs helps in many ways like identifying the geothermal gradient for exploration mapping, heat flow in geothermal region, lagging of borehole, difficulty, and design of the borehole and evaluate the properties of forming *in situ* thermo-physical [237].

The prediction of SFT in boreholes is executed by using the simplified method of analysis, that is based on the complicated heat transform method focused at the bottom-hole circumstances in which BHTs are in fact calculated. The calculations of the BHT appear to show the thermal anomalies [237]. There are many analysis methods like Brennand method [238],

Hornerplot method [239], Kutasov-Eppelbaum method [240], Leblanc method [241], and Manetti method [242]. Most of these models require minimum threw or even more observations of BHT in various shut-in times at the same depth of borehole. The SFT identification in this method is done through the mathematical modeling using the input of BHT and shut in time, data related to non-linear and linear part between BHT and each methods time function [243, 244]. Although the effective progress is achieved in recent years in this area, there is a wide difference between the results from the various methods [245]. Therefore, the advanced development of modern, reliable technique to predict SFT is still a difficult task. So, to overcome the complexity [246] in the prediction process, the ANN is developing as a new stable model to measure SFTs in geothermal wells.

ANN as the effective computational technique, applied in various sciences as a modeling tool, addressed many real-world complex issues mainly as a forecasting tool [247]. In the recent research, the application of ANN is found to be increasing drastically in earth sciences [248–252], geothermal, and petroleum engineering [252–256]. The new three-layer ANN was developed to predict the SFT in geothermal wells. It was trained with the database related to the estimated SFT (statistically normal) in geothermal borehole that includes data related to the build-up thermal recovery analyzed during the borehole drilling [237]. The build-up thermal recovery data contains shunt in time and BHT values and transient gradient of temperature. The estimated calculation of SFT value is done through seven analytical methods [237]. The normalization of SFT is done using statistical tests [245], mean SFT, and regular estimated deviations are measured using enhanced outlier identification/statistical process of rejection [257]. The statistical method integrated with ANN approach helps to detect the errors in the result and it also rejects prior to choosing a suitable SFT estimates [237]. The evaluation of the ANN model developed is done using set of four BHU data, for which the SFT was already known. The accuracy assessment of the ANN model was carried out using these validation tests [237].

The new ANN model developed using the multilayer layer and feed-forward architecture has more advantages than analytical method, as it requires BHT and shut-in time as the input mainly [237]. The prediction model is validated by comparing SFT measured and stimulated, that shows the errors less than ±5%. The ANN model proposed can be a functional method for estimating SFT in boreholes. The forecasting accuracy of the ANN model can be increased by using the patterns with more BHT data. The concept of introducing ANN for SFT prediction enables new faster and practical tool for geothermal industry [237].

2.6   Conclusion

This chapter is an overview of the proper utilization of renewable resources like water, solar, wind, and geothermal energy. It also discusses the various forecasting methods using AI approaches in the monitoring, analyses, modeling, and optimization of these renewable sources. The critical findings of this review are summarized as follows.

- WOA has found to be more promising in ground water level forecasting due to its capability of handling many parameters at a time and can be easily paired with other algorithms.
- A back-propagation model with three layers acts as an effective supportive system for drought management.
- LMA gives effective results in ground water level prediction where limited information of hydrological parameters is available.
- GDX method is the most supportive system for long term (1 week) prediction of ground water that helps in effective planning and utilization of groundwater.
- RBFN exhibits better accuracy for rainfall-runoff analysis.
- BR algorithm works well when there is increase of neurons in the hidden layer and performs well for small and big networks.
- Radial basis function networkalong with SOM is found to be the one of the most accurate algorithms in forecasting the output power of PV systems.
- MLP with three-layer structure designed using Feed-Forward Back-Propagation provides better forecasting of solar radiation in remote areas that has less solar measurement sources.
- NARX ANN model is one of the best suitable models for continuous monitoring of wind turbine in which the fault is predicted 26 hours in advance.
- A combined approach of type 2 FNN accompanied by PSO in the SCADA input data of a MLP can be utilized for better estimation of wind power.
- ABC algorithm provides better thermal efficiency in geothermal plants.

This chapter presents a comprehensive work on the restoration of renewable sources using various AI techniques. As a future scope, the research should be focused on more AI algorithms which can provide improved performance methods with enhanced predictions.

References

1. Marques, A.C. and Fuinhas, J.A., Is renewable energy effective in promoting growth? *Energy Policy*, 46, 434–442, 2012.
2. Gielen, D., Boshell, F., Saygin, D., Bazilian, M.D., Wagner, N., Gorini, R., The role of renewable energy in the global energy transformation. *Energy Strategy Rev.*, 24, 38–50, 2019.
3. Sinha, S. and Chandel, S.S., Review of software tools for hybrid renewable energy systems. *Renewable Sustainable Energy Rev.*, 32, 192–205, 2014.
4. Şen, Z., Solar energy in progress and future research trends. *Prog. Energy Combust. Sci.*, 30, 4, 367–416, 2004.
5. Demirbaş, A., Global Renewable Energy Resources. *Energy Sources Part A: Recovery Util. Environ. Eff.*, 28, 8, 779–792, 2006.
6. Scheierling, S.M., Loomis, J.B., Young, R.A., Irrigation water demand: A meta-analysis of price elasticities. *Water Resour. Res.*, 42, 1, 1–9, 2006.
7. Wisser, D., Frolking, S., Douglas, E.M., Fekete, B.M., Vörösmarty, C.J., Schumann, A.H., Global irrigation water demand: Variability and uncertainties arising from agricultural and climate data sets. *Geophys. Res. Lett.*, 35, 24, 1–5, 2008.
8. Sharma, S.K. and Vairavamoorthy, K., Urban water demand management: prospects and challenges for the developing countries. *Water Environ. J.*, 23, 3, 210–218, 2009.
9. Wada, Y., van Beek, L.P.H., Viviroli, D., Dürr, H.H., Weingartner, R., Bierkens, M.F.P., Global monthly water stress: 2. Water demand and severity of water stress. *Water Resour. Res.*, 47, 7, 1–17 2011.
10. Giwa, A., Alabi, A., Yusuf, A., Olukan, T., A comprehensive review on biomass and solar energy for sustainable energy generation in Nigeria. *Renewable Sustainable Energy Rev.*, 69, 620–641, 2017.
11. Dike, V.N., Chineke, T.C., Nwofor, O.K., Okoro, U.K., Optimal angles for harvesting solar electricity in some African cities. *Renewable Energy*, 39, 433–9, 2012.
12. Onuegbu, T.U., Ilochi, N.O., Ogbu, I.M., Obumselu, F.O., Okafor, I., Preparation of environmental friendly bio-coal briquette from groundnut shell and maize cob biomass waste: comparative effects of ignition time and water boiling studies. *Curr. Res. Chem.*, 4, 110–8, 2012.
13. Ayodele, O.O. and Dawodu, F.A., Production of biodiesel from Calophylluminophyllum oil using a cellulose-derived catalyst. *Biomass- Bioenergy*, 70, 239–48, 2014.

14. Jha, S.K., Bilalovic, J., Jha, A., Patel, N., Zhang, H., Renewable energy: Present research and future scope of Artificial Intelligence. *Renewable Sustainable Energy Rev.*, 77, 297–317, 2017.

15. Karki, R. and Billinton, R., Reliability/cost implications of PV and wind energy utilization in small isolated power systems. *IEEE Trans. Energy Convers.*, 16, 4, 368–373, Dec. 2001.

16. Murat, A.Y. and Ozyildirim, S., Artificial Intelligence (AI) studies in water resources. *Nat. Eng. Sci.*, 3, 2, 187–195, 2018.

17. Sheldon, R.A., Utilisation of biomass for sustainable fuels and chemicals: Molecules, methods and metrics. *Catal. Today*, 167, 1, 3–13, 2011.

18. Ehteram, M., Afan, H.A., Dianatikhah, M., Ahmed, A.N., Fai, C.M., Hossain, M.S. *et al.*, Assessing the predictability of an improved ANFIS model for monthly streamflow using lagged climate indices as predictors. *Water*, 11, 6, 1130, 2019a.

19. Ehteram, M., Singh, V.P., Ferdowsi, A., Mousavi, S.F., Farzin, S., Karami, H. *et al.*, An improved model based on the support vector machine and cuckoo algorithm for simulating reference evapotranspiration. *PLoS One*, 14, 5, e0217499, 2019b.

20. Ghorbani, M.A., Deo, R.C., Karimi, V., Yaseen, Z.M., Terzi, O., Implementation of a hybrid MLP-FFA model for water level prediction of Lake Egirdir, Turkey. *Stochastic Environ. Res. Risk Assess.*, 32, 6, 1683–1697, 2018.

21. Lee, S., Lee, K.-K., Yoon, H., Using artificial neural network models for groundwater level forecasting and assessment of the relative impacts of influencing factors. *Hydrogeol. J.*, 27, 2, 567–579, 2018.

22. Nistor, M.-M., Vulnerability of groundwater resources under climate change in the Pannonian basin. *Geo-Spatial Inf. Sci.*, 22, 4, 345–358, 2019.

23. Yaseen, Z.M., Allawi, M.F., Karami, H., Ehteram, M., Farzin, S., Ahmed, A.N. *et al.*, A hybrid bat–swarm algorithm for optimizing dam and reservoir operation. *Neural Comput. Appl.*, 31, 1–15, 2019.

24. Mehne, H.H. and Mirjalili, S., A parallel numerical method for solving optimal control problems based on whale optimization algorithm. *Knowledge-Based Syst.*, 151, 114–123, 2018.

25. Hasanien, H.M., Performance improvement of photovoltaic power systems using an optimal control strategy based on whale optimization algorithm. *Electr. Power Syst. Res.*, 157, 168–176, 2018.

26. Yıldız, B.S. and Yıldız, A.R., Comparison of grey wolf, whale, water cycle, ant lion and sine-cosine algorithms for the optimization of a vehicle engine connecting rod. *Mater. Test.*, 60, 3, 311–315, 2018.

27. Banadkooki, F.B., Ehteram, M., Ahmed, A.N. *et al.*, Enhancement of Groundwater-Level Prediction Using an Integrated Machine Learning Model Optimized by Whale Algorithm. *Nat. Resour. Res.*, 29, 3233–3252, 2020.

28. Sahu, P.R., Hota, P.K., Panda, S., Modified whale optimization algorithm for fractional-order multi-input SSSC-based controller design. *Optim. Control Appl. Methods*, 39, 5, 1802–1817, 2018.
29. Dracup, J.A., Lee, K.S., Paulson, E.G., Jr, on the definition of droughts. *Water Resour. Res.*, 16, 2, 297–302, 1980.
30. Wilhite, D.A. and Dinar, A., Understanding the drought phenomenon: the role of definitions. *Water Int.*, 10, 3, 111–120, 1985.
31. Vaux, H.J. and Pruit, W.O., Crop–water production functions, in: *Advances in irrigation*, vol. 2, D. Hillel (Ed.), pp. 61–97, Academic, New York, 1983.
32. Howell, T., Relationship between crop production and transpiration, evaporation and irrigation, in: *Irrigation of agricultural crops, agronomy monograph No. 30 ASA*, B.A. Steward and D.R. Neilson (Eds.), pp. 391–434, CSSA and SSSA, Madison, WI, 1990.
33. Carson, D.J., Seasonal forecasting. *J. R. Meteorol. Soc.*, 124, 1–26, 1998.
34. Goddard, L., Mason, S.J., Zebiak, S.E., Ropelewski, C.F., Basher, R., Cane, M.A., Current approaches to seasonal-to-interannual climate predictions. *Int. J. Climatol.*, 21, 1111–1152, 2001.
35. Desalegn, C.E., Babel, M.S., Gupta, A.D., Seleshi, B.A., Merrey, D., Farmers' perception of water management under drought conditions in the Upper Awash Basin, Ethiopia. *Int. J. Water Resour. Dev.*, 22, 4, 589–602, 2006.
36. Desalegn, C.E., Babel, M.S., Gupta, A.D., Drought analysis in the Awash River Basin, Ethiopia. *Water Resour. Manage.*, 24, 7, 1441–1460, 2010.
37. Edossa, D.C. and Babel, M.S., Application of ANN-Based Streamflow Forecasting Model for Agricultural Water Management in the Awash River Basin, Ethiopia. *Water Resour. Manage.*, 25, 6, 1759–1773, 2011.
38. Yaseen, Z.M., El-shafie, A., Jaafar, O., Afan, H.A., Sayl, K.N., Artificial intelligence based models for stream-flow forecasting: 2000–2015. *J. Hydrol.*, 530, 829–844, 2015.
39. Ethiopian Valleys Development Studies Authority, *Amibara irrigation project II: inception report for technical support services*, Halcrow-ULG Ltd, UK, 1979.
40. Nash, J.E. and Sutcliffe, J.V., River flow forecasting through conceptual models. Part-I: A discussion of principles. *J. Hydrol.*, 10, 282–290, 1970.
41. Savic, D.A., Walters, G.A., Davidson, J.W., A Genetic Programming Approach to Rainfall-Runoff Modeling. *Water Resour. Manage.*, 13, 3, 219–231, 1999.
42. Tokar, A.S. and Markus, M., Precipitation runoff modeling using artificial neural network and conceptual models. *J. Hydrol. Eng.*, 2, 156–161, 2000.
43. Chen, Z., Stephen, E.G., Kirk, G.O., Predicting average annual groundwater levels from climatic variables: an empirical model. *J. Hydrol.*, 260, 102–117, 2002.
44. Bierkens, M.F.P., Modeling water table fluctuations by means of a stochastic differential equation. *Water Resour. Res.*, 34, 2485–2499, 1998.
45. Knotters, M. and Bierkens, M.F.P., Physical basis of time series models for water table depths. *Water Resour. Res.*, 36, 1, 181–188, 2000.

46. Daliakopoulos, I.N., Coulibaly, P., Tsanis, I.N., Groundwater level forecasting using artificial neural networks. *J. Hydrol.*, 309, 229–240, 2005.

47. Nayak, P.C., Satyaji Rao, Y.R., Sudheer, K.P., Groundwater level forecasting in a shallow aquifer using artificial neural network approach. *Water Resour. Manage.*, 20, 77–90, 2006.

48. Krishna, B., Satyaji Rao, Y.R., Vijaya, T., Modelling groundwater levels in an urban coastal aquifer using artificial neural networks. *Hydrol. Processes*, 22, 8, 1180–1188, 2008.

49. Du, K.-L. and Swamy, M.N.S., Radial Basis Function Networks, in: *Neural Networks and Statistical Learning*, pp. 299–335, 2013.

50. Do, L.N.N., Taherifar, N., Vu, H.L., Survey of neural network-based models for short-term traffic state prediction. *Wiley Interdiscip. Rev.: Data Min. Knowl. Discovery*, 9, e1285, 2018.

51. Alciaturi, C.E. and Quevedo, G., Bayesian regularization: application to calibration in NIR spectroscopy. *J. Chemom.*, 23, 11, 562–568, 2009.

52. Mirzaee, H., Long-term prediction of chaotic time series with multi-step prediction horizons by a neural network with Levenberg–Marquardt learningalgorithm. *Chaos, Solitons Fractals*, 41, 4, 1975–1979, 2009.

53. ASCE Task Committee, artificial neural networks in hydrology- I: preliminary concepts. *J. Hydrol. Eng. ASCE*, 5, 2, 115–123, 2000a.

54. Haykin, S., *Neural networks: a comprehensive foundation*, 2nd edn, Prentice Hall, Englewood Cliffs, 1999.

55. He, Z., Zhang, Y., Guo, Q., Zhao, X., Comparative study of artificial neural networks and wavelet artificial neural networks for groundwater depth data forecasting with various curve fractal dimensions. *Water Resour. Manage.*, 28, 5297–5317, 2014.

55. Coppola, E.A., Rana, A.J., Poulton, M.M., Szidarovszky, F., Uhl, V.W., A neural network model for predicting aquifer water level elevations. *Ground Water*, 43, 2, 231–241, 2005.

56. Mohanty, S., Jha, M.K., Raul, S.K., Panda, R.K., Sudheer, K.P., Using Artificial Neural Network Approach for Simultaneous Forecasting of Weekly Groundwater Levels at Multiple Sites. *Water Resour. Manage.*, 29, 15, 5521–5532, 2015.

57. Maier, H.R. and Dandy, G.C., neural networks for prediction and forecasting of water resources variables: a review of modeling issue and application. *Environ. Model. Software*, 15, 101–124, 2000.

58. Hou, A., Jin, S., Harmuth, H., Gruber, D., Thermal and Thermomechanical Responses Prediction of a Steel Ladle Using a Back-Propagation Artificial Neural Network Combining Multiple Orthogonal Arrays. *Steel Res. Int.*, 90, 1900116, 2019.

59. Rhoades, S. and Walski, T., Using Regression Analysis to Project Pumpage. *J. AWWA*, 83, 12:45, 1991.

60. Steiner, R.C. and Smith, J.A., Short-term Municipal Water Use Forecasting. *ASCE Natl. Specialty Conf.*, Tampa, Fla, 1983.

61. Garret, J.H. and Ghaboussi, X., Neural Networks, in: *Expert Systems for Civil Engineers: Knowledge Representation*, R.H. Allen (Ed.), ASCE, New York, 1991.
62. Crommelynck, V. *et al.*, Daily and Hourly Water Consumption Forecasting Tools Using Neural Networks. *Proc. 1992 AWWA Computer Specialty Conf.*, Nashville, Tenn, 1992.
63. Hegazy, T., Fazio, P., Moselhi, O., Developing Practical Neural Network Applications Using Back-Propagation. *Comput.-Aided Civ. Infrastruct. Eng.*, 9, 2, 145–159, 1994.
64. Ciampi, A. and Zhang, F., A new approach to training back-propagation artificial neural networks: empirical evaluation on ten data sets from clinical studies. *Stat. Med.*, 21, 9, 1309–1330, 2002.
65. Jain, A. and Ormsbee, L.E., Short-term water demand forecast modeling techniques-Conventional Methods versus AI. *J. Am. Water Works Assoc.*, 94, 7, 64–72, 2002.
66. Todd, D.K. and Mays, L.W., *Groundwater hydrology*, 3rd edn, Wiley, Hoboken, 2005.
67. IWMI, *The strategic plan for IWMI 2000-2005*, p. 28, International Water Management Institute (IWMI), Colombo, 2001.
68. Kalf, F.R.P. and Woolley, D.R., Applicability and methodology for determining sustainable yield in groundwater systems. *Hydrogeol. J.*, 13, 1, 295–312, 2005.
69. Alley, W.M. and Leake, S.A., The journey from safe yield to sustainability. *Ground Water*, 42, 1, 12–16, 2004.
70. Sophocleous, M., Groundwater recharge and sustainability in the high plains aquifer in Kansas, USA. *Hydrogeol. J.*, 13, 2, 351–365, 2005.
71. Coppola, E.A., Rana, A.J., Poulton, M.M., Szidarovszky, F., Uhl, V.W., A neural network model for predicting aquifer water level elevations. *Ground Water*, 43, 2, 231–241, 2005.
72. French, M.N., Krajewski, W.F., Cuykendall, R.R., Rainfall forecasting in space and time using neural network. *J. Hydrol.*, 137, 1–31, 1992.
73. Bishop, C.M., *Neural networks for pattern recognition*, Oxford University Press, New York, 1995.
74. Mackay, D.J.C., A practical Bayesian framework for backpropagation networks. *Neural Comput.*, 4, 3, 448–472, 1991.
75. Porter, D.W., Gibbs, P.G., Jones WF Huyakorn, P.S., Hamm, L.L., Flach, G.P., Data fusion modeling for groundwater systems. *J. Contam. Hydrol.*, 42, 303–335, 2000.
76. Mohanty, S., Jha, M.K., Kumar, A., Sudheer, K.P., Artificial Neural Network Modeling for Groundwater Level Forecasting in a River Island of Eastern India. *Water Resour. Manage.*, 24, 9, 1845–1865, 2009.
77. Mohanty, S., Jha, M.K., Kumar, A., James, B.K., Groundwater scenario in Kathajodi River basin of Orissa. *Proceedings of workshop on groundwater*

scenario and quality in Orissa, Bhubaneswar, Orissa, India, 6–7 March 2009, pp. 82–90, 2009.

78. Coulibaly, P., Anctil, F., Bobee, B., Daily reservoir inflow forecasting using artificial neural networks with stopped training approach. *J. Hydrol.*, 230, 244–257, 2000.

79. Coulibaly, P., Anctil, F., Aravena, R., Bobee, B., Artificial neural network modeling of water table depth fluctuations. *Water Resour. Res.*, 37, 4, 885–896, 2001.

80. Guan, C. and Yang, Y., Research of extraction behavior of heavy metal Cd in tea based on backpropagation neural network. *Food Sci. Nutr.*, 8, 2 , 1067–1074.

81. Hornik, K., Stinchcombe, M., White, H., Multilayer feedforward networks are universal approximators. *Neural Networks*, 2, 5, 359–366, 1989.

82. Sudheer, K.P., *Modeling hydrological processes using neural computing technique*. PhD thesis, Indian Institute of Technology, Delhi, India, 2000.

83. Fernando, D.A.K. and Jayawardena, A.W., Runoff Forecasting Using RBF Networks with OLS Algorithm. *J. Hydrol. Eng.*, 3, 3, 203–209, 1998.

84. Chen, S., Cowan, C.F.N., Grant, P.M., Orthogonal least squares learning algorithm for radial basis function networks. *IEEE Trans. Neural Networks*, 2, 2, 302–309, 1991.

85. Ferre, L. and Villa, N., Multilayer Perceptron with Functional Inputs: an Inverse Regression Approach. *Scand. J. Stat.*, 33, 4, 807–823, 2006.

86. Senthil Kumar, A.R., Sudheer, K.P., Jain, S.K., Agarwal, P.K., Rainfall-runoff modelling using artificial neural networks: comparison of network types. *Hydrol. Processes*, 19, 6, 1277–1291, 2005.

87. Sherstinsky, A. and Picard, R.W., On the efficiency of the orthogonal least squares training method for radial basis function networks. *IEEE Trans. Neural Networks*, 7, 1, 195–200, Jan. 1996.

88. Yadav, A.K., Malik, H., Chandel, S.S., Application of rapid miner in ANN based prediction of solar radiation for assessment of solar energy resource potential of 76 sites in Northwestern India. *Renewable Sustainable Energy Rev.*, 52, 1093–1106, 2015.

89. Curteanu, S. and Cartwright, H., Neural networks applied in chemistry. I. Determination of the optimal topology of multilayer perceptron neural networks. *J. Chemom.*, 25, 10, 527–549, 2011.

90. Azadeh, A., Maghsoudi, A., Sohrabkhani, S., Using an integrated artificial neural networks model for predicting global radiation: the case study of Iran. *Energy Convers. Manage.*, 50, 6, 1497–1505, 2009.

91. Hasni, A. *et al.*, Estimating global solar radiation using artificial neural network and climate data in the south-western region of Algeria. *Energy Proc.*, 18, 531–537, 2012.

92. Mellit, A. *et al.*, An adaptive model for predicting of global, direct and diffuse hourly solar irradiance. *Energy Convers. Manage.*, 51, 771–782, 2010.

93. Yao, X., A review of evolutionary artificial neural networks. *Int. J. Intell. Syst.*, 8, 4, 539–567, 1993.
94. Abraham, A., Artificial Neural Networks, in: *Handbook of Measuring System Design*, 2005.
95. Malik, H. and Garg, S., Long-Term Solar Irradiance Forecast Using Artificial Neural Network: Application for Performance Prediction of Indian Cities, in: *Applications of Artificial Intelligence Techniques in Engineering*, pp. 285–293, 2018.
96. Yadav, A.K., Malik, H., Chandel, S.S., Selection of most relevant input parameters using WEKA for artificial neural network based solar radiation prediction models. *Sustainable Energy Rev.*, 31, 509–519, 2014.
97. Yadav, A.K., Sharma, V., Malik, H., Chandel, S.S., Daily array yield prediction of grid-interactive photovoltaic plant using relief attribute evaluator based radial basis function neural network. *Renewable Sustainable Energy Rev.*, 81, 2, 2115–2127, 2018.
98. Malik, H., Yadav, A.K., Mishra, S., Mehto, T., Application of neuro-fuzzy scheme to investigate the winding insulation paper deterioration in oil-immersed power transformer. *Electr. Power Energy Syst.*, 53, 256–271, 2013.
99. https://eosweb.larc.nasa.gov–Atmospheric Science Data Center (ASDC) at NASA Langley Research Center. Retrieved on Jan 2021.
100. Wong, L.T. and Chow, W.K., Solar radiation model. *Appl. Energy*, 69, 3, 191–224, 2001.
101. Muneer, T., Younes, S., Munawwar, S., Discourses on solar radiation modeling. *Renewable Sustainable Energy Rev.*, 11, 4, 551–602, 2007.
102. Mellit, A. and Kalogirou, S.A., Artificial intelligence techniques for photovoltaic applications: A review. *Prog. Energy Combust. Sci.*, 34, 5, 574–632, 2008.
103. *Solar Energy Fundamentals and Modeling Techniques*, Springer Verlag, London, 2008.
104. Paulescu, M., Paulescu, E., Gravila, P., Badescu, V., Modeling Solar Radiation at the Earth Surface, in: *Green Energy and Technology*, pp. 127–179, 2012.
105. Computational Intelligence in Time Series Forecasting, in: *Advances in Industrial Control*, 2005.
106. Elizondo, D., Hoogenboom, G., McClendon, R., Development of a neural network model to predict daily solar radiation. *Agric. For. Meteorol.*, 71, 1–2, 115–132, 1994.
107. Mohandes, M., Rehman, S., Halawani, T.O., Estimation of global solar radiation using artificial neural networks. *Renewable Energy*, 14, 1–4, 179–184, 1998.
108. Şen, Z., Fuzzy algorithm for estimation of solar irradiation from sunshine duration. *Sol. Energy*, 63, 1, 39–49, 1998.
109. Al-Alawi, S.M. and Al-Hinai, H.A., An ANN-based approach for predicting global radiation in locations with no direct measurement instrumentation. *Renewable Energy*, 14, 1–4, 199–204, 1998.

110. Kemmoku, Y., Orita, S., Nakagawa, S., Sakakibara, T., Daily Insolation Forecasting Using a Multi-Stage Neural Network. *Sol. Energy*, 66, 3, 193–199, 1999.

111. Sfetsos, A. and Coonick, A.H., Univariate and multivariate forecasting of hourly solar radiation with artificial intelligence techniques. *Sol. Energy*, 68, 2, 169–178, 2000.

112. Mihalakakou, G., Santamouris, M., Asimakopoulos, D.N., The total solar radiation time series simulation in Athens, using neural networks. *Theor. Appl. Clim.*, 66, 3–4, 185–197, 2000.

113. Cao, S. and Cao, J., Forecast of solar irradiance using recurrent neural networks combined with wavelet analysis. *Appl. Therm. Eng.*, 25, 2–3, 161–172, 2005.

114. Hontoria, L., Aguilera, J., Zufiria, P., Generation of hourly irradiation synthetic series using the neural network multilayer perceptron. *Sol. Energy*, 72, 5, 441–446, 2002.

115. Hontoria, L., Aguilera, J., Zufiria, P., An application of the multilayer perceptron: Solar radiation maps in Spain. *Sol. Energy*, 79, 5, 523–530, 2005.

116. Mellit, A., Kalogirou, S.A., Shaari, S., Salhi, H., Hadj Arab, A., Methodology for predicting sequences of mean monthly clearness index and daily solar radiation data in remote areas: Application for sizing a stand-alone PV system. *Renewable Energy*, 33, 7, 1570–1590, 2008.

117. Mellit, A., Artificial Intelligence technique for modelling and forecasting of solar radiation data: a review. *Int. J. Artif. Intell. Soft Comput.*, 1, 1, 52, 2008.

118. Mellit, A. and Pavan, A.M., A 24-h forecast of solar irradiance using artificial neural network: Application for performance prediction of a grid-connected PV plant at Trieste, Italy. *Sol. Energy*, 84, 5, 807–821, 2010.

119. Chen, C., Duan, S., Cai, T., Liu, B., Online 24-h solar power forecasting based on weather type classification using artificial neural network. *Sol. Energy*, 85, 11, 2856–2870, 2011.

120. Bacher, P., Madsen, H., Nielsen, H.A., Online short-term solar power forecasting. *Sol. Energy*, 83, 10, 1772–1783, 2009.

121. Mellit, A., Benghanem, M., Arab, A.H., Guessoum, A., A simplified model for generating sequences of global solar radiation data for isolated sites: using artificial neural network and a library of Markov transition matrices approach. *Sol. Energy*, 79, 5, 469–482, 2005.

122. Yona, A., Senjyu, T., Funabashi, T., Application of recurrent neural network to short-term-ahead generating power forecasting for photovoltaic system. In: 2007. *IEEE Power Engineering Society General Meeting*, pp. 3659–3664, 2007.

123. Cao, J.C. and Cao, S.H., Study of forecasting solar irradiance using neural networks with preprocessing sample data by wavelet analysis. *Energy*, 31, 15, 3435–3445, 2006.

124. Kemmoku, Y., Orita, S., Nakagawa, S., Sakakibara, T., Daily insolation forecasting using a multi-stage neural network. *Sol. Energy*, 66, 3, 193–199, 1999.

125. Mellit, A., Benghanem, M., Arab, A.H., Guessoum, A., A simplified model for generating sequences of global solar radiation data for isolated sites: using artificial neural network and a library of Markov transition matrices approach. *Sol. Energy*, 79, 5, 469–482, 2005.

126. Hocaoglu, F.O., Gerek, O.N., Kurban, M., Hourly solar radiation forecasting using optimal coefficient 2-D linear filters and feed-forward neural networks. *Sol. Energy*, 82, 8, 714–726, 2008.

127. Cao, J. and Lin, X., Application of the diagonal recurrent wavelet neural network to solar irradiation forecast assisted with fuzzy technique. *Eng. Appl. Artif. Intell.*, 21, 8, 1255–1263, 2008.

128. Lambert, T. and Lilienthal, P., *HOMER: the micro-power optimisation model*, Software Produced by NREL, USA, Available from:2004; 2004.

129. Dalton, G.J., Lockington, D.A., Baldock, T.E., Feasibility analysis of renewable energy supply options for a grid-connected large hotel. *Renewable Energy*, 34, 4, 955–964, 2009.

130. Alamsyah, T.M.I., Sopian, K., Shahrir, A., Predicting average energy conversion of photovoltaic system in Malaysia using a simplified method. *Renewable Energy*, 29, 3, 403–411, 2004.

131. TRNSYS, A transient simulation program. EES Rep.38, University of Wisconsin, Madison, 1973.

132. Ropp, M.E., Begovic, M., Rohatgi, A., Long, R., Design Considerations for Large Roof-integrated Photovoltaic Arrays. *Prog. Photovoltaics: Res. Appl.*, 5, 1, 55–67, 1997.

133. Menicucci, D.F. and Fernandez, J.P., *User's Manual for PVFORM: Photovoltaic System Simulation Program for Stand-Alone and Grid-Interactive Applications*, Sandia National Laboratories Publication SAND85±0376, October 1989.

134. Zhou, W., Yang, H., Fang, Z., A novel model for photovoltaic array performance prediction. *Appl. Energy*, 84, 12, 1187–1198, 2007.

135. Chakraborty, S., Weiss, M.D., Simoes, M.G., Distributed Intelligent Energy Management System for a Single-Phase High-Frequency AC Microgrid. *IEEE Trans. Ind. Electron.*, 54, 1, 97–109, 2007.

136. Sideratos, G. and Hatziargyriou, N.D., An advanced statistical method for wind power forecasting. *IEEE Trans. Power Syst.*, 22, 1, 258–365, 2007.

137. Pelland, S., Remund, J., Kleissl, J., Oozeki, T., Brabandere, K.D., Photovoltaic and Solar Forecasting: State of the Art. IEA PVPS Task 14, Subtask 3.1, Report IEA-PVPS T14-01, The International Energy Agency (IEA), USA, October 2013.

138. Lorenz, E., Hurka, J., Heinemann, D., Beyer, H.G., Irradiance forecasting for the power prediction of grid-connected photovoltaic systems. *IEEE J. Sel. Top. Appl. Earth Obs. Remote Sens.*, 2, 1, 2–10, 2009.

139. Reikard, G., Predicting solar radiation at high resolutions: a comparison of time series forecasts. *Sol. Energy*, 83, 3, 342–349, 2009.

140. Al-Alawi, S. and Al-Hinai, H., An ANN-based approach for predicting global radiation in locations with no direct measurement instrumentation. *Renewable Energy*, 14, 14, 199–204, 1998.

141. Chaabene, M. and Ammar, M.B., Neuro-fuzzy dynamic model with Kalman filter to forecast irradiance and temperature for solar energy systems. *Renewable Energy*, 33, 7, 1435–1443, 2008.

142. Mandal, P., Madhira, S.T.S., Haque, A.U., Meng, J., Pineda, R.L., Forecasting power output of solar photovoltaic system using wavelet transform and artificial intelligence techniques. *Proc. Comput. Sci.*, 12, 332–337, 2012.

143. Cao, J. and Lin, X., Study of hourly and daily solar irradiation forecast using diagonal recurrent wavelet neural networks. *Energy Convers. Manage.*, 49, 6, 1396–1406, 2008.

144. Haque, A.U., Nehrir, M.H., Mandal, P., Solar PV power generation forecast using a hybrid intelligent approach. Paper presented at: *Power and Energy Society General Meeting (PES)*, Vancouver, BC, 2013.

145. Abedinia, O., Amjady, N., Ghasemi, A., A new meta-heuristic algorithm based on shark smell optimization. *Complex J.*, 21, 5, 97–116, 2016.

146. Abedinia, O., Amjady, N., Ghadimi, N., Solar energy forecasting based on hybrid neural network and improved metaheuristic algorithm. *Comput. Intell.*, 34, 1, 241–260, 2017, doi: 10.1111/coin.12145.

147. Amjady, N. and Keynia, F., A new prediction strategy for price spike forecasting of day-ahead electricity markets. *Appl. Soft Comput.*, 11, 6, 4246–4256, 2011.

148. Amjady, N. and Keynia, F., Day-ahead price forecasting of electricity markets by mutual information technique and cascaded neuro-evolutionary algorithm. *IEEE Trans. Power Syst.*, 24, 1, 306–318, 2009.

149. Amjady, N., *Electric Power Systems: Advanced Forecasting Techniques and Optimal Generation Scheduling*. Chapter 4, CRC Press, Taylor & Francis, Boca Raton, FL, 2012.

150. University of Oregon, Solar Radiation Monitoring Laboratory Website, 2012, http://solardat.uoregon.edu/, Access date 2021.

151. Zhang, Z.-Y. and Wang, K.-S., Wind turbine fault detection based on SCADA data analysis using ANN. *Adv. Manuf.*, 2, 1, 70–78, 2014.

152. Hansen, A.D., Wind Turbine Technologies, in: *Wind Energy Engineering*, pp. 145–160, 2017.

153. Bangalore, P., Letzgus, S., Karlsson, D., Patriksson, M., An artificial neural network-based condition monitoring method for wind turbines, with application to the monitoring of the gearbox. *Wind Energy*, 20, 8, 1421–1438, 2017.

154. Garcia, M.C., Sanz-Bobi, M.A., Del Pico, J., SIMAP: Intelligent System for Predictive Maintenance. *Comput. Ind.*, 57, 6, 552–568, 2006.

155. Zaher, A., McArthur, S.D.J., Infield, D.G., Patel, Y., Online wind turbine fault detection through automated SCADA data analysis. *Wind Energy*, 12, 6, 574–593, 2009, doi: 10.1002/we.319.

156. Karlsson, D., *Wind turbine performance monitoring using artificial neural networks with a multi-dimensional data filtering approach*, Masters' Thesis, Dept. of Energy and Environment, Chalmers University of Technology, Gothenburg, Sweden, 2015.

157. Zhu, X., Genton, M.G., Gu, Y., Xie, L., Space-time wind speed forecasting for improved power system dispatch. *TEST*, 23, 1, 1–25, 2014.

158. Govorov, M., Beconytė, G., Gienko, G., Putrenko, V., Spatially constrained regionalizationwith multilayer perceptron. *Trans. GIS*, 23, 5048–1077, 2019.

159. Moustris, K.P., Zafirakis, D., Alamo, D.H., 24-h Ahead Wind Speed Prediction for the Optimum Operation of Hybrid Power Stations with the Use of Artificial Neural Networks, in: *Perspectives on Atmospheric Sciences*, 2017.

160. Welch, R.L., Ruffing, S.M., Venayagamoorthy, G.K., Comparison of feedforward and feedback neural network architectures for short term wind speed prediction. *2009 International Joint Conference on Neural Networks*, 2009.

161. Li, P., Eickmeyer, J., Niggemann, O., Data Driven Condition Monitoring of Wind Power Plants Using Cluster Analysis. *2015 International conference on cyber-enabled Distributed computing and knowledge*, 2015.

162. Lawan, S.M., Abidin, W.A.W.Z., Chai, W.Y., Baharun, A., Masri, T., Some Methodologies of wind speed prediction: A Critical Review. *Int. J. Renew. Energy*, 9, 1, 41–56, January-June 2014.

163. El Shahat, A., Haddad, R.J., Kalaani, Y., An artificial Neural Network model for wind energy estimation. *SoutheastCon 2015*, 2015.

164. Li, Q., Li, R., Ji, K., Dai, W., Kalman Filter and Its Application. *2015 8th International Conference on Intelligent Networks and Intelligent Systems (ICINIS)*, 2015.

165. Sharma, D. and Lie, T.T., Wind speed forecasting using hybrid ANN-Kalman Filter techniques. *2012 10th International Power & Energy Conference (IPEC)*, 2012.

166. Sharifian, A., Ghadi, M.J., Ghavidel, S., Li, L., Zhang, J., A new method based on Type-2 fuzzy neural network for accurate wind power forecasting under uncertain data. *Renewable Energy*, 120, 220–230, 2018.

167. Chitsaz, H., Amjady, N., Zareipour, H., Wind power forecast using wavelet neural network trained by improved Clonal selection algorithm. *Energy Convers. Manage.*, 89, 588–598, 2015.

168. Kani, S.A.P. and Riahy, G.H., A new ANN-based methodology for very short-term wind speed prediction using Markov chain approach. *2008 IEEE Canada Electric Power Conference*, 2008.

169. Jain, V., Singh, A., Chauhan, V., Pandey, A., Analytical study of Wind power prediction system by using Feed Forward Neural Network. *2016 International Conference on Computation of Power, Energy Information and Communication (ICCPEIC)*, 2016.

170. Li, S., Wind power prediction using recurrent multilayer perceptron neural networks. *2003 IEEE Power Engineering Society General Meeting (IEEE Cat. No.03CH37491)*, 2003.

171. Melikoglu, M., Geothermal energy in Turkey and around the World: a review of the literature and an analysis based on Turkey's Vision 2023 energy targets. *Renewable Sustainable Energy Rev.*, 76, 485e92, 2017.

172. Bleicher, A. and Gross, M., Geothermal heat pumps and the vagaries of subterranean geology: energy independence at a household level as a real world experiment. *Renewable Sustainable Energy Rev.*, 64, 279e88, 2016.

173. Pfenninger, S. and Keirstead, J., Comparing concentrating solar and nuclear power as baseload providers using the example of South Africa. *Energy*, 87, 303e14, 2015.

174. Özkaraca, O., Keçebaş, A., Demircan, C., Comparative thermodynamic evaluation of a geothermal power plant by using the advanced exergy and artificial bee colony methods. *Energy*, 156, 169–180, 2018, doi: 10.1016/j.energy.2018.05.095.

175. Nicholson, M., Biegler, T., Brook, B.W., How carbon pricing changes the relative competitiveness of low-carbon baseload generating technologies. *Energy*, 36, 305e13, 2011.

176. Khublaryan, M.G., *Types and properties of waters. Encyclopedia of life support systems*, vol. 1, p. 1e159, EOLSS Publishers Co. Ltd, Oxford, United Kingdom, 2009.

177. Bertani, R., Geothermal power generation in the world 2010e2014 update report. *Geothermics*, 60, 31e43, 2016.

178. TEIAS. Turkish electricity Transmission Corporation, http://www.teias.gov.tr/, Accessed date: 15.04.2017.

179. Rosen, M.A. and Dincer, I., Exergy methods for assessing and comparing thermal storage systems. *Int. J. Energy Res.*, 27, 4, 415e30, 2003.

180. Tsatsaronis, G., Design optimization using exergoeconomics, in: *Thermodynamic optimization of complex energy systems*, Kluwer Academic Publishers, Dordrecht, 1999.

181. Keçebaş, A. and Gokgedik, H., Thermodynamic evaluation of a geothermal power € plant for advanced exergy analysis. *Energy*, 88, 746e55, 2015.

182. Gokgedik, H., Yürüsoy, M., Keçebaş, A., Improvement potential of a real geothermal power plant using advanced exergy analysis. *Energy*, 112, 254e63, 2016.

183. Nami, H., Nemati, A., Fard, F.J., Conventional and advanced exergy analyses of a geothermal driven dual fluid organic Rankine cycle (ORC). *Appl. Therm. Eng.*, 122, 59e70, 2017.

184. Sun, J. and Li, W.H., Operation optimization of an organic Rankine cycle (ORC) heat recovery power plant. *Appl. Therm. Eng.*, 31, 2032e41, 2011.

185. Dai, Y., Wang, J., Gao, L., Parametric optimization and comparative study of organic Rankine cycle (ORC) for low grade waste heat recovery. *Energy Convers. Manage.*, 50, 576e82, 2009.

186. Rashidi, M.M., Galanis, N., Nazari, F., Parsa, A.B., Shamekhi, L., Parametric analysis and optimization of regenerative Clausius and organic Rankine cycles with two feed water heaters using artificial bees colony and artificial neural network. *Energy*, 36, 5728e40, 2011.

187. Sadeghi, S., Saffari, H., Bahadormanesh, N., Optimization of a modified doubleturbineKalina cycle by using Artificial Bee Colony algorithm. *Appl. Therm. Eng.*, 91, 19e32, 2015.

188. Saffari, H., Sadeghi, S., Khoshzat, M., Mehregan, P., Thermodynamic analysis and optimization of a geothermal Kalina cycle system using Artificial Bee Colony algorithm. *Renewable Energy*, 89, 154e67, 2016.

189. Arslan, O. and Yetik, O., ANN based optimization of supercritical ORC-binary geothermal power plant: Simav case study. *Appl. Therm. Eng.*, 31, 3922e8, 2011.

190. Wang, J., Yan, Z., Wang, M., Li, M., Dai, Y., Multi-objective optimization of an organic Rankine cycle (ORC) for low grade waste heat recovery using evolutionary algorithm. *Energy Convers. Manage*, 71, 146e58, 2013.

191. Clarke, J. and McLeskey Jr., J.T., Multi-objective particle swarm optimization of binary geothermal power plants. *Appl. Energy*, 138, 302e14, 2015.

192. Clarke, J., McLay, L., McLeskey Jr., J.T., Comparison of genetic algorithm to particle swarm for constrained simulation-based optimization of a geothermal power plant. *Adv. Eng. Inf.*, 28, 81e90, 2014.

193. Sadeghi, S., Saffari, H., Bahadormanesh, N., Optimization of a modified doubleturbineKalina cycle by using Artificial Bee Colony algorithm. *Appl. Therm. Eng.*, 91, 19e32, 2015.

194. Saffari, H., Sadeghi, S., Khoshzat, M., Mehregan, P., Thermodynamic analysis and optimization of a geothermal Kalina cycle system using Artificial Bee Colony algorithm. *Renewable Energy*, 89, 154e67, 2016.

195. Karaboga, D., An ideal based on honey bee swarm for numerical optimization, Technical Report e TR06, Erciyes University, Engineering, Kayseri, Turkey, 2005.

196. Karaboga, D. and Akay, B., A comparative study of artificial bee colony algorithm. *Appl. Math. Comput.*, 214, 1, 108e32, 2009.

197. Shokati, N., Ranjbar, F., Yari, M., Exergoeconomic analysis and optimization of basic, dual-pressure and dual-fluid ORCs and Kalina geothermal power plants: a comparative study. *Renewable Energy*, 83, 527e542, 2015.

198. Yamankaradeniz, N., Thermodynamic performance assessments of a district heating system with geothermal by using advanced exergy analysis. *Renewable Energy*, 85, 965e972, 2016.

199. Valdimarsson, P. and Eliasson, L., Factors influencing the economics of the Kalina power cycle and situations of superior performance, in: *International Geothermal Conference*, Reykjavik, Iceland, 2003.

200. Sadeghi, S., Saffari, H., Bahadormanesh, N., Optimization of a modified doubleturbineKalina cycle by using Artificial Bee Colony algorithm. *Appl. Therm. Eng.*, 91, 19e32, 2015.

201. Bombarda, P., Invernizzi, C.M., Pietra, C., Heat recovery from diesel engines: a thermodynamic comparison between Kalina and ORC cycles. *Appl. Therm. Eng.*, 30, 2, 212e219, 2010.
202. Velez, F., Segovia, J.J., Martín, M.C., Antolín, G., Chejne, F., Quijano, A., A technical, economical and market review of organic rankine cycles for the conversion of low-grade heat for power generation. *Renewable Sustainable Energy Rev.*, 16, 6, 4175e4189, 2012.
203. Wang, J., Yan, Z., Wang, M., Dai, Y., Thermodynamic analysis and optimization of an ammonia-water power system with LNG (liquefied natural gas) as its heat sink. *Energy*, 50, 513e522, 2013.
204. Shi, X. and Che, D., A combined power cycle utilizing low-temperature waste heat and LNG cold energy. *Energy Convers. Manage.*, 50, 3, 567e575, 2009.
205. Wang, H., Shi, X., Che, D., Thermodynamic optimization of the operating parameters for a combined power cycle utilizing low-temperature waste heat and LNG cold energy. *Appl. Therm. Eng.*, 59, 1, 490e497, 2013.
206. Zhang, X., He, M., Zhang, Y., A review of research on the Kalina cycle. *Renewable Sustainable Energy Rev.*, 16, 7, 5309e5318, 2012.
207. Chen, Y., Guo, Z., Wu, J., Zhang, Z., Hua, J., Energy and exergy analysis of integrated system of ammonia-water Kalina-Rankine cycle. *Energy*, 90, 2028–2037, 2015. 2028e2037.
208. Zhang, N. and Lior, N., Methodology for thermal design of novel combined refrigeration/power binary fluid systems. *Int. J. Refrig.*, 30, 6, 1072e1085, 2007.
209. Tillner-Roth, R. and Friend, D.G., A Helmholtz free energy formulation of the thermodynamic properties of the mixture {waterþ ammonia}, *J. Phys. Chem. Ref. Data*, 27, 1, 63e96, 1998.
210. El-Sayed, Y.M. and Tribus, M., A theoretical comparison of the Rankine and Kalina cycles, in: *Winter Annual Meeting of the American Society of Mechanical Engineers*, Miami, USA, 1985.
211. Ziegler, B. and Trepp, C., Equation of state for ammonia-water mixtures. *Int. J. Refrig.*, 7, 2, 101e106, 1984.
212. Xu, F. and Goswami, D.Y., Thermodynamic properties of ammoniaewater mixtures for power-cycle applications. *Energy*, 24, 6, 525e536, 1999.
213. Lolos, P.A. and Rogdakis, E.D., A Kalina power cycle driven by renewable energy sources. *Energy*, 34, 4, 457e464, 2009.
214. Ogriseck, S., Integration of Kalina cycle in a combined heat and power plant, a case study. *Appl. Therm. Eng.*, 29, 2843e2848, 2009.
215. Thorin, E., *Power Cycles with Ammonia-water Mixtures as Working Fluid*, Doctoral thesis, Department of Chemical Engineering and Technology, Energy Processes, Royal Institute of Technology, Stockholm, Sweden, 2000.
216. Larsen, U., Nguyen, T., Knudsen, T., Haglind, F., System analysis and optimization of a Kalina split-cycle for waste heat recovery on large marine diesel engines. *Energy*, 64, 484e494, 2014.

217. He, J., Liu, C., Xu, X., Li, Y., Wu, S., Xu, J., Performance research on modified KCS (Kalina cycle system) 11 without throttle valve. *Energy*, 64, 389e397, 2014.

218. Abdous, M.A., Saffari, H., Avval, H.B., Khoshzat, M., Investigation of entropy generation in a helically coiled tube in flow boiling condition under a constant heat flux. *Int. J. Refrig.*, 60, 217e233, 2015.

219. Saffari, H., Sadeghi, S., Khoshzat, M., Mehregan, P., Thermodynamic analysis and optimization of a geothermal Kalina cycle system using Artificial Bee Colony algorithm. *Renewable Energy*, 89, 154–167, 2016, doi: 10.1016/j. renene.2015.11.087.

220. Bui, K.-H.N., Agbehadji, I.E., Millham, R., Camacho, D., Jung, J.J., Distributed artificial bee colony approach for connected appliances in smart home energy management system. *Expert Syst.*, 37, e12521, 2020.

221. Ahmadi, P., Pouria, I., Dincer, M., Rosen, A., Thermoeconomic multiobjective optimization of a novel biomass-based integrated energy system. *Energy*, 68, 958e970, 2014.

222. Ahmadi, P., Dincer, I., Rosen, M.A., Exergy, exergoeconomic and environmental analyses and evolutionary algorithm based multi-objective optimization of combined cycle power plants. *Energy*, 36, 10, 5886e5898, 2011.

223. Karaboga, D. and Basturk, B., A powerful and efficient algorithm for numerical function optimization: artificial bee colony (ABC) algorithm. *J. Glob. Optim.*, 39, 3, 459e471, 2007.

224. Karaboga, D. and Akay, B., A comparative study of artificial bee colony algorithm. *Appl. Math. Comput.*, 214, 1, 108e132, 2009.

225. Basturk, B. and Karaboga, D., An artificial bee colony (ABC) algorithm for numeric function optimization. *IEEE Swarm Intelligence Symposium*, Indianapolis, IN, USA, May 12e14, 2006.

226. Baykasoglu, A., Ozbakir, L., Tapkan, P., Artificial bee colony algorithm and its application to generalized assignment problem, in: *Swarm Intelligence: Focus on Ant and Particle Swarm Optimization*, F.T.S. Chan and M.K. Tiwari (Eds.), p. 113e144, ITech Education and Publishing, Vienna, Austria, 2007.

227. Ibrahim, O.M. and Klein, S.A., Absorption power cycles. *Energy*, 21, 1, 21e27, 1996.

228. Davis, A.P. and Michaelides, E.E., Geothermal power production from abandoned oil wells. *Energy*, 34, 866–872, 2009.

229. Saito, S., Sakuma, S., Uchida, T., Drilling procedures, techniques and test results for a 3.7 km deep, 500 1C exploration well, Kakkonda, Japan. *Geothermics*, 27, 573–590, 1998.

230. Fomin, S., Chugunov, V., Hashida, T., Analytical modelling of the formation temperature stabilization during the borehole shut-in period. *Geophys. J. Int.*, 155, 469–478, 2003.

231. Santoyo, E., García, A., Espinosa, G., Hernández, I., Santoyo, S., STATIC_TEMP: a useful computer code for calculating static formation temperatures in geothermal wells. *Comput. Geosci.*, 26, 201–217, 2000.

232. Espinosa-Paredes, G. and Espinosa-Martinez, E.G., A feedback-based inverse heat transfer method to estimate unperturbed temperatures in wellbores. *Energy Convers. Manage.*, 50, 140–148, 2009.

233. Wisian, K.W., Blackwell, D.D., Bellani, S., Henfling, J.A., Normann, R.A., Lysne, P.C., Forster, A., Schrotter, J., Field comparison of conventional and new technology temperature logging systems. *Geothermics*, 27, 131–141, 1998.

234. Fomin, S., Hashida, T., Chugunov, V., Kuznetsov, A.V., A borehole temperature during drilling in a fractured rock formation. *Int. J. Heat Mass Transfer*, 48, 385–394, 2005.

235. Kutasov, I.M. and Eppelbaum, L.V., Prediction of formation temperatures in permafrost regions from temperature logs in deep wells-field cases. *Permafrost Periglacial Processes*, 14, 247–258, 2003.

236. Espinosa, G., Garcia, A., Santoyo, E., Hernandez, I., TEMLOPI/V.2: a computer program for estimation of fully transient temperatures in geothermal wells during circulation and shut-in. *Comput. Geosci.*, 27, 327–344, 2001.

237. Bassam, A., Santoyo, E., Andaverde, J., Hernández, J.A., Espinoza-Ojeda, O.M., Estimation of static formation temperatures in geothermal wells by using an artificial neural network approach. *Comput. Geosci.*, 36, 9, 1191–1199, 2010.

238. Brennand, A.W., A new method for the analysis of static formation temperature test, in: *Proceedings of the 6th New Zealand Geothermal Workshop*, Auckland, New Zealand, pp. 45–47, 1984.

239. Dowdle, W.L. and Cobb, W.M., Static formation temperature from well logs—an empirical method. *J. Pet. Technol.*, 11, 1326–1330, 1975.

240. Kutasov, I.M. and Eppelbaum, L.V., Determination of formation temperature from bottom-hole temperature logs—a generalized Horner method. *J. Geophys. Eng.*, 2, 90–96, 2005.

241. Leblanc, Y., Pascoe, L.J., Jones, F.W., The temperature stabilization of a borehole. *Geophysics*, 46, 1301–1303, 1981.

242. Manetti, G., Attainment of temperature equilibrium in holes during drilling. *Geothermics*, 2, 94–100, 1973.

243. Verma, S.P., Andaverde, J., Santoyo, E., Application of the error propagation theory in estimates of static formation temperatures in geothermal and petroleum boreholes. *Energy Convers. Manage.*, 47, 3659–3671, 2006a.

244. Verma, S.P., Andaverde, J., Santoyo, E., Statistical evaluation of methods for the calculation of static formation temperatures in geothermal and oil wells using an extension of the error propagation theory. *J. Geochem. Explor.*, 89, 398–404, 2006b.

245. Andaverde, J., Verma, S.P., Santoyo, E., Uncertainty estimates of static formation temperature in borehole and evaluation of regression models. *Geophys. J. Int.*, 160, 1112–1122, 2005.

246. Hermanrud, C., Cao, S., Lerche, I., Estimates of virgin rock temperature derived from BHT measurements: bias and error. *Geophysics*, 55, 924–931, 1990.

247. Zhang, G., Patuwo, B.E., Hu, M.Y., Forecasting with artificial neural networks: the state of the art. *Int. J. Forecasting*, 14, 35–62, 1998.
248. Goutorbe, B., Lucazeau, F., Bonneville, A., Using neural networks to predict thermal conductivity from geophysical well logs. *Geophys. J. Int.*, 166, 115–125, 2006.
249. Hsieh, B.Z., Wang, C.W., Lin, Z.S., Estimation of formation strength index of aquifer from neural networks. *Comput. Geosci.*, 35, 1933–1939, 2009.
250. Leite, E.P. and de Souza Filho, C.R., Probabilistic neural networks applied to mineral potential mapping for platinum group elements in the Serra Leste region, Caraja's mineral province, Brazil. *Comput. Geosci.*, 35, 675–687, 2009a.
251. Leite, E.P. and de Souza Filho, C.R., TEXTNN—a MATLAB program for textural classification using neural networks. *Comput. Geosci.*, 35, 2084–2094, 2009b.
252. Morton, J.C., Boosting a fast neural network for supervised land cover classification. *Comput. Geosci.*, 35, 1280–1295, 2009.
253. Farshad, F.F., Garber, J.D., Lorde, J.L., Predicting temperature profiles in producing oil wells using artificial neural networks. *Eng. Comput.*, 17, 735–754, 2000.
254. Bayram, A.F., Application of an artificial neural network model to a Na/K geothermometer. *J. Volcanol. Geotherm. Res.*, 112, 75–81, 2001.
255. Spichak, V.V., Estimating temperature distributions in geothermal areas using a neuronet approach. *Geothermics*, 35, 181–197, 2006.
256. Serpen, G., Palabiyik, Y., Serpen, U., An artificial neural network model for Na/K geothermometer, in: *Proceedings of the 34th Workshop on Geothermal Reservoir Engineering*, Stanford University, Stanford, USA, pp. 1–12, 2009.
257. Verma, S.P., Díaz-González, L., González-Ramírez, R., Relative efficiency of single-outlier discordancy tests for processing geochemical data on reference materials. *Geostand. Geoanal. Res.*, 33, 29–49, 2009.

3

Artificial Intelligence–Based Energy-Efficient Clustering and Routing in IoT-Assisted Wireless Sensor Network

Nitesh Chouhan

Department of IT, MLV Textile & Engineering College, Bhilwara, India

Abstract

Two well-known optimization problems are energy-efficient routing and clustering which have been studied widely to extend lifetime of Internet of Things (IoT)–assisted wireless sensor networks (WSNs). An advancement made in wireless technologies has developed a greater impact over the IoT systems. For connected people and objects, IoT have become popular for exchanging and collecting data based on sensors. Communication between entities plays a vital role to develop a sustainable environment. In IoT-assisted WSNs, there are several ways in which the nodes are considered as the resource parameters, like energy resources, storage resources, and computing resources for achieving higher energy utilization and for maintaining long network lifetime. Clustering is one of the efficient approaches that connects and organizes the sensor nodes by balancing the loads and maximizing the lifespan of the network.

At first, the nodes are simulated together in IoT-assisted WSN. Using optimization algorithm, this performs the cluster head selection, after that on the basis of optimization the routing process is done. By considering the fitness, the routing path is selected parameters, like QoS parameters, and trust factors. The QoS parameters include the energy, delay, distance, as well as link lifetime. Using fitness parameter, the optimal path with the minimum distance path is selected.

The industrial operations have been transformed by Artificial Intelligence (AI). AI is using for reducing the computational costs of optimization this is one of the effective and important applications of AI. In this chapter, firstly, optimization concept is fully explained. Then, various optimization algorithms explained used

Email: niteshchouhan_9@yahoo.com

Ajay Kumar Vyas, S. Balamurugan, Kamal Kant Hiran and Harsh S. Dhiman (eds.) *Artificial Intelligence for Renewable Energy Systems*, (79–92) © 2022 Scrivener Publishing LLC

in the clustering and routing. These algorithms optimize the problem of study. At the end, various models are fully discussed. The results of the algorithms show that by better clustering and routing, the conditions can be improved.

Keywords: Clustering, IoT, WSNs, hierarchical routing, AI, energy efficient, routing, fuzzy C-mean approach

3.1   Introduction

Advances made in the wireless sensor networks (WSNs) have attracted and gained momentum in the various fields of real-time applications like medicine, military, monitoring systems, and tracking systems. The different aspects and requirements of the applications have led to the development of low-cost and power consumption wireless devices. Decision-making process is one of the supporting tools which help to take action by analyzing several parameters. The incorporation of different devices exposes a different form of information, and thus, the decision-making process becomes quite complex tasks [1]. In specific, information obtained from the WSNs has the potentiality of associating toward different devices which can lead to delayed information transfer processes. In spite of those unique features rendered by WSNs, despite its application in real world is limited. In general, the radio range is used to connect the different devices. Relied upon the requirement of application, the sensor nodes are deployed and communicated. Nodes form networks by organizing among themselves to reachable and great value information from the physical environment [2].

The nodes are managed by the clustering approach. It is performed in two ways, namely, centralized and distributed [3]. In the viewpoint of centralized clustering approach, the sink node takes charge of collecting the information from wireless networks. Each sensor node is provided with the global knowledge since the sink node is limited from the aspects like energy constraints and storage constraints. Finally, the sink node estimates the cluster heads (CHs) and also its members. However, it is not suitable for the optimal-based large-scale environment [4]. The distributed clustering approach makes use of local knowledge wherein each sensor node is capable of electing the CHs on the basis of requirements. In the case of heterogeneous sensor networks, the deployment of static and dynamic clustering approach has brought the challenges like network congestion, heavy traffic rate, and undersampling and oversampling of the cluster centers.

3.2   Related Study

This segment discusses the reviews of existing techniques. Different sensor nodes are placed on the wireless environment under multi-hop communications [5]. Sink nodes have consumed an additional energy to transmit/receive the data packets. Energy hole issue is one of the vital concepts which was evaluated under AODV, DSR, and TORA protocols. The results have stated that the AODV and DSR protocols performed better than the TORA from the aspects of packet delivery ratio, throughput, and overheads. Though it has improved the network lifetime, the increased sensors node in the topology has lowered the performance. Reaching the base station (BS) has become quite complex in large-scale networks. This leads to the routing problem which was resolved by the protocol, named On-Hole Children Reconnection (OHCR) and On-Hole Alert (OHA) [6]. The connectivity factor between the sensor nodes was efficiently handled under energy metrics. Compared to Shortest-Path Tree (SPT) and Degree-Constrained Tree (DCT), the suggested technique has achieved 75% increased network lifetime. Further, an energy-efficient LEACH protocol [7] was studied to improve the residual energy. Each deployed sensor node was projected into a clustering process. Depending on the instruction given by CHs, the resources are optimized. Though it has reduced the energy-consumption rate, the traffic flow between sensors under the clustering process is not explored.

Quality-of-Service (QoS)–based routing protocols [8] were introduced under multi-objective functions. Here, heuristic-based neighbor selection models were formulated under geographic-based routing models. It has followed the distance, delay, and path-based metrics to obtain optimal routing path. It has significantly reduced the network consumption, yet the network congestion rate becomes increased. Several offloading computational algorithms [9] were introduced to effectively utilize the route-discovery mechanisms for building topologies, CH formation, and CH selection. The time taken for CH selection is higher while discovering the routes. It develops an overhead over the protocol. Owing to it, several clustering-based routing protocols were developed using non-deterministic approaches [10]. PSO protocol for Hierarchical Clustering (PSO-HC) was designed to improve the lifetime of the CHs as well as network scalability. System has reduced the CH, and the link quality of networks cannot be studied.

With the baseline of PSO, multiple-sink placement algorithm [11] was suggested for encoding the particles and evaluating the fitness. Depending on the hop count, the multiple hop count was employed for energy-efficient systems. The position of the sink has significantly depleted the energy and thus, heuristics models were used for finding the minimum sink utilization. Then, Enhanced PSO-Based Clustering Energy Optimization (EPSO-CEO) algorithm [12] was suggested to improve the local searching algorithms for CH selection. With the help of multi-hop routing protocols, the network lifetime and the consumed energy were enhanced. The data collection and aggregation methods have to be enhanced. Delay-sensitive–based multi-hop routing protocols were established by [13]. Here, an end-to-end delay was improvised using probability blocking mechanisms. Different numerical simulations were formulated for relay nodes and thus reduced the end-to-end delay. Though QoS models are improved, the probability of the hop count was increased in small-scale networks.

Different optimization techniques were studied by different researchers. Since the energy transmission/consumption [14] remains to be challenged, a different numerical solver was suggested. CH selection was done by the clusters rate, hop-count rate, and the relay nodes. Cluster-based aggregation mechanisms were designed for inter-cluster and intra-cluster communication. Network overloads [15] were re-formulated to reduce the congestion near cluster nodes. However, extracting the CH nodes is not properly defined. Energy consumption rate was improvised the position of the sink nodes. Ring routing protocols were introduced to reduce the overhead of the mobile sinks. System has increased the packet delivery rate on small-scale networks. Along with the similar objectives, genetic algorithm [16] was studied for network lifetime enhancement and the cost minimization. A protocol, named Genetic Algorithm–based Energy-efficient Clustering Hierarchy (GAECH) was designed from three aspects, viz., First Node Die (FND), Half Node Die (HND), and Last Node Die (LND). The estimated fitness function ensured a well-balanced cluster formation which increased the lifetime and stability of the node. While, the degree of a node might affect the performance of the network lifetime, which is not focused.

In the case of virtual networks, wireless connectivity plays a key role in CH formation. The deployment of Weakly Connected Dominating Set (WCDS) [17] has explored the proper utilization of the CH selection. The network edge and balancing of loads were improved in this study. The system has obtained better utilization of CHs, irrespective of the node size. Similar approaches were explored in the game theory applications [18]. Most of the routing protocols were designed to overcome the issues of energy consumption, delay, and throughput rate. In coordination to this, game theory was used to enhance the packet delivery rate. By optimizing the route establishment time incessantly using hierarchical routing protocols. Though it improved packet delivery, multi-objective–based decision-making process is not focused. Wireless network application is widely inclined in the field of Internet of Things (IoT). Again, the clustering algorithm has been stimulated in the IoT applications. It was explored in the LEACH protocol [19] and obtained 60% development in throughput, network span and residual energy. Similarly, game theory–based energy-efficient clustering routing protocol (GEEC) [20] was developed to balance the energy efficiency and the lifespan without compromising the QoS of wireless networks. Topology formation has resolved the energy repletion issue with better cluster forming. Evolutionary game models have significantly detected the behavior of the nodes that has resulted in better control messages.

Owing to it, an energy-efficient data aggregation scheme for clustered WSN (EEDAC-WSN) [21] was established for small-sized control frames of cluster member nodes. By monitoring the stability of the node, the member nodes are efficiently communicated in the networks. Compared to the LEACH protocol, the suggested protocols have lowered the delay rate even for small-scale networks as well as large scale networks. Induction trees in hierarchical-based clustering nodes [22] have been studied to resolve the inference problems during induced tree formation. Induced tree of the crossed cube (ITCC) was designed on the basis of the degree of the graph nodes. It was understood that the Voronoi cell has monitored the node's behavior. Though it claims for reduced delay rate, the use of relay nodes is higher. Since the WSNs are decentralized, the information transformation takes via a clustering algorithm. During clustering-based communication process, the sensor node takes maximized energy which was resolved by WEMER protocol [23]. Though it was concentrated on improvising the gateway nodes, the congestion between those nodes are not concentrated. To makes the other pervasive more effective WSN technologies growth perceived a demand for IoT applications. Over world-wide IoT [19] is utilizing for providing the consistently to network. In addition, for guaranteeing the ubiquitous communications, the IoT follows the principle [20]. Moreover, the IoT engaged with applications, which includes smart home, cities, and agriculture military [21]. In various IoT applications, for improving the data transmission, scalability, and the energy efficiency in the WSNs, the BS received the sensed data that sensor node passes to that makes network more possible. Based on the above-mentioned requirement, that may guarantee latency, loss rate, the minimal energy consumption, and delay in IoT with the development of multipath-aware routing protocol is the essential prerequisite [4].

For the IoT application, the WSN is responsible to collect sensed data for the IoT application [12]. The sensor nodes are here, initially scattered in the IoT, and then sensed data to the sink (gateway) node of the Wireless Sensor Node, the sensor nodes periodically forward back this. After that, the sink node utilizes gathered data for producing fruitful information. Therefore, those routing protocols are classified into two categories, namely, flat-based and cluster routing protocols. While comparing the energy consumption on both, the cluster-enabled protocols have big advantage [14]. In the sensor nodes cluster, one node is selected as the CH, and the remaining are cluster members. To forward the data directly to the sink node, these cluster members not able [13].

Wireless Sensor Node consists of these constraints, such as power, processing memory, transmission range, and bandwidth availability. To improve nodes lifetime as well as energy is the challenge [16]. In this environment, the resources should be follow by the routing protocol, such as manage enable fast convergence, lossy links, energy saving, and prevent routing loops. The secure routing protocol is introduced for effective data routing more, to improve the clustering performance and sensors positioning [15, 18]. In addition, due to adaptive communication patterns, sensors, and lightweight routing protocols, the existing routing protocols failed to apply the WSN directly. As *ad hoc* topology used by WSNs without identifying path, infrastructure, and then forwarding data to the sink is the quite difficult and interesting task [7]. Moreover, for extending heterogeneous WSNs, lifetime effective device placement, routing protocol, and the topology management techniques are introduced [17]. Nowadays, various protocols, namely, gradient-based routing, rumor, and energy, are introduced, termed as the data center–oriented protocol [18].

3.3   Clustering in WSN

Clustering technologies play a major role in the WSNs which have assisted in improving the performance of the network. The WSNs are classified into two networks, *viz.*, flat networks and clustered networks. The clustered networks are widely adopted to enhance the scalability, reliability, and availability of the wireless networks. Figure 3.1 presents the clustered WSNs [24].

Initially, the sensor nodes are distributed arbitrarily in the wireless environment. CH is selected by the deployed sensor nodes based on the energy parameter. It helps to collect, aggregate, and transmit the data to the sink nodes. This takes the hierarchy structure of the sensor nodes. It also diversifies the member nodes and the CHs. The other parameters in clustering are the cluster number/size, complexity of algorithms, overlapping,

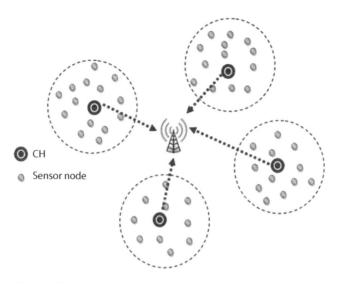

Figure 3.1 Clustered WSNs.

relay-overhead in inter-cluster, and routing policies. The clustering algorithms were divided into two types: probabilistic and non-probabilistic algorithms. The CHs are elected by its co-sensor nodes of assigned probabilities known as probabilistic algorithms. Whereas, CHs are selected under a certain criteria as well as proximity of sensor nodes known as non-probabilistic algorithms. In the perspective of a collaborative environment, with the help of nearest cluster nodes, the data is collected, aggregated, and transmitted to its sink node.

3.4 Research Methodology

This section presents the methodology of the research study. A novel routing protocol, using Artificial Intelligence (AI) uses with the objectives of enhancement of network lifetime and reduced usage of cluster number/size. The proposed phases are presented as follows:

3.4.1 Creating Wireless Sensor–Based IoT Environment

Consider a set of sensor nodes, as $S = \{N_1, N_2 \ldots N_n\}$ deployed in the IoT environment which are randomly associated with each other. Initially, the sensor nodes and the sink nodes are discrete in nature. All sensor nodes are equipped with a similar amount of energy. By the use of signal strength obtained value, the distance between the nodes is computed.

3.4.2   Clustering Approach

This phase aim is to increase the network lifetime of the deployed sensor nodes. It follows the static as well as dynamic wireless environment. Here, the clustering has been done on demand basis, i.e., whenever a specific sensor area initiates for transmission purpose, at that time, the CH has elected. Let us assume, network lifetime of a sensor node is denoted as, $N_{Lifetime(i)}$. The elapsed time taken by nodes until the first node depletes its energy is given as $N_{ElapTime}$. Collectively, it is represented as follows:

$$N_{ElapTime} = min \tag{3.1}$$

The AI-based clustering eliminates the demerits of static and dynamic clustering approaches, by not performing clustering at each round. Based on the sync_pulse window, the clustering process is initiated for the particular sensor area. The below pseudo-code depicts the working of AI-based clustering approach. Algorithm 3.1 explains how clustering is performed using AI technique.

Algorithm 3.1 AI-based clustering approach.

Setup stage:
  The residual energy of a cluster head node$\rightarrow R_{CH}$
        β: $constant val ueranges\ 0 \leq \beta \leq 1$
            $S = \{N \in S_{CH} \lor R_N > 0\}$
$\forall N \in S$: If $R_N < \beta R_{CH}(N)$. Then
      The node N with data packets allocates the time bits.
      Collects the data packets
      Transmits to the Sink node in a multi-hop manner.
If the sync_ pulse has obtained then
      The node N gets ready to do the clustering process.
Once the sink node obtains data packet:
      If time_bits (T) = true then
      Sink node broadcasts the sync_ pulse per round in the specified
      sensor area.

Once the lifetime of a network is preserved, a CH node has been selected. Here, AI-based clustering approach is employed as an energy-efficient routing process in WSNs. The objective of the AI approach is to elect the CH from the set of sensor nodes. In association with the above process, the nodes are aware of when to initiate the clustering process. Let us assume that set of clusters is represented as $C = \{c_1, c_2 \dots c_n\}$. The deployment of AI-based clustering is to efficiently utilize the energy of the sensor nodes. Thus, objective function of energy minimization is given as follows:

$$E_M = \sum_{i=1}^{c} \sum_{j=1}^{N} degree_{ij}^{M} distance_{ij}^{2}$$

(3.2)

where

$degree_{ij}^{M}$ is the j's degree of a node on cluster i.

$distance_{ij}^{2}$ is the distance between node j and the midpoint of cluster i.

Once the distance between nodes is minimized, then the energy consumption is also minimized. Since the CH election is done by rounds, each round performs data transmission operation. Initially, the nodes are assigned with the degree, and thus, it is used for the formation of a clustering process. The proximity value of each node is estimated. If the value of a node is closer to the proximity value, then it is labeled as cluster C_1. Likewise, all sensor nodes in the application area are examined. Once the clusters are formed, the sink node selects the nearest cluster center C_i to become CH and then the information of CH node was broadcasted. The total number of clusters C is computed as follows:

$$C = \frac{\sqrt{N}}{\sqrt{2 * \pi}} \sqrt{\frac{E_{fa}}{E_M}} \frac{M}{distance_{Sink\ Node}^{2}}$$

(3.3)

In some cases, the non-CH at particular time T may attempt to transmit the data packets to sink nodes. Thus, it can deplete the energy. In order to eliminate this scenario, an optimal CH has been elected by the present CH at each round. At the initial round, the sink node selects the CH. The CH is selected, and then, the data transmission process is scheduled by TDMA.

3.4.3   AI-Based Energy-Aware Routing Protocol

It is found that some rounds are suffering from overloads of cluster members, which leads to heavy congestions as well as unwanted energy consumption. Therefore, the need of finding the shortest route path has reduced the effects of energy consumption rate. Algorithm 3.2 explains the working of AI-based energy-aware routing Protocol. This protocol reduced the CHs overload and also enhanced the lifetime of the network.

Algorithm 3.2

Input: $C = \{c_1, c_2 \ldots c_n\}$, Neighborhood hop and simulation measurements
Begin
Function Clusters
      Estimate the cluster midpoint by getting spatial information of
      nodes
for (n = 1; n< = S; n++)
Do
        If R_N >optimum $_{threshold}$
set list_of_cluster_centers []
End if
end for
for (n = 1; n< = list_of_cluste_centers;n++)
        Estimate the midpoint of N_n
        set the max(proximal value of N_n) as CH_n
end for
end procedure
Function Route detection
for each N_n
    Do
        call optimized_routing_protocol ()
  while (y! = destination)
        N_i sets next-hop by using highest FP_n
          FP_n Reply to y
            y = FP_n
  if y_n. sync_pulse is high
call route_restore ()
end if
end while
end for
end procedure
Function Nodes_status
      if (RE_C <μ*RE_{init})
        initiate re-routing ()
      if (Δt _ Sync_Pulse _expired) then
        initiate re-routing ()
end if
end if
end procedure
End

3.5 Conclusion

Rapid innovations of wireless technologies have impressed the researchers to delve into the study of wireless-based IoT systems. A unique feature is the reliable monitoring services, increased network lifetime, and minimized energy consumption rate. However, a complete solution is possible due to the issues like congestion and overload of the network scenarios. In this study, an energy-efficient hybrid hierarchical clustering algorithm for wireless sensor devices in IoT is designed. It is explored by two phases, namely, CH selection using AI approach and shortest route path finding using AI-based energy-aware routing protocol. Our main novelty is the clustering process is initiated on the received request from the sensor nodes. It eliminates the traffic analysis caused during clustering analysis.

References

1. Thein, M.C.M. and Thein, T., An Energy Efficient Cluster-Head Selection for Wireless Sensor Networks. *International Conference on Intelligent Systems, Modeling and Simulation*, pp. 287–291, 2010.
2. Lee, J.S. and Cheng, W.L., Fuzzy-logic-based clustering approach for wireless sensor networks using energy prediction. *IEEE Sens. J.*, 12, 2891–2897, 2012.
3. Attea, B.A.A. and Khalil, E.A., A new evolutionary based routing protocol for clustered heterogeneous wireless sensor networks. *Appl. Soft Comput.*, 12, 1950–1957, 2012.
4. Kuila, P. and Jana, P.K., A novel differential evolution based clustering algorithm for wireless sensor networks. *Appl. Soft Comput.*, 25, 414–425, 2014.
5. Shokouhifar, M. and Jalali, A., A new evolutionary based application specific routing protocol for clustered wireless sensor networks. *AEU-Int. J. Electron. Commun.*, 69, 432–441, 2015.
6. Rohini, S. and Lobiyal, D.K., Proficiency analysis of AODV, DSR and TORA Ad- hoc routing protocols for energy holes problem in wireless sensor networks. *Proc. Comput. Sci.*, 57, 2015, 1057–1066, 2015.
7. Mohemed, R.E., Saleh, A.I., Abdelrazzak, M., Samra, A.S., Energy-efficient routing protocols for solving energy hole problem in Wireless Sensor Networks. *Comput. Netw.*, 114, 2017, 51–66, 2017.
8. Arumugam, G.S. and Ponnuchamy, T., EE-LEACH: development of energy-efficient LEACH protocol for data gathering in WSN. *EURASIP J. Wirel. Commun. Netw.*, 2015, 1, 1–9, 2015.
9. Mazaheri, M.R., Homayounfar, B., Mazinani, S.M., QoS based and energy aware multipath hierarchical routing algorithms in WSNs. *Wirel. Sens. Netw.*, 4, 31–39, 2012.

10. Sharma, S., Jena, Kumar, S., Cluster based multipath routing protocol for wireless sensor networks. *ACM SIGCOMM Comput. Commun. Rev.*, 45, 2, 15–20, 2015.

11. Elhabyan, R.S. and Yagoub, M.C.E., PSO-HC: Particle Swarm Optimization Protocol for Hierarchical Clustering in Wireless Sensor Networks 978-1-63190-043-3, in: *10th IEEE International Conference on Collaborative Computing: Networking, Applications and Worksharing (CollaborateCom 2014)*, pp. 417–424, 2014.

12. Srinivasa Rao, P.C. *et al.*, PSO-based multiple-sink placement algorithm for protracting the lifetime of Wireless Sensor Networks, in: *Proc. of the Second International Conference on Computer and Communication Technologies*, Springer, pp. 605–616, 2016.

13. Vimalarani, C., Subramanian, R., Sivanandam, S.N., An enhanced PSO-based clustering energy optimization algorithm for wireless sensor network. *Sci. World J.*, 2016, 1–11, 2016.

14. Hyadi, A., Afify, L., Shihada, B., End-to-end delay analysis in wireless sensor networks with service vacation. *IEEE Conference on Wireless Communications and Networking*, Istanbul, Turkey, 2014.

15. Abu-Baker, A.K., Energy-Efficient Routing in Cluster-Based Wireless Sensor Networks: Optimization and Analysis. *Jordan J. Electr. Eng.*, 2, 2, 146–159, 2016.

16. Kumbhar, A.D. and Chavan, M.K., An Energy Efficient Ring routing Protocol for Wireless Sensor Network. *International conference on I-SMAC (IoT in Social, Mobile, Analytics and Cloud) (I-SMAC 2017)*.

17. Baranidharan, B. and Santhi, B., GAECH: Genetic Algorithm Based Energy Efficient Clustering Hierarchy in Wireless Sensor Networks. *Hindawi Publishing Corporation J. Sens.*, 15, 20–35, 2015.

18. Dou, C., Chang, Y.-H., Ruan, J.-S., On the Performance of Weakly Connected Dominating Set and Loosely Coupled Dominating Set for Wireless Sensor/Mesh Networks. *Appl. Mech. Mater.*, 764–765, 929–935, 2015.

19. Arafat Habib, Md and Moh, S., Game theory-based Routing for Wireless Sensor Networks: A Comparative Survey. *Appl. Sci.*, 9, 2896, 2019.

20. Behera, T.M., Mohapatra, S.K., Samal, U.C., Khan, M.S., Daneshmand, M., Gandomi, A.H., Residual Energy Based Cluster-head Selection in WSNs for IoT Application. *IEEE Internet Things J.*, 6, 3, 5132–5139, 2019.

21. Lin, D. and Wang, Q., A game theory based energy efficient clustering routing protocol for WSNs. *J. Wirel. Netw.*, 23, 4, 1101–1111, 2017.

22. Roy, N.R. and Chandra, P., EEDAC-WSN: Energy Efficient Data Aggregation in Clustered WSN. *International Conference on Automation, Computational and Technology Management (ICACTM)*, 2019.

23. Zhang, J., Xu, L., Ye, X., An efficient connected dominating set algorithm in wsns based on the induced tree of the crossed cube. *Appl. Math. Comput. Sci.*, 25, 2, 295–309, 2015.

24. Bello, A.D. and Lamba, O.S., Energy Efficient for Data Aggregation in Wireless Sensor Networks. *Int. J. Eng. Res. Technol. (IJERT)*, 9, 1, 110–120, 2020.

.

4

Artificial Intelligence for Modeling and Optimization of the Biogas Production

Narendra Khatri[1]* and Kamal Kishore Khatri[2]

[1]Department of Mechatronics, Manipal Institute of Technology, Manipal Academy of Higher Education, Manipal, India
[2]Department of Mechanical-Mechatronics Engineering, The LNM Institute of Information Technology, Jaipur, Rajasthan, India

Abstract

The artificial intelligence (AI) is emerging nowadays, making human life easier. As the area of renewable energy is growing significantly for the sustainable development, the deployment of AI can help greatly to achieve its goals. The biogas is source of renewable energy, which is generated from the anaerobic digestion of the biomass, cow dung, wastewater sludge, and kitchen waste, etc. Anaerobic digestion is a non-linear biological process where biomass is digested to generate biogas and slurry in the absence of oxygen. AI models have been developed for the prediction of yield and energy content of the produced biogas. This chapter presents a comprehensive review of AI techniques for the modeling of the biogas production process. The literature on the applications of artificial neural network models and evolutionary algorithms related to anaerobic digestion has been compiled and synthesized. The integration of appropriate AI technique in biogas has been reviewed for optimum biogas production round the year.

Keywords: Artificial intelligence, artificial neural network, evolutionary algorithms, genetic algorithm, particle swarm optimization, ant colony optimization

4.1 Introduction

Artificial intelligence (AI) is an emerging area of research. The application of AI is continuously increasing in the area of renewable energy.

---

*Corresponding author: narkhatri@gmail.com

Ajay Kumar Vyas, S. Balamurugan, Kamal Kant Hiran and Harsh S. Dhiman (eds.) *Artificial Intelligence for Renewable Energy Systems*, (93–114) © 2022 Scrivener Publishing LLC

Various renewable energy sources are explored till now and many more in pipeline. The biofuels are produced for the biomass. These are good sources of renewable energy and can be used to replace the fossil fuels. The biogas is derived by anaerobic digestion/co-digestion of the biomass, cow dung, wastewater sludge, and kitchen waste. The biogas generation is a biological process in which the biomass is digested through biochemical method; it coverts organic matter to biogas and slurry using bacterial consortium in the absence of oxygen [1]. The generated gas is a mixture of methane, carbon dioxide, and trace amount of other gases such as hydrogen sulfide, ammonia, and hydrogen. The slurry generated in the process has valuable agronomical features [2].

Anaerobic digestion process of biomass for generation of biogas is also known as biomethanization. It is a natural biochemical process and takes place under the controlled environment without oxygen. Biomethanization takes place in main four steps, *viz.*, hydrolysis, acidogenesis, acetogenesis, and methanogenesis. During the biomethanization process various complex organic compounds are formed, and formation of end product as methane along with nutritious effluents. Figure 4.1 shows the principal of biogas generation. Once the biomass is fed to the bioreactor, first biochemical process (hydrolysis) of the biomass gets started. The biomass

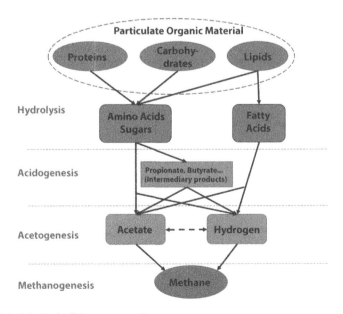

Figure 4.1 Principal of biogas generation.

is composed of proteins, carbohydrates, and lipids which are transformed into amino acids, sugars and fatty acids in hydrolysis process. The amino acids and sugars are being converted in to propionate and butyrate (intermediary products) during the acidogenesis process. Acetogenesis is a chemical process in which intermediary products are converted to acetate and hydrogen. During the methanogenesis process the acetate and hydrogen compounds are transformed into methane. Figure 4.2 shows the pictorial view of biogas generation plant at the LNMIIT, Jaipur.

Anaerobic digestion is strongly dependent on environmental parameters, such as temperature, pH, alkalinity, acidity, ammonia concentration, and organic load [3–5]. Therefore, control of operational parameter is a priority for bioprocess optimization. The small changes in the operational parameters results in significant change in the biogas yield and composition. Hence various models of anaerobic digestion process have been developed to optimize the process [6]. The mechanism of anaerobic digestion is very complex since it relies on both endogenous and exogenous variables. The researchers have conducted various studies to identify and assess the effect of various parameters [7–9].

The application of AI for modeling to optimize biogas yield, to control and diagnose faults in AD system are critical aspects of the biogas production process. Various types of ANN models have been developed for prediction of yield, energy content and composition of the produced biogas.

Figure 4.2 Biogas generation plant at the LNMIIT, Jaipur.

Nature inspired algorithms are also used along with the ANN models to optimize the biogas yield [10–14].

This chapter is an overview of the integration of AI in the area of biogas production. This chapter is organized into four main sections. The first section gives a brief overview of the biogas production process, need of modeling, and identification of critical parameters which are modeled and controlled for biogas production and optimization. The second section presents artificial neural network (ANN) architecture, training algorithms, and application of ANNs in biogas production processes. In the third section, evolutionary algorithms, *viz.*, GA, ACO, and PSO, are briefly presented and discussed. This chapter covers important AI techniques for optimization of biogas production.

4.2   Artificial Neural Network

ANN is a well known AI technique used for modeling and optimization of complex nonlinear processes. ANN is one of the most used techniques for modeling the nonlinear processes. ANN models are data driven. The real-time or experimental data is used for the model development. The experimental dataset is divided into three different sets, i.e., training, testing, and validation datasets. These datasets are used to train, test and validate the model respectively. Once an ANN-based process model with reasonably good generalization potential is developed, it is possible to optimise its input space effectively to obtain the desired (optimum) values of process variables.

4.2.1   ANN Architecture

ANNs are complex structure which can take several inputs, process it, and produce the single/multiple output. ANN's work is to mutate the input information into consequential useful output. Figure 4.3 represents the basic architecture of the ANN; it can have three types of layers, i.e., input, output, and one or multiple hidden layers within. The neurons are the fundamental unit of the neural network. These neurons receive inputs from other nodes of the network or an external source. Each node of the input layer is connected to each node of the hidden layer, equally all the nodes of the hidden layer are connected to each node of the output layer, and each connection between these nodes has a specific weight. Weights are allocated to a neuron depending on its perceived worth to other inputs.

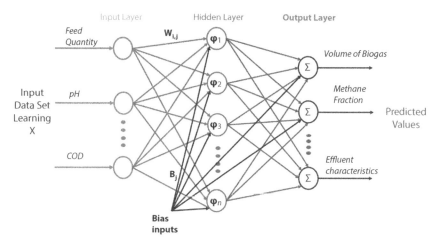

Figure 4.3 Basic artificial neural network architecture.

All input layer node values are multiplied with the assigned weight to their interconnection and summarized to generate the first hidden layer value. Mathematically: The inputs of pth neuron ($Y_{i,p}$ i = 1, 2, ..., q where q is the number of neurons linked to the pth neuron) are multiplied by their weights ($W_{i,p}$) and summed. This generated sum is added with the bias input of pth neuron (B_p) to form Σ_p [Equation (4.1)]

$$\Sigma_p = B_p + \sum_{i=1}^{q} W_{i,p} Y_{i,p} \qquad (4.1)$$

The resultant value (Σ_p) is fed to activation function, i.e., $f_a(\Sigma_p)$. Each neuron is connected to other by the weighted connection; the weight of these connections is updated during neural network training [15]. The hidden layer of neural network performs main computation; therefore, it collects all the input from the input layer and processes these inputs through the respective weights and performs necessary calculations to generate meaningful results. The computed results are processed and presented through the output layer for user understanding.

In ANN, flow of information takes place in two ways, i.e., feedforward and feedback. In feedforward network, the flow of information is unidirectional. In feedback network, it uses the internal memory to process the sequence of input data. In feedback network, information can travel in both forward and backward direction. Figure 4.4 shows the backpropagation

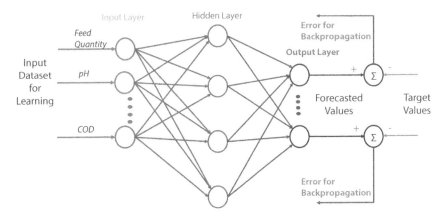

Figure 4.4 Feedback propagation artificial neural network.

type neural network. The reference signal feedback enables the neural network to predict more close to the actual value.

The ANN model is modeled in three steps, i.e., training, testing, and validation. The input data is divided into three sets to perform these operations. To train the neural network, training datasets are used; in training, the weights between the nodes are updated. Validation data sets are used to fine tune neural network performance and test data sets are used to assess neural network precision and error margin. Neural network algorithms are implemented for training after classification of the data in these three sets. Optimizer is used to facilitate the training optimization. The optimization algorithm is chosen based on model's specifications such as memory, numerical precision and processing speed.

4.2.2   Training Algorithms

The identification of the fastest training algorithm is very difficult for the given problem. The speed of the training algorithm depends upon various factors, *viz.*, problem complexity, training data set size, the number of weights and biases in the network, the error goal, and the application area of the network. The most used ANN training algorithms are Levenberg-Marquardt, Resilient backpropagation, and BFGS Quasi-Newton.

4.2.3   Performance Parameters for Analysis of the ANN Model

The developed ANN models are assessed using statistical parameters, *viz.*, mean absolute deviation (MAD), mean square error (MSE), root mean square error (RMSE), and correlation coefficient (R) [16, 17]. Equations (4.2) to (4.5) represent the mathematics behind these statistical parameters.

$$MAD = \frac{1}{n}\sum_{j=1}^{n}|z'_j - z_j| \qquad (4.2)$$

$$MSQ = \frac{1}{n}\sum_{j=1}^{n}(z'_j - z_j)^2 \qquad (4.3)$$

$$RMSE = \sqrt{\frac{1}{n}\sum_{j=1}^{n}(z'_j - z_j)^2} \qquad (4.4)$$

$$R = \frac{\sum_{i=1}^{n}(z_i - \bar{z}_i) \times (z'_i - \bar{z}'_i)}{\sqrt{\sum_{i=1}^{n}(z_i - \bar{z}_i)^2 \times \sum_{i=1}^{n}(z'_i - \bar{z}'_i)^2}} \qquad (4.5)$$

where z and z' represent actual and predicted data.

4.2.4 Application of ANN for Biogas Production Modeling

ANNs are used to model the behavior of different linear and non-linear processes with higher accuracy. ANN models are developed to predict biogas yield and composition of produced biogas from the bioreactor. The model efficiency is depending upon the data quality and quantity for model training. The wider the data set (collection of input data points along with the proportional outputs) better the model performance. Researchers have developed various ANN models for the prediction of biogas production.

Dahunsi et al. have predicted the biogas production potential in the anaerobic digester using ANN model with HLR, HRT, TS, T_{op}, VS, and pH [18]. Similarly, Holubar et al. developed a model to predict the biogas yield and composition of the produced biogas by the anaerobic digestion of lingocellulosic. The prominent input parameters for modeling are pH, VFAs, COD, and VS [20]. Clercq et al. have developed a software tool based on machine learning for biogas yield prediction in industrial scale bioreactor. Logistic regression, support vector machine (SVM), random forest, and k-nearest neighbors (KNN) are used for the biogas yield prediction. The KNN is predicting the biogas yield with the accuracy of 87%, which is highest among all the models developed [21].

Table 4.1 Some important applications of ANN technology for the development of biogas predication model in anaerobic digestion process.

S. no.	Name of artificial neural network model	Objective	Input parameter(s)	Output parameter(s)	Optimum model(s)	Result(s)	Ref.
1	Hierarchical neural networks	To design and develop artificial neural network based prediction model to control anaerobic digestion process	Feeding rate, pH, chemical oxygen demand, VFA concentration, redox potential, VSS, biogas composition, methane production rate, and effluent	Optimum feed composition, composition of produced biogas, rate of methane production	FFBP ANN with 9-3-2 for the biogas composition and methane production rate	The developed model could be used for forecasting and control of anaerobic digestion process.	[19]
2	Feedforward neural network	To forecast trace compounds in anaerobic digestion biogas	In H_2S model: Sulfate loading rate, OLR, and H_2S in biogas (ppm). In NH_3 model: total nitrogen loading rate, OLR and NH_3 in biogas (ppm), biogas productivity, pH, ammonia in the digester	Proportion of H_2S (ppm) and ammonia (ppm) in biogas	For prediction of H_2S- 5 neurons in the hidden layer For prediction of NH_3-7 neurons in the hidden layer.	The developed models predicted H_2S and NH_3 traces satisfactorily in the produced biogas.	[24]

(Continued)

Table 4.1 Some important applications of ANN technology for the development of biogas predication model in anaerobic digestion process. (*Continued*)

S. no.	Name of artificial neural network model	Objective	Input parameter(s)	Output parameter(s)	Optimum model(s)	Result(s)	Ref.
3	Three-layer ANN model	To predict the methane proportion and biogas yield from the molasses wastewater treatment using pilot-scale mesophilic UASB reactor.	Organic loading rate, pH volatile fatty acid concentrations, Temperature, alkalinity, COD for influent, and effluent.	Methane percentage in produced biogas and biogas yield	Biogas model: 8-9-1 with SCG (train-scg) algorithm Methane model: 8-12-1 with SCG (train-scg) algorithm	The ANN models developed with SCG training algorithm have estimated biogas and methane production.	[20]
4	BPNN	To forecast the percentage of methane in biogas produced from landfill upon injection of liquid organic waste	Rate of extraction of landfill gas in (m³/h) and landfill leachate: food waste leachate	Percentage Methane content (%)	Extreme learning machine based ANN with high R value and minimum MAPE	The developed model performance is exceptionally high and significant.	[25]

(*Continued*)

Table 4.1 Some important applications of ANN technology for the development of biogas predication model in anaerobic digestion process. (*Continued*)

S. no.	Name of artificial neural network model	Objective	Input parameter(s)	Output parameter(s)	Optimum model(s)	Result(s)	Ref.
5	ANN and Principal component analysis ANN (PC-ANN)	To forecast carbon (C) and nitrogen (N) in different blends of seven substrates.	C/N ratio, VS Loading, protein, VFA, lipid, Carbohydrate, lignin, TKN and TAN in the substrates	Methane vields, concentration of COD and $NH_4^+ - N$ concentrations	Principal component analysis ANN (PC-ANN)	The developed model can predict and optimize the nutrient recycling in anaerobic digestion process.	[26]

Sakiewics *et al.* developed an ANN model for the integrated wastewater treatment facility of 27 MLD at Rybnik, Poland. ANN model is developed with seven main plant operational parameters for the prediction of biogas; it is observed that five out of seven are affecting the biogas yield. Simultaneously, sensitivity analysis is performed; it is observed that COD, BOD, TSS, P, and N concentration of wastewater are the parameters which effects the biogas yield [22]. Almomani developed an ANN-based prediction model for biogas yield in chemically treated co-digested agriculture waste. The prediction accuracy of cumulative methane percentage is more than 90% [23].

The literature review reveals that ANN is an efficient technique for modeling and predicting impact of different process parameters on biogas yield and composition under mesophilic or thermophilic conditions. The production of biogas can be optimized by optimization of parameters under favorable digestive conditions once the parameter effects have been identified. Table 4.1 shows some of the important applications of the ANN modeling for the prediction and control of biogas production through anaerobic digestion process.

4.3   Evolutionary Algorithms

Nature evolution has profoundly impressed scientists with the ideology underlying it to establish methods of evolutionary optimization process. The evolutionary algorithms are created by materializing the behavior of different species into mathematical patterns [27]. The most famous are genetic algorithm (GA), ant colony optimization (ACO), and particle swarm optimization (PSO).

4.3.1   Genetic Algorithm

The GAs are biologically inspired and effective domain-independent search methods, developed in the 1970s by John Holland at University of Michigan. These methods can facilitate the efficient solution of problems in various application domains. From the AI research viewpoint, it offers an outstanding learning mechanism. GAs are a special class of evolutionary algorithms; typical strategies in all GAs are inheritance-birth traits, mutation-change to prevent resemblance, natural selection-variation improve longevity, and crossover recombination. Best use of GAs has been found when the objective function is discontinuous, strongly nonlinear, high dimensional, stochastic, undefined, and inconsistent derivatives.

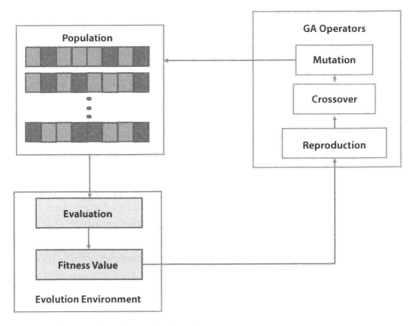

Figure 4.5 Genetic algorithm evaluation flow.

GAs are not too fast, but they cover a wide variety of features, are capable of rapidly identifying promising areas of search space but can take a reasonably long time to achieve an optimum solution. For combinational problems, GAs are good heuristic, generally emphasizing the combination of good parent (crossover) information. Different GAs use different representation, mutation crossover, and selection mechanism, Figure 4.5 represents the evolution flow of GAs.

4.3.2 Ant Colony Optimization

ACO is a component of swarm intelligence used for optimization of computational problems; it is probabilistic technique uses graphs to find the optimum path. Ants lay a trail of pheromones to inform other ants to follow the path in search of food. Once a food source is found, the ant who discovered it communicates this information to its peers and they follow the pheromones trail of that ant. As more number of ants travels to the food source, they also lay their own pheromone on the path, which makes it thicker resulting more and more ants get attracted. If an obstacle arrives along the desired route, then the ants quickly change the path and take the next most efficient path to the food presented in Figure 4.6. A high

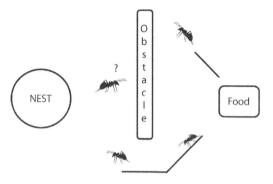

Figure 4.6 Path of ant when there is an obstruction.

pheromone level on the correct path provides a better stimulus to the ant and has a greater chance of turning right.

Artificial ants reflect multi-agent strategies that are inspired by the behavior of real ants. Pheromone is deposited by ants as they travel, and successive ants prefer pathways of more pheromone. Without any direct communication between them, the ants quickly leave other trails to focus on the shortest, as presented in Figure 4.7 [28].

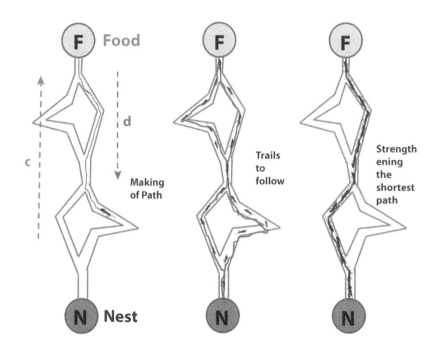

Figure 4.7 Ant colony optimization.

Figure 4.8 Swarm of birds [30].

4.3.3   Particle Swarm Optimization

PSO is one of the most popular and efficient algorithms. It is proposed by Kennedy and Eberhart [29]. It is inspired by swarm behavior, such as fish or birds (Figure 4.8) and is highly effective in a number of optimization problems. Each candidate solution is called as particle. The population is set of vector and is called swarm. Particle changes their components and move (fly) in space. They can evaluate their actual position using the function to be optimized. The function is called as fitness evaluation.

In PSO, possible particles travel to reach the global optimum in the search field. This movement is based on right control parameter combinations and a substitution formula. Particles also modify their positions with their own location called P_{best} (particle best) and the best position of the swarm G_{best} (global best). When a better solution is found by any particle, all particles augment their position in the search space for this better solution [31]. The flowchart for PSO is given in Figure 4.9.

4.3.4   Application of Hybrid Models (ANN and Evolutionary Algorithms) for Biogas Production Modeling

The integration of the ANN along with the evolutionary algorithms is used for the prediction and optimization of various nonlinear biological processes such as anaerobic digestion process. Popular evolutionary algorithms used are GA, ACO, and PSO. The combination of these algorithms

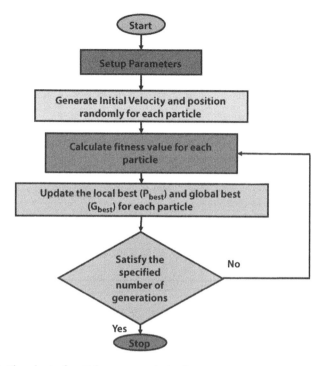

Figure 4.9 Flowchart of particle swarm optimization.

and ANN model is to model the complex engineering problem, *viz.*, estimation of the biogas yield and percentage of methane content in the produced gas. These hybrid models are used to optimize and select the input values to produce the optimum output. Table 4.2 presents some important applications of combinational models of ANN along with the evolutionary algorithms for optimizing the anaerobic digestion processes.

4.4   Conclusion

Various AI techniques were used to model and optimise biogas production processes due to its capacity to manage complexity, nonlinearity, and digestion uncertainty. The researchers are applying these advanced computational modeling techniques on the biogas processes due to the need of quick and precise control of the biogas production system. AI and evolutionary algorithms can act as promising techniques to model, optimise and govern biogas production processes. Although these advanced techniques have very seldom been used in real time to monitor and control digestion

Table 4.2 Some important applications of combination of artificial neural network models along with the evolutionary algorithms for optimizing the anaerobic digestion processes.

S. no.	Type of feed stoke	Objective(s)	Model(s) for prediction	Algorithm used for optimization	Optimal value of model inputs	Optimal value of the model outputs	Ref.
1	Karanja Seed Cake and Cattle Dung	To model and optimize the biogas production through ANN and GA	A multi-layered feed-forward neural network	GA	pH 6.68, digestion time of 14.22 days, C/N (24.1:1)	Biogas yield, 89.8%; Methane yield, 73%.	[32]
2	Wastewater sludge	To model the anaerobic digestion process and optimize biogas yield for wastewater sludge in Hurma WWTP Antalya, Turkey	Multi-layer perceptron neural network	PSO	pH, 6.87; T (°C) 35.8; SLR (m³/day) 371.5; TS (mg/l) 22,090; TVS (mg/l) 18,361; VFA (mg/l) 17.04; ALK (mg/l) 3,934; SRT (day) 18.05; OLR (kg/m³ day) 2.02	Biogas yield, 3,322m³/day; max methane percentage, 66.8%; rise in methane percentage with respect to avg. value, 4.8%; rise in biogas yield with respect to the avg. value, 64%; decrease in CO_2 and other contents, 8.5%.	[31]

(Continued)

Table 4.2 Some important applications of combination of artificial neural network models along with the evolutionary algorithms for optimizing the anaerobic digestion processes. (*Continued*)

S. no.	Type of feed stoke	Objective(s)	Model(s) for prediction	Algorithm used for optimization	Optimal value of model inputs	Optimal value of the model outputs	Ref.
3	Banana stem, paper waste, rice bran, saw dust, and Cow dung	To optimize best co-substrate combination for optimum biogas yield	Feedforward multilayer ANN	GA	Concentration of paper waste 25%, rice bran 5%, saw dust 20%, cow dung 25%, and banana stem 25%.	Biogas yield of 10,280 ml which is 8.64% higher in comparison with non-optimized yield.	[10]
4	Agriculture Substrate	To develop a quick and accurate model for biogas yield prediction	A two-layer FFANN	ACO	Concentration of Pheromone Inert particulates, 0.71; Long chain fatty acids, 0.81; Inorganic nitrogen, 0.74; Amino acids, 0.86; Sugars, 0.76; Inert solutes, 0.69; Proteins, 0.87; Acetic acid, 0.74; Composites, 0.78; Lipids, 0.81; Carbohydrates, 0.95.	R^2 of 0.89 for the biogas production and error of 5.1%	[33]

(*Continued*)

Table 4.2 Some important applications of combination of artificial neural network models along with the evolutionary algorithms for optimizing the anaerobic digestion processes. (*Continued*)

S. no.	Type of feed stoke	Objective(s)	Model(s) for prediction	Algorithm used for optimization	Optimal value of model inputs	Optimal value of the model outputs	Ref.
5	Agriculture Substrate	To predict the biogas yield based on feature selection through ANN and GA-ACO	Multi-layered ANN	GA-ACO	Neutral detergent fiber (NDF), HRT, TS, n-butyric acid, and Acid detergent lignin (ADL)	R^2 of 0.90 and Prediction error of 6.24%	[34]
6	Cattle manure (CM) and Palm oil mill effluent (POME)	To predict and optimize biogas generation in solar based AD of POME and CM	FF-ANN	PSO	POME: CM (50:50) OHP doses (%) 1.00% NH_4HCO_3 doses (mg/L) - 0	Biogas yield 2,462.72 ml	[13]

processes. So, in future, it is aimed to use these advanced modeling and optimization algorithms to control and monitor anaerobic digestion process in real-time for the biogas production and optimization.

References

1. Khatri, N. and Khatri, K.K., Hydrogen enrichment on diesel engine with biogas in dual fuel mode. *Int. J. Hydrogen Energy*, 45, 11, 7128–7140, Feb. 2020,.
2. Demirbas, A., Taylan, O., Kaya, D., Biogas production from municipal sewage sludge (MSS). *Energy Sources Part A Recovery Util. Environ. Eff.*, 38, 20, 3027–3033, 2016.
3. Cuadros, F., López-Rodríguez, F., Ruiz-Celma, A., Rubiales, F., González-González, A., Recycling, reuse and energetic valuation of meat industry wastes in extremadura (Spain). *Resour. Conserv. Recycl.*, 55, 4, 393–399, 2011.
4. Mata-Alvarez, J., Dosta, J., Romero-Güiza, M.S., Fonoll, X., Peces, M., Astals, S., A critical review on anaerobic co-digestion achievements between 2010 and 2013. *Renewable Sustainable Energy Rev.*, 36, 412–427, 2014.
5. Yadvika, S., Sreekrishnan, T.R., Kohli, S., Rana, V., Enhancement of biogas production from solid substrates using different techniques - A review. *Bioresour. Technol.*, 95, 1, 1–10, 2004.
6. Kythreotou, N., Florides, G., Tassou, S.A., A review of simple to scientific models for anaerobic digestion. *Renewable Energy*, 71, 701–714, 2014.
7. Carrère, H. *et al.*, Pretreatment methods to improve sludge anaerobic degradability: A review. *J. Hazard. Mater.*, 183, 1–3, 1–15, 2010.
8. Khalid, A., Arshad, M., Anjum, M., Mahmood, T., Dawson, L., The anaerobic digestion of solid organic waste. *Waste Manage.*, 31, 8, 1737–1744, 2011.
9. Horváth, I.S., Tabatabaei, M., Karimi, K., Kumar, R., Recent updates on biogas production - A review. *Biofuel Res. J.*, 3, 2, 394–402, 2016.
10. Gueguim Kana, E.B., Oloke, J.K., Lateef, A., Adesiyan, M.O., Modeling and optimization of biogas production on saw dust and other co-substrates using Artificial Neural network and Genetic Algorithm. *Renewable Energy*, 46, 276–281, 2012.
11. Rego, A.S.C., Leite, S.A.F., Leite, B.S., Grillo, A.V., Santos, B.F., Artificial neural network modelling for biogas production in biodigesters. *Chem. Eng. Trans.*, 74, March, 25–30, 2019.
12. Ramachandran, A., Rustum, R., Adeloye, A.J., Review of anaerobic digestion modeling and optimization using nature-inspired techniques. *Processes*, 7, 12, 1–12, 2019.
13. Zaied, B.K. *et al.*, Prediction and optimization of biogas production from POME co-digestion in solar bioreactor using artificial neural network coupled with particle swarm optimization (ANN-PSO). *Biomass Convers. Biorefin.*, 10, 1–16, 2020.

14. Li, X., Sha, J., liang Wang, Z., A comparative study of multiple linear regression, artificial neural network and support vector machine for the prediction of dissolved oxygen. *Hydrol. Res.*, 48, 5, 1214–1225, 2017.

15. Almasi, F., Soltanian, S., Hosseinpour, S., Aghbashlo, M., Tabatabaei, M., Advanced Soft Computing Techniques in Biogas Production Technology, in: *Biogas: Fundamentals, Process, and Operation*, M. Tabatabaei and H. Ghanavati (Eds.), pp. 387–417, Springer International Publishing, Cham, 2018.

16. Khatri, N., Khatri, K.K., Sharma, A., Prediction of effluent quality in ICEAS-sequential batch reactor using feedforward artificial neural network. *Water Sci. Technol.*, 80, 2, 213–222, 2019.

17. Khatri, N., Khatri, K.K., Sharma, A., Artificial neural network modelling of faecal coliform removal in an intermittent cycle extended aeration system-sequential batch reactor based wastewater treatment plant. *J. Water Process Eng.*, 37, March, 101477, 2020.

18. Dahunsi, S.O., Oranusi, S., Owolabi, J.B., Efeovbokhan, V.E., Comparative biogas generation from fruit peels of fluted pumpkin (Telfairia occidentalis) and its optimization. *Bioresour. Technol.*, 221, 517–525, 2016.

19. Holubar, P., Zani, L., Hager, M., Fröschl, W., Radak, Z., Braun, R., Advanced controlling of anaerobic digestion by means of hierarchical neural networks. *Water Res.*, 36, 10, 2582–2588, 2002.

20. Yetilmezsoy, K., Turkdogan, F.I., Temizel, I., Gunay, A., Development of ann-based models to predict biogas and methane productions in anaerobic treatment of molasses wastewater. *Int. J. Green Energy*, 10, 9, 885–907, 2013.

21. De Clercq, D. *et al.*, Machine learning powered software for accurate prediction of biogas production: A case study on industrial-scale Chinese production data. *J. Cleaner Prod.*, 218, 390–399, 2019.

22. Sakiewicz, P., Piotrowski, K., Ober, J., Karwot, J., Innovative artificial neural network approach for integrated biogas – wastewater treatment system modelling: Effect of plant operating parameters on process intensification. *Renewable Sustainable Energy Rev.*, 124, 109784, 2020.

23. Almomani, F., Prediction of biogas production from chemically treated co-digested agricultural waste using artificial neural network. *Fuel*, 280, April, 118573, 2020.

24. Strik, D. P. B. T. B., Domnanovich, A.M., Zani, L., Braun, R., Holubar, P., Prediction of trace compounds in biogas from anaerobic digestion using the MATLAB Neural Network Toolbox. *Environ. Model. Software*, 20, 6, 803–810, 2005.

25. Behera, S.K., Meher, S.K., Park, H.S., Artificial neural network model for predicting methane percentage in biogas recovered from a landfill upon injection of liquid organic waste. *Clean Technol. Environ. Policy*, 17, 2, 443–453, 2015.

26. Li, H. *et al.*, Estimating the Fates of C and N in Various Anaerobic Codigestions of Manure and Lignocellulosic Biomass Based on Artificial Neural Networks. *Energy Fuels*, 30, 11, 9490–9501, 2016.
27. Gazi, V. and Passino, K.M., *Swarm stability and optimization*, Springer-Verlag, and Berlin Heidelberg, 2011.
28. Goodwin, M., Granmo, O.C., Radianti, J., Sarshar, P., Glimsdal, S., Ant colony optimisation for planning safe escape routes. *Lect. Notes Comput. Sci. (including Subser. Lect. Notes Artif. Intell. Lect. Notes Bioinformatics)*, 7906 LNAI, 53–62, 2013.
29. Kennedy, J.F., Eberhart, R.C., Shi, Y., *Swarm intelligence*, Morgan Kaufmann Publishers, USA, 2001.
30. Bird folk, 2021, Pinterest, Inc., San Francisco, California [Online]. Available: https://in.pinterest.com/. [Accessed: 14-Feb-2021].
31. Akbaş, H., Bilgen, B., Turhan, A.M., An integrated prediction and optimization model of biogas production system at a wastewater treatment facility. *Bioresour. Technol.*, 196, 566–576, 2015.
32. Barik, D. and Murugan, S., An Artificial Neural Network and Genetic Algorithm Optimized Model for Biogas Production from Co-digestion of Seed Cake of Karanja and Cattle Dung. *Waste Biomass Valorization*, 6, 6, 1015–1027, 2015.
33. Beltramo, T., Ranzan, C., Hinrichs, J., Hitzmann, B., Artificial neural network prediction of the biogas flow rate optimised with an ant colony algorithm. *Biosyst. Eng.*, 143, 68–78, 2016.
34. Beltramo, T., Klocke, M., Hitzmann, B., Prediction of the biogas production using GA and ACO input features selection method for ANN model. *Inf. Process. Agric.*, 6, 3, 349–356, 2019.

Battery State-of-Charge Modeling for Solar PV Array Using Polynomial Regression

Siddhi Vinayak Pandey*, Jeet Patel and Harsh S. Dhiman

Dept. of Electrical Engineering, Adani Institute of Infrastructure Engineering, Ahmedabad, India

Abstract

Due to the increased demand of solar photovoltaic (PV) arrays, its integration with a battery and modeling of precise State of Charge (SoC) is a consequential parameter to understand the available battery capacity in real time domain. In this paper, the integration of solar PV array with the first-order RC circuit has been implemented utilizing the MATLAB (Simulink Library). For experimentation, the open-circuit voltage (V_{oc}) and the short-circuit current (I_{sc}) of the solar panel is considered as 36.3 volts and 7.84 amperes, respectively. The continuous fluctuating irradiance from 110,580 W/m^2 leads in the variation of output voltage of the solar PV arrays. Also, the variations of battery charging current, voltage across battery, and battery SOC due to variations in irradiance are examined in detail. The proposed methodology of this manuscript explains the authentic time modeling of SoC utilizing the second, third, fourth, and fifth order of a polynomial regression technique. The comparative relationship between the OCV and SoC during the charging of the model with solar PV array has been also obtained for different orders of polynomials. Quantitatively, fifth-order model outperforms second, third, and fourth by 27.5%, 26.7%, and 21.3%, respectively.

Keywords: Battery, SoC, modeling, solar PV, kalman filter, regression, forecasting, capacity

5.1 Introduction

Sustainable energy sources lead to reduction in carbon footprint and thus increase the reliability of a system [1–4]. The State of Charge (SoC) is a

---

Corresponding author: siddhipandey.ele17@aii.ac.in

Ajay Kumar Vyas, S. Balamurugan, Kamal Kant Hiran and Harsh S. Dhiman (eds.) *Artificial Intelligence for Renewable Energy Systems*, (115–128) © 2022 Scrivener Publishing LLC

parameter by which users can get details about the availability of battery capacity. The precise calculation and estimation of the available energy within a battery has always been a challenging task. Mathematically, SoC is a ratio of current capacity $Q(t)$ to nominal capacity Q_n given as

$$SoC(t) = \frac{Q(t)}{Q_n} \qquad (5.1)$$

The precise calculation and modeling of the SoC will not only increases the system performance but also impacts cycle life in a longer run. Measurement and estimation of SoC remains one of the challenging tasks. SoC estimation is based on various sensor-based, filter-based, and data-driven techniques out of which Coulomb counting is the fundamental one. In [5], authors use Coulomb counting where current is integrated with respect to time. However, this method is inefficient due to the effect of temperature, discharge current, and cycle life of the battery. In order to overcome this, filter-based and data-driven estimation algorithms are utilized to estimate the SoC of the battery. In [6], authors use a Kalman Filter technique for SoC estimation. The Kalman filter is an estimator used to estimate the linear and nonlinear systems. Based on the present data of voltage, current, and temperature, it estimates the SoC with good accuracy and precision. While the estimation error of fully and partially charged battery is found to be around 0.5%. Apart from the Kalman filter, machine learning–based algorithms are also used to estimate the SoC of a battery. In [7], authors use a Support Vector Machine (SVM) approach, which is a statistical learning method used for estimating the SoC of a battery. The SoC of a Lithium Iron Manganese Phosphate (LiFeMnPO$_4$) battery is estimated under the constant charging and variable load condition. The error in the proposed model is less than 4%, while the RMSE is 0.4% throughout the whole experiment. Apart from SVM, various other data-driven methods such as Neural Networks (NNs), Deep Neural Networks (DNNs), and Reinforcement Learning (RL) approach are used for the estimation of SoC.

Due to green gas emissions, the world is perpetually shifting toward renewable energy sources. Solar and wind energy being the pioneers in power portfolio. The on-field efficiency of solar panels is near about 18% to 21% [8]. However, due to the recent advancement in perovskite solar cells, reflectors, photonic crystals, and recycling photovoltaic (PV) cells, the efficiency of the solar cells is increasing drastically. Further, it is expected that, till 2030, the on-field efficiency of solar-based PV cells will be near about 30% [9].

Nowadays, the integration of solar PV arrays with batteries is gaining tremendous importance due to intermittency posed. Regarding this, many electric conveyances, grids, and space satellites are directly charging their batteries through solar PV arrays [10]. Mainly, two topologies exist for solar PV array with battery. The first one being stand-alone system, while the other being the grid-tied system. In the stand-alone system, solar PV is connected to the load via a battery. While in a grid-tied system, the load is supplied by a grid in case of failure in PV side [11].

In order to implement solar PV arrays in applications such as electric vehicles, space satellites, and drones, the weight of the module plays a very crucial role. The huge weight of solar panels can increase the overall pay-load capacity of the vehicles, and to overcome this, installation of thin-film crystalline–based solar panels is suggested. The thin-film crystalline–based solar cells are very light in weight. However, they are less efficient in their PV operation. Majority of the research is focused to enhance the efficiency of thin-film crystalline solar panels [12]. The selection of battery while implementing the solar PV arrays is also a consequential parameter for the efficient and vigorous performance of the system. In [13], authors discuss the case of LFP (Lithium Ion Phosphate) and LCO (Lithium Cobalt Oxide) batteries which, when tested at 45°C, observed an optimistic operation for the PV battery integrated module.

The energy generated through solar PV arrays is directly dependent on the irradiance and surface temperature of solar panels as variation in irradiance and surface temperature can impact power generation of the solar PV plant [14]. This type of change can directly affect the voltage and current level of the plant. Furthermore, this also impacts the SoC level of the interconnected battery. In [15], authors proposed a study based on the effect of variation in irradiance and surface temperature for solar PV arrays. In the proposed model, factors such as fill factor, efficiency, open-circuit voltage (OCV), and maximum power are the parameters get affected due to the variation in irradiance and surface temperature of a solar predicated PV arrays. The increment in irradiance increases the OCV and overall efficiency of the system. While increase in the surface temperature of the PV cell decreases the OCV, fill factor, efficiency, and a maximum power of a system. Apart from these factors, the construction of a battery is dependent upon the materials, modeling, and effect of the age-ing mechanism during the real-time charging and discharging of a battery. Due to the escalating demand for energy storage systems, batteries play an important role in storing bulk power. As a matter of fact, an elevated research is going on in the field of eco-friendly–based battery material that gets recycled easily. Variants such as Lead acid, Nickel, Lithium, Cadmium,

Table 5.1 Brief summary of current research in battery energy storage systems.

SoC estimation [16]	Dynamic battery modeling [17]	Ageing mechanism [18]
• Direct measurement methods 1. Coulomb counting 2. Open-circuit voltage	• Electrochemical model It uses electrochemical parameters and variables to define a battery model	• Loss of active material The positive electrode of the battery undergoes contraction and relaxation constantly which causes the material to deteriorate slowly loses lithium absorbing capacity.
• Filter-based methods 1. Kalman filter 2. Extended Kalman filter	• Equivalent first-order battery model The first-order model has a resistance R_0 which represents internal battery resistance of the battery along with one RC network.	• Loss of Lithium inventory While forming the SEI layer, large amount of lithium is consumed which is the main reason for LLI. The high rate charging and discharging connected with it or low-temperature, lithium plating may occur on the negative electrode and form lithium crystal branches which cause further loss of Li-ion.
• Data-driven methods 1. Support Vector Machines 2. Neural Network	• Equivalent second-order battery model A second-order system has a similar circuit connected with it, but with an extra (one more) RC network.	Almost all positive electrodes are made up of carbon. An SEI (solid electrolyte interface) layer is formed and diminished during the charging and discharging process of the battery.

alkaline, Mercury, and Nickel Metal Hydride are toxic elements often used in fabrication process. A summary of the methods for estimating the SoC of a battery, dynamic battery modeling, and ageing mechanism of Li-ion battery is depicted in Table 5.1.

In this manuscript, the first-order RC circuit is implemented under the variation of irradiance on the solar PV array. The variation of SoC during the charging of a battery has been obtained using the Kalman Filter technique, and based on the charging response of a first-order model, the second, third, fourth, and fifth degree of polynomial regression technique is used to obtain the relationship between OCV and SoC. The comparative analysis of regression between the OCV and SoC at different degrees of the polynomial is investigated in detail.

The remainder of the manuscript is organized as follows. Section 5.2 describes the simulation setup of our proposed methodology. Section 5.3 gives insights about modeling, comparisons of regression techniques and results of our proposed methodology. While the conclusions and references are presented in Section 5.4.

5.2   Dynamic Battery Modeling

In order to simulate the dynamic characteristics of a battery, the values of an input voltage source, resistor, and capacitor play an important role [19]. In this manuscript, the first-order RC model has been used to store the energy generated by the solar PV array. Given the simulation setup, the dynamic first-order model of the battery is illustrated in Figure 5.1.

In Figure 5.1, the terms V_{oc} and V_{batt} are OCV and terminal voltage, R_0 is the internal resistance, while R_1 and C_1 are the external polarizing resistor and capacitance of the battery. During the operation, the capacitor

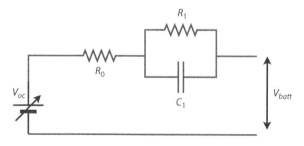

Figure 5.1 First-order battery model.

gets energized and stores the energy which was supplied through voltage source (V_s). This dynamic model works in close approximation to the battery being used in real-time applications. Mathematically, charging of a capacitor with respect to time is given as

$$V_{batt} = V_{oc} - IR_1 e^{-t/\tau} \tag{5.2}$$

$$i(t) = \frac{V_{batt}}{R_1} e^{-t/\tau} \tag{5.3}$$

The terms V_{batt} and $i(t)$ in (5.2) and (5.3) represent voltage across and current through the capacitor. While the $\tau = R_1 C_1$ denotes the time constant of the model. This time constant requires five steps (five times constant) to charge the capacitor. During the charging conditions, the demeanor of the system remains exponential.

5.2.1   Proposed Methodology

The proposed methodology of our experimental setup aims to determine the relationship between the SoC and OCV of a battery. The direct charging of a battery using the solar PV arrays under the variable irradiance and surface temperature of a PV cell is used to charge the battery. The proposed experimental setup is explained using the following block diagram.

The schematic block diagram in Figure 5.2 consists of basic blocks which are interconnected together to perform the intended task. The solar PV array is kept under the variable irradiance and temperature. The variability between irradiance and temperature affects the output voltage generation of a solar PV array. This variable voltage is directly stored in the battery.

The battery connected with solar PV array gets charged when a sophisticated amount of voltage generated across the solar PV array. The measurement block is interconnected with such sensors, which can measure the value

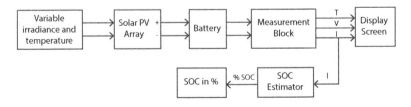

Figure 5.2 Block diagram for the simulation setup.

of voltage, current, and temperature of a dynamic battery model during the charging condition. These measurements are clearly visible on the display screen, which is connected next to the measurement block. In order to estimate the SoC of a battery during the charging condition; the SoC estimator is used. In our case, the Kalman Filter is used for the SoC estimation of a battery during a direct charging condition with a solar PV array.

The Kalman Filter is a state estimator, used to estimate and track the data in the real-time domain. In our case, it takes the input current of a battery during the charging condition with a solar PV array for estimating the SoC of a battery in the real-time domain. The Kalman filter takes the state-space values and inputs current of a battery. Based on these data, it estimates the SoC of a battery. The mathematical representation of the Kalman filter [20] is as

$$
\begin{aligned}
x_{k+1} &= A_k x_k + B_k u_k + w_k \\
y_k &= C_k x_k + D_k u_k + v_k,
\end{aligned}
\tag{5.4}
$$

where A_k, B_k, C_k, and D_k represent state matrices of the first-order battery model. The term x_k represents initial state (state vector), while y_k is the set of observed data (observable at time k) in Kalman filter. During these estimations, it is required to know the noise of the initial system by which the filter received data for estimation. The term w_k represents the process noise, and v_k represents the measurement noise in a system. Due to modeling approximations and model integration errors, the process noise (w_k) is a consequential parameter to include in a model. Initialization for, k = 0, set

$$
\hat{x}_0^+ = E[x_0]
$$

$$
P_{x,0}^+ = E\left[(x_0 - x_0^+)(x_0 - x_0^+)^T\right]
$$

State estimate time update given as

$$
\hat{x}_0^- = A_{k-1}\hat{x}_{k-1}^- + B_{k-1}u_{k-1}
\tag{5.5}
$$

Error covariance time update

$$
P_{x,0}^- = A_{k-1}P_{x-0}^+ A_{k-1}^T + Q_w
\tag{5.6}
$$

Kalman gain matrix

$$k_k = P_{\tilde{x},k}^- C_k^T \left[C_k P_{\tilde{x}_0}^- C_k^T + R_v \right]^T \qquad (5.7)$$

State estimate measurement update

$$Q_k^* = 8_k^- + K_k \left[y_k - C_k \cdot \varepsilon_k^- - D_k u_k \right] \qquad (5.8)$$

Error covariance measurement update

$$P_{\hat{X}_k}^+ = \left(I - K_k C_k \right) P_{\tilde{X}_k}^- \qquad (5.9)$$

The state space matrices for the first-order battery model are given as

$$x = \begin{bmatrix} v_1 \\ x_{SoC}^+ \\ x_{SoC}^- \end{bmatrix} \quad x_0 = \begin{bmatrix} 0 \\ 0 \\ 0 \end{bmatrix} \quad y = \begin{bmatrix} V_{batt} \\ x_{SoC} \end{bmatrix} \quad u = \begin{bmatrix} i_d \\ i_c \end{bmatrix}$$

$$A_k = \begin{bmatrix} -1/(R_1 C_1) & 0 & 0 \\ 0 & 0 & 0 \\ 0 & 0 & 0 \end{bmatrix} \quad B_k = \begin{bmatrix} 1/C_1 & 1/C_1 \\ 1/C_{cap} & 0 \\ 0 & \eta_c/C_{cap} \end{bmatrix}$$

$$C_k = \begin{bmatrix} 1 & \gamma & \gamma \\ 0 & 1 & 1 \end{bmatrix} \quad D_k = \begin{bmatrix} R_0 & R_0 \\ 0 & 0 \end{bmatrix}$$

5.3   Results and Discussion

The entire simulation setup has is analyzed in MATLAB 2015b, core-i5 CPU environment. For simulation analysis, a "1Soltech 1STH-215-p Solar PV module" with the connection of 3 parallel and 1 series string has been utilized. The maximum power of the selected module is 213.15 W. The value of modeling parameters has been mentioned in Table 5.2, while the I-V and P-V characteristics of the PV array are illustrated in Figure 5.3.

Table 5.2 Model parameters for SoC estimation [20].

Parameters	Values
R_0	143 mΩ
R_1	0.15 mΩ
C_1	3.4kF
C_{cap}	1,000 Ah
γ	0.635V%SoC
η_c	99%
Q	diag([5 0.1 0.1])
R	diag([14 5])

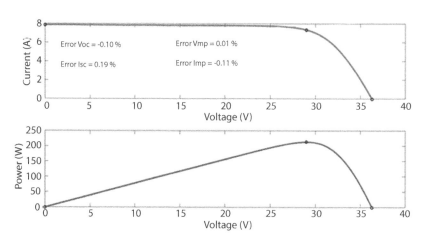

Figure 5.3 I-V and P-V curve for solar PV array.

In order to replicate the practical scenario, the irradiance level for PV array is kept variable rather than a constant one. Figure 5.4 illustrates the solar irradiance (W/m²) for simulation environment considered in this analysis. The irradiance plot in Figure 5.4 is shown for first 6 seconds of the simulation, while Figure 5.5 depicts the curve fitting result for OCV-SoC based on second, third, fourth & fifth order polynomials.

It is evident that output voltage and current for solar PV array will vary due to the variation of irradiance. These variations directly affect the charging characteristics of our dynamic battery model. In this section,

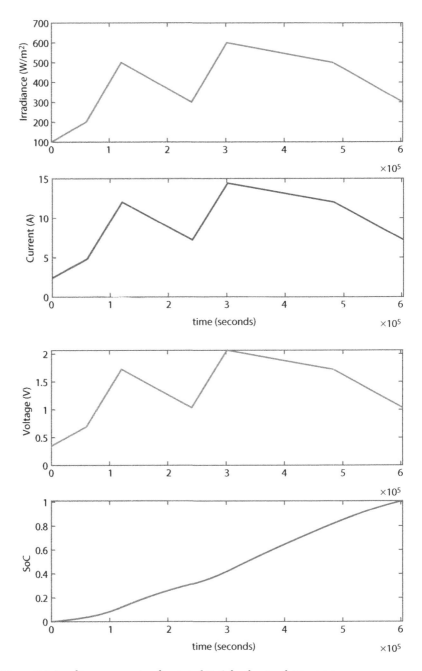

Figure 5.4 Irradiance, current, voltage, and SoC for the simulation setup.

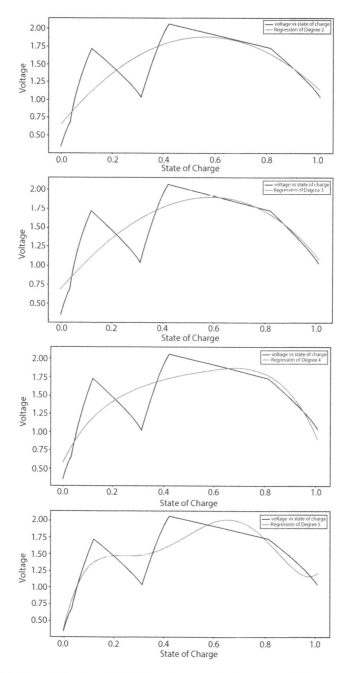

Figure 5.5 Curve fitting for OCV-SoC based on second-, third-, 4, and fifth-order polynomials.

Table 5.3 Performance metrics for regression models.

Degree of the polynomials	R^2	RMSE
2	0.7278	0.2289
3	0.7309	0.2276
4	0.7532	0.2179
5	0.8326	0.1795

a relationship between voltage and SoC of a battery utilizing the polynomial regression approach is obtained. The curve fitting utilizing the polynomial regression technique engenders the values of the coefficient for the equations, which defines the relationship between the two curves given as an input. Polynomials of order second, third, fourth, and fifth degree are analyzed based on their R^2 and RMSE values.

The value of R^2 for degree 2 is 0.7278 while for degree 5 it is 0.8326. Further, RMSE of 0.2289 for degree 2 and 0.1795 for degree 5 is observed. The term R^2 gives an idea of how well the output of a process fits the set of input observations. It is statistics data of the closeness of the data and the fitting regression line. The quality of the fitting will increase with an increase in the value of the degree of a polynomial. From Table 5.3, it is observed that increase in the degree of polynomial the relationship between SoC and voltage increases fitting accuracy. The regression method is also used to predict the future values of voltage or SoC given that any one of them is given. A polynomial equation of degree at which the value of R-square is maximum (close to 1) can be used as a base parameter to predict variables provided that the usage of the battery is not changed. Similarly, RMSE decreases in magnitude for higher-order polynomials.

5.4   Conclusion

In this manuscript, we have investigated the response of the SoC and the OCV across the dynamic battery model under the variable voltage and current during the charging cycle of the battery. These variable input voltage and current have been obtained using the variable irradiance and surface temperature of a solar PV array which is connected as an input of the dynamic battery model to store the energy within it. In order to match the simulation result with reality, these variable irradiance and surface temperature of solar PV array with respect to time has been simulated.

After forming and storing the energy within the dynamic battery model; the SoC of the battery has been estimated using the Kalman filter approach. After the successful estimation of SoC, the OCV and SoC have been plotted using the polynomial regression technique. The regression plots between the OCV and SoC have been drawn for the polynomial degree of 2, 3, 4, and 5. Results reveal that R^2 keeps increasing as we increase the degrees of regression. Simultaneously, the value of RMSE keeps decreasing as we increase the degree of the polynomial regression.

References

1. Dhiman, H.S., Deb, D., Foley, A.M., Bilateral gaussian wake model formulation for wind farms: A forecasting based approach. *Renewable Sustainable Energy Rev.*, 127, 109873, Jul. 2020.

2. Dhiman, H.S., Deb, D., Guerrero, J.M., Hybrid machine intelligent SVR variants for wind forecasting and ramp events. *Renewable Sustainable Energy Rev.*, 108, 369–379, Jul. 2019.

3. Dhiman, H.S., Deb, D., Foley, A.M., Lidar assisted wake redirection in wind farms: A data driven approach. *Renewable Energy*, 152, 484–493, Jan. 2020.

4. Dhiman, H.S. and Deb, D., *Decision and Control in Hybrid Wind Farms*, Gateway East, Springer Singapore, 2020.

5. Chang, W.-Y., The state of charge estimating methods for battery: A review. *ISRN Appl. Math.*, 2013, 1–7, 2013, [Online]. Available: https://doi.org/10.1155/2013/953792.

6. Yu, Z., Huai, R., Xiao, L., State-of-charge estimation for lithium-ion batteries using a kalman filter based on local linearization. *Energies*, 8, 8, 7854–7873, Jul. 2015, [Online]. Available: https://doi.org/10.3390/en8087854.

7. Anton, J.C.A., Nieto, P.J.G., Viejo, C.B., Vilan, J.A.V., Support vector machines used to estimate the battery state of charge. *IEEE Trans. Power Electron.*, 28, 12, 5919–5926, Dec. 2013, [Online]. Available: https://doi.org/10.1109/tpel.2013.2243918.

8. Almasoud, A. and Gandayh, H.M., Future of solar energy in Saudi Arabia. *J. King Saud Univ. – Eng. Sci.*, 27, 2, 153–157, Jul. 2015, [Online]. Available: https://doi.org/10.1016/j.jksues.2014.03.007.

9. Arshad, R., Tariq, S., Niaz, M.U., Jamil, M., Improvement in solar panel efficiency using solar concentration by simple mirrors and by cooling, in: *2014 International Conference on Robotics and Emerging Allied Technologies in Engineering (iCREATE)*, Apr. 2014, IEEE, [Online]. Available: https://doi.org/10.1109/icreate.2014.6828382.

10. Zhu, T. and Wang, L., *State Energy Transition*, Gateway East, Springer Singapore, 2020, [Online]. Available: https://doi.org/10.1007/978-981-32-9499-8.

11. Glavin, M. and Hurley, W., Battery management system for solar energy applications, in: *Proceedings of the 41st International Universities Power Engineering Conference*, Sep. 2006, IEEE, [Online]. Available: https://doi. org/10.1109/upec.2006.367719.

12. Kaundinya, D.P., Balachandra, P., Ravindranath, N., Grid-connected versus stand-alone energy systems for decentralized power—a review of literature. *Renewable Sustainable Energy Rev.*, 13, 8, 2041–2050, Oct. 2009, [Online]. Available: https://doi.org/10.1016/j.rser.2009.02.002.

13. Powalla, M., Paetel, S., Hariskos, D., Wuerz, R., Kessler, F., Lechner, P., Wischmann, W., Friedlmeier, T.M., Advances in cost-efficient thin-film photovoltaics based on cu(in, ga)se 2. *Engineering*, 3, 4, 445–451, Aug. 2017, [Online]. Available: https://doi.org/10.1016/j.eng.2017.04.015.

14. Vega-Garita, V., Hanif, A., Narayan, N., Ramirez-Elizondo, L., Bauer, P., Selecting a suitable battery technology for the photovoltaic battery integrated module. *J. Power Sources*, 438, 227011, Oct. 2019, [Online]. Available: https://doi.org/10.1016/j.jpowsour.2019.227011.

15. Abed, K., Bahgat, A., Badr, M., El-Bayoumi, M., Ragheb, A., Experimental study of battery state of charge effect on battery charging/discharging performance and battery output power in pv energy system. *ARPN J. Eng. Appl. Sci.*, 13, 739–745, 01 2018.

16. Musanga, L.M., Barasa, W.H., Maxwell, M., The effect of irradiance and temperature on the performance of monocrystalline silicon solar module in kakamega. *Phys. Sci. Int. J.*, 19, 4, 1–9, Oct. 2018, [Online]. Available: https://doi.org/10.9734/psij/2018/44862.

17. L.C., Electrochemical model parameter identification of lithium-ion battery with temperature and current dependence. *Int. J. Electrochem. Sci.*, 14, 4124–4143, Apr. 2019, [Online]. Available: https://doi.org/10.20964/2019.05.05.

18. Lyu, C., Zhao, Y., Luo, W., Wang, L., Aging mechanism analysis and its impact on capacity loss of lithium ion batteries, in: *2019 14th IEEE Conference on Industrial Electronics and Applications (ICIEA)*, Jun. 2019, IEEE, [Online]. Available: https://doi.org/10.1109/iciea.2019.8833827.

19. Zhang, L., Peng, H., Ning, Z., Mu, Z., Sun, C., Comparative research on RC equivalent circuit models for lithium-ion batteries of electric vehicles. *Appl. Sci.*, 7, 10, 1002, Sep. 2017, [Online]. Available: https://doi.org/10.3390/app7101002.

20. Rosewater, D., Ferreira, S., Schoenwald, D., Hawkins, J., Santoso, S., Battery energy storage state-of-charge forecasting: Models, optimization, and accuracy. *IEEE Trans. Smart Grid*, 10, 3, 2453–2462, May 2018.

6

Deep Learning Algorithms for Wind Forecasting: An Overview

M. Lydia[1]* and G. Edwin Prem Kumar[2]

*[1]Dept. of Mechatronics Engineering,
Sri Krishna College of Engineering and Technology, Coimbatore, India
[2]Dept. of Information Technology,
Sri Krishna College of Engineering and Technology, Coimbatore, India*

Abstract

India, having the fourth largest installed capacity of wind power, is poised to grow in leaps and bounds in renewable energy utilization. The stochastic nature of wind has been a constant challenge in integration of wind power to the grid. According to the National Institute of Wind Energy (NIWE), the estimated wind potential of India at 120 m above ground level is around 695 GW. In order to effectively tap this power and to enhance wind power penetration in the grid, it is imperative that efficient wind speed and wind power forecasting models are in place. Forecasting of wind power aids in effective grid operations, planning of economic dispatch, estimation of candidate sites for wind farms and in scheduling operation and maintenance of wind farms. Deep learning models for wind forecasting have recently challenged the conventionally used forecasting models in terms of their accuracy, robust nature, and ability to handle huge volumes of data at a much lower computational cost. An exhaustive review of all the deep learning models used for wind speed/power forecasting is reviewed in this chapter. The research challenges faced and future research directions are also presented.

Keywords: Deep learning, forecasting, wind speed, wind power, accuracy

Nomenclature

AR	Autoregressive
ARMA	Autoregressive with moving average
ARX	Autoregressive with exogenous input

*Corresponding author: lydiaedwin.05@gmail.com

Ajay Kumar Vyas, S. Balamurugan, Kamal Kant Hiran and Harsh S. Dhiman (eds.) *Artificial Intelligence for Renewable Energy Systems*, (129–146) © 2022 Scrivener Publishing LLC

CEEMDAN	Complete ensemble empirical mode decomposition with adaptive noise
CRPS	Continuous ranked probability score
CNN	Convolutional neural network
DAE	Denoising autoencoder
DBN	Deep belief network
DGF	Double Gaussian function
DL	Deep learning
DLNN	Deep learning neural networks
DRNN	Deep recurrent neural networks
ELM	Extreme learning machine
EMD	Empirical mode decomposition
ENN	Elman neural network
ESN	Echo state network
GD	Gradient descent
GRU	Gated recurrent unit
HBSA	Hybrid backtracking search algorithm
IRAE	Independent recurrent autoencoder
kNN	k-nearest neighbor
LASSO	Least absolute shrinkage selector operator
LSTM	Long short-term memory
LUBE	Lower and upper bound estimation
ML	Machine learning
MAE	Mean absolute error
MAPE	Mean absolute percentage error
MLP	Multi-layer perceptron
MTL	Multi-task learning
MSE	Mean squared error
NN	Neural network
NWP	Numerical weather prediction
PSO	Particle swarm optimization
RBF	Radial basis function
RF	Random forest
RMSE	Root mean squared error
RMSLE	Root mean squared log error
RNN	Recurrent neural network
R-NNs	Rough NN
SAE	Stacked autoencoder
SCADA	Supervisory control and data acquisition
SDAE	Stacked denoising autoencoder
SIRAE	Stacked independently recurrent autoencoder
sMAPE	Symmetric mean absolute percentage error
SSA	Single spectrum analysis
STL	Single task learning

SVM	Support vector machine
SVR	Support vector regression
TL	Transfer learning
VMD	Variational mode decomposition
WF	Wind forecasting
WPF	Wind power forecasting
WPRE	Wind power ramp event
WSF	Wind speed forecasting
WT	Wind turbines
xGBoost	Extreme gradient boost

6.1 Introduction

Increasing use of renewable energy has become a mandatory alternative to mitigate the impact of environmental degradation caused by fossil fuels. Non-conventional energy resources like wind energy help in reduction of the carbon footprint globally, emission of green-house gases, and other pollutants. Accurate forecasting models are necessary for ensuring increased penetration of renewable energy in the power grid. Forecasting in offshore scenario is more challenging due to severe and unpredictable weather conditions that the wind turbines (WT) are exposed to.

Wind forecasting is classified into ultra-short-term, very short-term, short-term, and long-term wind forecasting based on the forecasting horizon. Ultra-short-term forecasting models spanning few seconds have been used to build accurate models for onshore and offshore WT models. Very short-term forecasting can span for few minutes and is very helpful in power prediction in intra-day and real-time markets. Short-term forecasting can span for few minutes to hours or days and is helpful in day-ahead markets, reserve setting, unit commitment, and economic dispatch. Long-term forecasts which usually span from days to weeks are useful for scheduling operation and maintenance activities.

The wind speed or power data used to build forecasting models can be 10-minute averaged data or hourly averaged data or daily data, depending on the availability of data for the site under consideration. Recent literature includes the use of high-frequency SCADA data, sampled for every 1 second.

Forecasting models for wind speed or wind power have been essentially built using three different approaches, namely, physical, statistical, and learning models [1]. The physical models include the numerical weather prediction (NWP) models which include the mathematical description of physical processes taking place in the earth's atmosphere (Figure 6.1). Statistical approach involves in quantitatively defining the relationship between meteorological predictions and historical data. Statistical modeling involves mathematical relationships between the dependent and independent variables. They include autoregressive (AR), auto regressive with moving average (ARMA), auto regressive with exogenous variables (ARX), and autoregressive integrated moving average (ARIMA). Learning approach include soft computing-based methods including artificial intelligence, fuzzy logic, support vector machine, and neural networks.

The methodologies used for wind forecasting can also be classified as model-driven, data-driven, and ensemble methods [2]. Model-based methods are built based on NWP models and meteorological data, whereas data-driven models attempt to learn relationships between the identified input variables. Data-driven models include statistical and artificial intelligence-based approaches like AR, ARMA, ANN, and ELM. A combination of model-based and data-driven models result in the ensemble methods. These methods incorporate signal processing techniques like wavelets and optimization algorithms like PSO, along with other prediction models like ANN and SVM.

Deep learning (DL) algorithms have proved to outperform traditional NNs and other conventional models with improved feature extraction and enhanced ability to learn complex non-linear relationships. According to literature, DL models for wind power forecasting includes hybrid ensemble deep reinforcement learning model, DL neural network, Bayesian DL model, convolutional gated recurrent unit vector, and support vector regression. The accuracy of these forecasting models can be ascertained

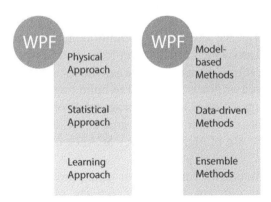

Figure 6.1 Classification of WPF models.

using suitable performance metrics like root mean squared error, mean absolute error, and mean absolute percentage error.

6.2 Models for Wind Forecasting

Models for WPF are primarily based on the relationship of wind power and important features like wind speed at hub height, wind direction, wind shear, and other atmospheric parameters like relative humidity, atmospheric pressure, and temperature. Models for WSF have been realized using time series modeling and various others statistical and ML models. The various WPF models are outlined in Figure 6.2.

6.2.1 Persistence Model

The persistence model works on the assumption that wind at a future instant will take the same value as the wind at current instant. These models have proven to work best for ultra-short-term horizons. However, their performance is relatively bad for longer time horizons.

6.2.2 Point vs. Probabilistic Forecasting

Point forecasting gives a single value for the wind power forecast. Most of the statistical approaches, time series models, and learning approaches like MLP, SVM, RNN, and ELM perform best to provide point forecast of wind speed or power. Due to the intermittent nature of wind, forecast

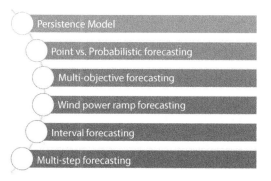

Persistence Model

Point vs. Probabilistic forecasting

Multi-objective forecasting

Wind power ramp forecasting

Interval forecasting

Multi-step forecasting

Figure 6.2 Wind forecasting methodologies.

error occurs which hamper the operation cost and supply consistency [3]. However, the uncertainties in wind power can be effectively captured using probabilistic forecast methods. These methods generate pdfs, quantiles, or intervals of future wind speed or power.

6.2.3   Multi-Objective Forecasting

Multi-objective optimization generally considers multiple criteria for the process of decision making. Zhou *et al.* proposed a multi-objective framework for wind power forecast intervals. They examined the relationship between the average width of forecast interval and its approximation error [3].

6.2.4   Wind Power Ramp Forecasting

Morena *et al.* [4] proposed a DLNN for prediction of wind power ramp events (WPREs). WPREs refer to sudden increase or decrease in wind power that may affect the WT operation. WPREs are spatially related events and their prediction aids in protection of WTs and in penetration of wind power to the grid.

6.2.5   Interval Forecasting

Wind speed interval prediction plays a significant role in WSF and WPF. Wind being a stochastic resource, needs nonlinear temporal parameters for prediction of intervals. Gaussian process, fuzzy inference, and beta distribution function are the conventional methods used for interval forecasting. Zhou *et al.* developed an LSTM based model for interval forecast. The prediction intervals were computed using the LUBE method. Gan *et al.* proposed the use of temporal CNN for interval prediction [5]. GD optimization–based DL model was developed by Li *et al.*, short-term interval forecasting of wind power [6].

6.2.6   Multi-Step Forecasting

The dynamic characteristic of wind power generated in a wind farm is very successfully captured by multi-step forecasting models. These models are based on three approaches, namely recursive approach, direct approach, and multi-input and multi-output approach [2]. The DL methods used for multi-step forecasting have been tabulated in Table 6.1.

Table 6.1 Models for multi-step wind forecasting.

Author	DL models
Chen *et al.* [7]	Predictive stacked autoencoders
Liu *et al.* [8]	Variational mode decomposition, SSA, LSTM, and ELM
Zhang *et al.* [9]	Deep Boltzmann machine
Xiang *et al.* [10]	Secondary decomposition, phase space reconstruction-bidirectional GRU, and chicken swarm optimization
Yan *et al.* [11]	Improved singular spectrum decomposition, LSTM, and grasshopper optimization algorithm–based deep belief network

6.3   The Deep Learning Paradigm

DL is a subset of machine learning which, in turn, is a subset of artificial intelligence. DL has the immense ability to learn without human intervention, extract significant features, and can handle unstructured and unlabelled data as well. The various paradigms of DL are depicted in Figure 6.3.

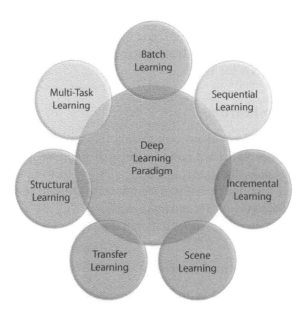

Figure 6.3 Deep learning paradigm.

6.3.1   Batch Learning

Batch represents a group of training samples used in one iteration. In batch learning, the batch size can either be equal to the total dataset or slightly lesser than the dataset.

6.3.2   Sequential Learning

Sequential learning is a paradigm of DL, where one part of a task is learnt before the next. Niu *et al.* proposed a sequence-to-sequence prediction model based on GRU. This kind of learning guaranteed stability in multi-step forecasting and ensured reliable power system operation [2]. Zhang *et al.* developed a sequence-to-sequence model for WPF [12]. They used NWP data for building the model and compared its performance with DBN and RF.

6.3.3   Incremental Learning

In this kind of learning, the knowledge of the existing model is continuously updated based on the input data. Hence, the learning process happens at the instant when a new input emerges.

6.3.4   Scene Learning

Yu *et al.* proposed the concept of scene learning, by embedding the WTs into the grid space [13]. Spatio-temporal features were extracted and given as input to deep CNN for WPF.

6.3.5   Transfer Learning

Transfer learning (TL) is about transferring the knowledge gained in one problem to another associated problem. Hu *et al.* implemented TK for WSF, by transferring knowledge from older farms rich in data to newer farms [14]. WF errors were found to be reduced significantly. Qureshi *et al.* proposed a WPF method based on DLNN and meta regression TL [15]. They found that TL significantly reduced the computational time of the DL algorithms.

6.3.6   Neural Structural Learning

Neural structured learning is about training NN using structured signals along with other inputs. Structure can either be in the form of graph or induced by perturbation. Mi and Zhao proposed a WSF model based on SSA and neural structural learning [16].

6.3.7 Multi-Task Learning

This kind of learning is believed to have widespread applicability to real world problems. It involves multiple related problems and exploits the data collected for all the tasks. Hence, it is proven to enhance generalization. A multi-task learning (MTL) for WPRE forecasting has been developed in [4]. MTL for simultaneous forecast of wind energy and demand was developed by Qin *et al.*, using a single NN method [17]. When compared with STL methods, the MTL methods resulted in more authentic results due to the presence of joint layers in its configuration.

6.4 Deep Learning Approaches for Wind Forecasting

6.4.1 Deep Neural Network

A DLNN for forecasting wind power in a 7-MW offshore WT was proposed by Lin and Liu. They used 1-s sampled SCADA data for building the model. They used eleven features including wind speed at four different heights, pitch angles of each blade, mean pitch angle, temperature, yaw

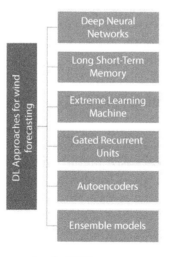

Figure 6.4 Deep learning approaches for WPF.

error, and orientation of nacelle [18]. A CNN-based wind speed forecasting model was proposed by Hong and Satriani for an offshore WT near Taiwan [19]. The model was used for day-ahead forecasting and was based on historic spatial and temporal data. Hong and Rioflorida proposed a hybrid CNN-RBF NN for day-ahead WSF [1]. Lin *et al.* developed a DLNN model for WPF in offshore WTs. The hostile effect of outliers was reduced using isolation forest algorithms [20]. A short-term WSF algorithm based on graph convolution DLNN was developed by Khodayar and Wang [21]. The proposed spatio-temporal model used the application of DL, graph theory, and rough set theory. The spatio-temporal features were robust and could tolerate uncertainties and noise and the proposed model outperformed DBNs and SAE networks (Figure 6.4).

6.4.2   Long Short-Term Memory

Qin *et al.* developed a fusion model of forecasting, using LSTM and DLNN [17]. Using CNN which exploited the spatial features of the wind field and LSTM that trained on the dynamic features, the prediction of wind signal was effectively made. Liu *et al.* proposed a hybrid combination of SDAE-LSTM for forecasting wind speed. This novel combination built on big data, outperformed the conventional MLP network [22]. The suitability of optimal LSTM networks for forecasting wind in long-term was ascertained by Pujari *et al.* [23]. A short-term WSF model based on LSTM was proposed based on four modules [24]. It included the application of crow search algorithm, wavelet transform, feature selection and LSTM based DL time series prediction. A hybrid WSF methodology was developed by Liu *et al.* incorporating the functionalities of wavelet transforms, LSTM, and ENN [25]. The efficacy of the model for multi-step prediction was also tested and was found to be excellent.

6.4.3   Extreme Learning Machine

Time series modeling utilizes time stamped data, to model the future values of the series as a function of present and past values. Yang and Chen developed a fusion model based on the combination of EMD, SAE, and ELM for accurate wind speed forecasting [26]. They also evaluated the impact of shared-hidden-layer style, which was responsible for enriching data-poor sources. Tahmasebifar *et al.* proposed hybrid models for point and probabilistic forecasting of wind power based on ELM [27]. The other techniques used in the fusion include, mutual information, bootstrap approach, and PSO.

6.4.4   Gated Recurrent Units

A GRU is similar to LSTM with a forget gate but has lesser parameters than LSTM. Niu *et al.* developed an attention-based GRU for WPF [2]. The attention mechanism aids in identifying the most significant input variable. Kisvari *et al.* proposed a GRU based WPF method [28]. They used the isolation forest algorithm for filtering options. The results obtained outperformed the LSTM model. Liu *et al.* proposed a novel fusion methodology for WPF by combining SSA, CNN, GRU and SVR method [29]. The proposed multi-step prediction model outperformed conventional forecasting models.

6.4.5   Autoencoders

Autoencoders belong to a family of NN, whose output is same as the input. They output is reconstructed by compressing the input on to a latent-space representation. Wang *et al.* developed SIRAE for efficient ultra-short-term WPF [30]. Variable mode decomposition technique was used to decompose the original sequence into sub-sequences, which were then used as input variables. Jahangir *et al.* proposed a novel WPF algorithm, in which DAE were used for denoising the inputs and R-NNs were used for forecasting [31]. A neuron-pair known as upper and lower bound neurons comprise rough neuron.

6.4.6   Ensemble Models

The research works carried out in developing ensemble models used for wind forecasting has been tabulated in Table 6.2.

6.4.7   Other Miscellaneous Models

The research works that are carried out using various other DL algorithms have been described in Table 6.3.

6.5   Research Challenges

Forecasting with increased accuracy with an aim to reduce the operational cost of WT is required. Forecasting algorithms exclusively aimed at offshore environmental conditions will be a definite boost to the budding offshore wind energy generation.

Table 6.2 Ensemble models for WPF.

Author	Proposed model	Algorithms used
H. H. H. Aly [32]	Intelligent clustered hybrid model	Recurrent Kalman filter, Fourier series, wavelet neural network, ANN
Peng et al. [33]	DL ensemble model	Wavelet soft threshold denoising, GRU
Wang et al. [34]	DL based ensemble model	Wavelet transform, deep CNN, ensemble technique
Liu et al. [35]	Time-variant multi-resolution ensemble model	Outlier robust ELM, multi-objective multi-verse optimizer algorithm, clustering autoencoder
Liu et al. [36]	Deep reinforcement learning model	Wavelet transform, LSTM, DBN, ESN, reinforcement learning
Chen et al. [37]	Nonlinear-learning ensemble	LSTM, SVR machine, external optimization algorithm
Jiajun et al. [38]	Ultra-short-term wind prediction	Wavelet transform, DBN, Light gradient boosting machine, random forest
Liu et al. [39]	Smart DL ensemble model	Wavelet packet decomposition, CNN, convolutional LSTM network

Development of DL models for prediction interval forecasting for wind farm clusters is identified as an area of future research. Development of top-quality prediction models for WPRE forecasting for wind farm clusters in a particular geographical area is an area yet to be explored. Autotuning of DRNN is an essential area of research. Wind forecasting algorithms with an ultimate aim of aiding effective charging of Plug-in electric vehicle, energy storage, and integration to the power grid should be built, taking into consideration the need and specifications of these applications.

The application of various DL paradigms in WF should be exploited to get more precise forecasting, suitable for various applications. A significant improvement in the efficiency of captured energy from wind will go a long way in transforming wind farms to wind power plants.

Table 6.3 Miscellaneous DL models for WF.

Proposed model	Algorithms used	Metric for forecast accuracy
Two-stage DL WSF [40]	Wavelet packet decomposition, CNN, bivariate Dirichlet process mixture model	MAE, MAPE, RMSE, coverage width-based criterion
Time series prediction of wind power generation [41]	Deep feed forward network, deep CNN, RNN, attention mechanism, LSTM	MSE, RMSE, RMSLE
Forecasting energy consumption and wind power generation [42]	Deep ESN	MAE, RMSE, MAPE, sMAPE
Interval DGNN for WSF [43]	ELM-HBSA	RMSE, MAPE
Short-term WSF [44]	CEEMDAN-LSTM, CEEMDAN-error-VMD-LSTM	RMSE, MAPE, MAE
WPF [45]	LASSO, kNN, xGBoost, SVR, RF	R^2, RMSE, MAE
Cascaded DL WPF [46]	EMD-VMD-CNN-LSTM	RMSE, MAE
Short-term WSF [47]	Rough deep neural architecture with SAE, SDAE	RMSE, MAE
Probabilistic spatiotemporal WSF [48]	Convolutional GRU, 3D-CNN, variational Bayesian DL	RMSE, CRPS

6.6   Conclusion

This chapter presents an exhaustive review on DL models for WF. The need for WPF models, the algorithms used to model, their applications, and their classification were described. The various DL paradigms were also presented with their application in WPF and WSF. An overview of research works undertaken in WF, based on DLNN, LSTM, ELM, GRU,

SAE, ensemble models, and other assorted models was presented in detail. The research challenges that are yet to be explored in this area have also been included to serve as inputs for future researchers.

References

1. Hong, Y.Y. and Rioflorido, C.L.P.P., A hybrid deep learning-based neural network for 24-h ahead wind power forecasting. *Appl. Energy*, 250, 530–539, 2019.
2. Niu, Z., Yu, Z., Tang, W., Wu, Q., Reformat, M., Wind power forecasting using attention-based gated recurrent unit network. *Energy*, 196, 117081, 2020.
3. Zhou, M., Wang, B., Guo, S., Watada, J., Multi-objective prediction intervals for wind power forecast based on deep neural networks. *Inf. Sci.*, 550, 207–220, 2021.
4. Moreno, M.D., Navarin, N., Gutierrez, P.A., Prieto, L., Sperduti, A., Sanz, S.S., Martinez, C.H., Multi-task learning for the prediction of wind power ramp events with deep neural networks. *Neural Networks*, 123, 401–411, 2020.
5. Gan, Z., Li, C., Zhou, J., Tang, G., Temporal convolutional networks interval prediction model for wind speed forecasting. *Electr. Power Syst. Res.*, 191, 106865, 2021.
6. Li, C., Tang, G., Xue, X., Chen, X., Wang, R., Zhang, C., The short-term interval prediction of wind power using the deep learning model with gradient descend optimization. *Renewable Energy*, 155, 197–211, 2020.
7. Chen, J., Zhu, Q., Li, H., Zhu, L., Shi, D., Li, Y., Duan, X., Liu, Y., Learning heterogeneous features jointly: A deep end-to-end framework for multi-step short-term wind power prediction. *IEEE Trans. Sustainable Energy*, 11, 3, 2020.
8. Liu, H., Mi, X., Li, Y., Smart multi-step deep learning model for wind speed forecasting based on variational mode decomposition, singular spectrum analysis, LSTM network and ELM. *Energy Convers. Manage.*, 159, 54–64, 2018.
9. Zhang, C., Chen, C.L.P., Gan, M., Chen, L., Predictive Deep Boltzmann Machine for multiperiod wind speed forecasting. *IEEE Trans. Sustainable Energy*, 6, 4, 2015.
10. Xiang, L., Li, J., Hu, A., Zhang, Y., Deterministic and probabilistic multi-step forecasting for short-term wind speed based on secondary decomposition and a deep learning method. *Energy Convers. Manage.*, 220, 113098, 2020.
11. Yan, X., Liu, Y., Xu, Y., Jia, M., Multistep forecasting for diurnal wind speed based on hybrid deep learning model with improved singular spectrum decomposition. *Energy Convers. Manage.*, 225, 113456, 2020.

12. Zhang, Y., Li, Y., Zhang, G., Short-term wind power forecasting approach based on Seq2Seq model using NWP data. *Energy*, 213, 118371, 2020.

13. Yu, R., Liu, Z., Li, X., Lu, W., Ma, D., Yu, M., Wang, J., Li, B., Scene learning: Deep convolutional networks for wind power prediction by embedding turbines into grid space. *Appl. Energy*, 238, 249–257, 2019.

14. Hu, Q., Zhang, R., Zhou, Y., Transfer learning for short-term wind speed prediction with deep neural networks. *Renewable Energy*, 85, 83–95, 2016.

15. Qureshi, A.S., Khan, A., Zameer, A., Usman, A., Wind power prediction using deep neural network based meta regression and transfer learning. *Appl. Soft Comput.*, 58, 742–755, 2017.

16. Mi, X. and Zhao, S., Wind speed prediction based on singular spectrum analysis and neural network structural learning. *Energy Convers. Manage.*, 216, 112956, 2020.

17. Qin, Y., Li, K., Liang, Z., Lee, B., Zhang, F., Gu, Y., Zhang, L., Wu, F., Rodriguez, D., Hybrid forecasting model based on long short-term memory network and deep learning neural network for wind signal. *Appl. Energy*, 236, 262–272, 2019.

18. Lin, Z. and Liu, X., Wind power forecasting of an offshore wind turbine based on high frequency SCADA data and deep learning neural network. *Energy*, 201, 117693, 2020.

19. Hong, Y.Y. and Satriani, T.R.A., Day-ahead spatiotemporal wind speed forecasting using robust design-based deep learning neural network. *Energy*, 209, 118441, 2020.

20. Lin, Z., Liu, X., Collu, M., Wind power prediction based on high-frequency SCADA data along with isolation forest and deep learning neural networks. *Electr. Power Energy Syst.*, 118, 105835, 2020.

21. Khodayar, M. and Wang, J., Spatio-temporal Graph Deep Neural Network for Short-term Wind Speed Forecasting. *IEEE Trans. Sustainable Energy*, 10, 2, 2019.

22. Liu, X., Zhang, H., Kong, X., Lee, K.Y., Wind speed forecasting using deep neural network with feature selection. *Neurocomputing*, 397, 393–403, 2020.

23. Pujari, K.N., Miriyala, S.S., Mittal, P., Mitra, K., Optimal Long Short-Term Memory Networks for long-term forecasting for real wind characteristics. *IFAC PapersOnLine*, 53-1, 648–653, 2020.

24. Memarzadeh, G. and Keynia, F., A new short-term wind speed forecasting method based on fine-tuned LSTM neural network and optimal input sets. *Energy Convers. Manage.*, 213, 112824, 2020.

25. Liu, H., Mi, X., Li, Y., Wind speed forecasting method based on deep learning strategy using empirical wavelet transform, long short-term memory neural network and Elman neural network. *Energy Convers. Manage.*, 156, 498–514, 2018.

26. Yang, H.F. and Chen, Y.P., Representation learning with extreme learning machines and empirical mode decomposition for wind speed forecasting methods. *Artif. Intell.*, 277, 103176, 2019.

27. Tahmasebifar, R., Moghaddam, M.P., Sheikh-El-Eslami, M.K., Kheirollahi, R., A new hybrid model for point and probabilistic forecasting of wind power. *Energy*, 211, 119016, 2020.

28. Kisvari, A., Lin, Z., Liu, X., Wind power forecasting – A data-driven method along with gated recurrent neural network. *Renewable Energy*, 163, 1895–1909, 2021.

29. Liu, H., Mi, X., Li, Y., Duan, Z., Xu, Y., Smart wind speed deep learning based multi-step forecasting model using singular spectrum analysis, convolutional Gated Recurrent Unit network and Support Vector Regression. *Renewable Energy*, 143, 842–854, 2019.

30. Wang, L., Tao, R., Hu, H., Zeng, Y., Effective wind power prediction using novel deep learning network: Stacked independently recurrent autoencoder. *Renewable Energy*, 164, 642–655, 2021.

31. Jahangir, H., Golkar, M.A., Alhameli, F., Mazouz, A., Ahmadian, A., Elkamel, A., Short-term wind speed forecasting framework based on stacked denoising auto-encoders with rough ANN. *Sustain. Energy Technol. Assess.*, 38, 100601, 2020.

32. Aly, II.H.H., A novel deep learning intelligent clustered hybrid models for wind speed and power forecasting. *Energy*, 213, 118773, 2020.

33. Peng, Z., Peng, S., Fu, L., Lu, B., Tang, J., Wang, K., Li, W., A novel deep learning ensemble model with data denoising for short-term wind speed forecasting. *Energy Convers. Manage.*, 207, 112524, 2020.

34. Wang, H., Li, G., Wang, G., Peng, J., Jiang, H., Liu, Y., Deep learning-based ensemble approach for probabilistic wind power forecasting. *Appl. Energy*, 188, 56–70, 2017.

35. Liu, H., Duan, Z., Chen, C., Wind speed big data forecasting using time-variant multi-resolution ensemble model with clustering auto-encoder. *Appl. Energy*, 280, 115975, 2020.

36. Liu, H., Yu, C., Wu, H., Duan, Z., Yan, G., A new hybrid ensemble deep reinforcement learning model for wind speed short term forecasting. *Energy*, 202, 117794, 2020.

37. Chen, J., Zeng, G., Zhou, W., Du, W., Lu, K., Wind speed forecasting using nonlinear-learning ensemble of deep learning time series prediction and extremal optimization. *Energy Convers. Manage.*, 165, 681–695, 2018.

38. Jiajun, H., Chuanjin, Y., Yongle, L., Huoyue, X., Ultra-short-term wind prediction with wavelet transform, deep belief network and ensemble learning. *Energy Convers. Manage.*, 205, 112418, 2020.

39. Liu, H., Mi, X., Li, Y., Smart deep learning-based wind speed prediction model using wavelet packet decomposition, convolutional neural network and convolutional long short-term memory network. *Energy Convers. Manage.*, 166, 120–131, 2018.

40. Liu, H., Duan, Z., Chen, C., Wu, H., A novel two-stage deep learning wind speed forecasting method with adaptive multiple error corrections and

bivariate Dirichlet process mixture model. *Energy Convers. Manage.*, 199, 11975, 2019.

41. Mishra, S., Bordin, C., Taharaguchi, K., Palu, I., Comparison of deep learning models for multivariate prediction of time series wind power generation and temperature. *Energy Rep.*, 6, 273–286, 2020.

42. Hu, H., Wang, L., Lv, S., Forecasting energy consumption and wind power generation using deep echo state network. *Renewable Energy*, 154, 598–613, 2020.

43. Khodayar, M., Wang, J., Manthouri, M., Interval deep generative neural network for wind speed forecasting. *IEEE Trans. Smart Grid*, 10, 4, 2019.

44. Ma, Z., Chen, H., Wang, J., Yang, X., Yan, R., Jia, J., Xu, W., Application of hybrid model based on double decomposition, error correction and deep learning in short-term wind speed prediction. *Energy Convers. Manage.*, 205, 112345, 2020.

45. Demolli, H., Dokuz, A.S., Ecemis, A., Gokcek, M., Wind power forecasting based on daily wind speed data using machine learning algorithms. *Energy Convers. Manage.*, 198, 111823, 2020.

46. Yin, H., Ou, Z., Huang, S., Meng, A., A cascaded deep learning wind power prediction approach based on a two-layer of mode decomposition. *Energy*, 189, 116316, 2019.

47. Khodayar, M., Kaynak, O., Khodayar, M.E., Rough deep neural architecture for short-term wind speed forecasting. *IEEE Trans. Industr. Inform.*, 13, 6, 2017.

48. Liu, Y., Qin, H., Zhang, Z., Pei, S., Jiang, Z., Feng, Z., Zhou, J., Probabilistic spatiotemporal wind speed forecasting based on a variational Bayesian deep learning model. *Appl. Energy*, 260, 114259, 2020.

7

Deep Feature Selection for Wind Forecasting-I

C. Ramakrishnan[1]*, S. Sridhar[2], Kusumika Krori Dutta[2],
R. Karthick[1] and C. Janamejaya[2]

1Dept. of EEE, SNS College of Technology, Coimbatore, India
2Dept. of EEE, M S Ramaiah Institute of Technology, Bangalore, India

Abstract

The existence of abundant renewable energy and fast growing technologies in wind energy extraction creates extensive attention on the wind forecasting. The forecastings are generally very short-term forecasting (few seconds to 30 minutes ahead), short-term forecasting (30 minutes to several hour ahead), medium-term forecasting (several hours to 1 week ahead), and long-term forecasting (from 1 week to 1 year or more). The forecasting involves extraction of single or multiple features from the time series data for more accurate prediction. The different wind speed and power forecasting model include physical model, statistical model, computational model, and hybrid model. Pre-processing the raw data, feature extraction, and prediction are the steps involved in forecasting of wind speed and wind energy. The accuracy in prediction cannot be as expected due to complex computations when mathematical models have been used though it is simple. To improve the performance of prediction and reduce the computational time, computational intelligence (CI) methods like artificial neural networks, evolutionary computation, fuzzy logic, and probabilistic methods are employed for analyzing, decision-making, and optimizing the data. The performance of DL techniques for the big dataset is significantly high when compare to other computational techniques like fuzzy logic, evolutionary computation, and support vector machine.

Keywords: Computational intelligence, deep learning, modeling, wind speed, wind power, wind forecasting

Corresponding author: ramramki.krishnan@gmail.com

Ajay Kumar Vyas, S. Balamurugan, Kamal Kant Hiran and Harsh S. Dhiman (eds.) *Artificial Intelligence for Renewable Energy Systems*, (147–180) © 2022 Scrivener Publishing LLC

7.1   Introduction

Fast depleting fossil fuels and the concerns regarding CO_2 emissions has shifted the thinking of energy policy makers and governments toward renewable energy. These fuels are cleaner and free of cost and do not cause any adverse climate change as the fossil fuels does. The key drivers for this energy transformation include the following:

- Cheaper renewable energy cost
- Reduction in CO_2 emission
- Increase in employability
- Sustainable energy and improved energy security

Among the various renewable energy sources available, wind energy is considered as a promising source because it is clean and available throughout the day [1]. One of the major drawbacks of wind energy is that it is interim in nature and a seasonal source. This drawback has imposed a major challenge in planning and operations of wind power systems. Also, the wind power output is directly related to its wind speed. Therefore, it becomes a necessity for policy makers to forecast the wind speed accurately to make wind energy a dominant source for microgrid and utilities to supply clean energy at reasonable cost.

As per the data available with various agencies, the wind installed capacity has grown tremendously from 100 GW in 2008 to 651 GW in 2019 [2]. The wind energy has expanded by leaps and bounds in last 20 years and is expected to grow at a rate of 7% year on year. This projection implies that the wind energy capacity would increase by 3-fold (about 1,900 GW) and nearly 10-fold by 2050 (about 6500GW). The year on year growth of wind energy is shown as graph in Figure 7.1a and the top 10 countries installed capacity is shown in Figure 7.1b.

With this trend of massive growth, there is a serious concern regarding various areas of wind energy systems including evacuation of power, quality of power and in particular the wind speed prediction. With technological advancement (a single 10-MW generator) and government policies, more and more wind energy integration is possible in future. Since the source of energy is intermittent and highly variable, it can cause instability in the power grid and hence the customers are not ensured with reliable power. In order to overcome these drawbacks, it is necessary to predict the

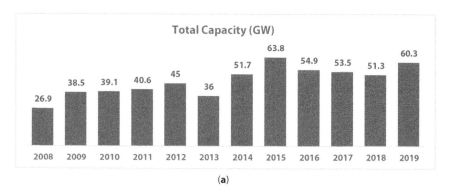

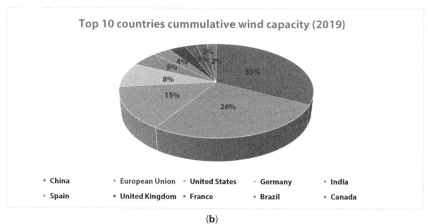

Figure 7.1 (a) Total installed wind capacity around the world. (b) Total installed wind capacity nation wise.

wind energy output which is possible with accurate wind speed forecasting to ensure technical and financial benefits.

Before discussing the forecasting techniques, it is necessary to recall few basic concepts regarding the wind energy conversion system. Basically, kinetic energy (KE) is converted through wind energy transformation systems, where KE is available in air to mechanical power by the wind turbine and next the electrical energy is achieved by transforming mechanical energy using an electrical generator. All kinds of renewable energy come from the Sun. Wind is produced as long as the sun exists and heats the atmosphere. The wind blows because the heating of atmosphere differs at different locations on earth in other words the uneven heating of atmosphere.

The wind generated blows past a turbine, the KE in it turns the turbine blades, thereby creating a mechanical energy. The turbine, in turn, is coupled to an electrical generator through a mechanical gear system where the mechanical energy is transformed into electrical energy. Therefore, the wind energy conversion system consists of various mechanical and electrical components through which the KE is converted into electrical energy as shown in Figure 7.2 [3, 4].

Therefore, it is clear that the output electrical energy depends on the KE of wind, in other words the wind speed.

The wind power output is given by

$$P_{air} = \frac{1}{2}(air\ mass\ per\ unit\ volume)(wind\ velocity)^2 \qquad (7.1)$$

$$= \frac{1}{2}(\rho A V_w)(V_w)^2$$
$$= \frac{1}{2}\rho A V_w^3 \qquad (7.2)$$

where P_{air} = power obtained from wind (W)
ρ = air density (1.225 kg/m³ at 15°C and normal pressure)
A = swept area in m²
V_w = wind speed in m/s.

The power available and power transferred is not same though equation shows wind power availability but it reduces by power coefficient C_p as

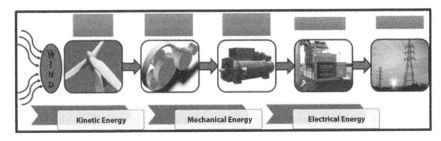

Figure 7.2 Components of wind energy conversion system.

stated by the scientist Albert Betz during transfer to the wind turbine rotor. The power available at the rotor is given by

$$P_T = \frac{1}{2}\rho A V_w^3 C_p \qquad (7.3)$$

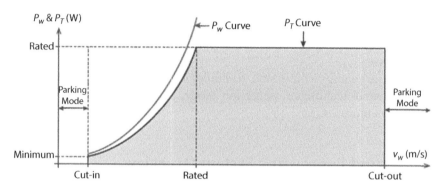

Figure 7.3 Wind power characteristics curve.

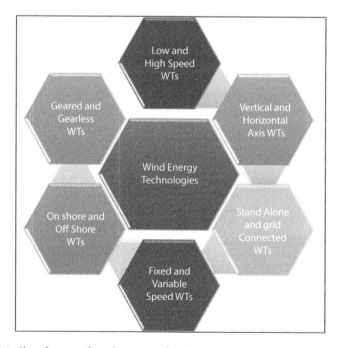

Figure 7.4 Classification of wind energy technologies.

The theoretical value of C_p in Equation (7.3) according to Betz is 0.593 known as the Betz's limit. The power speed characteristics which are a curve of P_{air} and P_T curves with respect to wind speed are shown in Figure 7.3. The minimum speed at which the turbine starts to generate power is also known as cut in speed, which is about 10 to 15 m/s. Below this speed, the turbine is safe in parking mode. The cut-out speed is the speed at which the generator is stopped to avoid damages and put the turbine in parking mode. This speed ranges between 25 and 30 m/s. As shown in Figure 7.3, the P_T curve is always less than the P_{air} curve because of the aerodynamic power losses.

The wind energy conversion technologies are classified based on the speed, control techniques, operation mode, and type of construction as shown in Figure 7.4.

7.2   Wind Forecasting System Overview

Wind power forecast generally refers to an estimation of energy production from a wind farm as shown in Figure 7.5. Non-conventional energy sources have become inevitable, to fulfill the energy crisis due to the shortage of fossil fuels [5]. Energy developed from wind is one of the clean and sustainable sources of energy, has created much attention in recent days, and is contributing to the economic growth.

The most important requirement for wind power generation is wind speed forecasting since it has the prediction capabilities. The high accuracy in wind speed forecasting helps to minimize the operating cost (better grid

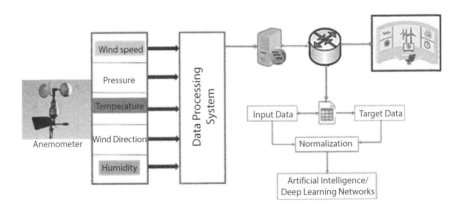

Figure 7.5 Wind forecasting system [4].

planning and integration of wind energy) of wind power plant and increases the reliability of electricity system [6]. The advantage of exact wind speed prediction increases the competition of wind power in the electricity market by timely operation of dispatching centers tuned to the program which reduces the impact of varying wind power on the grid [7, 8].

Power quality in the power grid must be an important issue when supplied from renewable and non-renewable energy power plants and also a balance between generation and loads. The behavior of the wind changes very often does not allow this source to synchronize with the grid permanently. The prediction of correct wind speed enhances the performance of wind power generation systems. In wind forecasting, the accuracy and stability are mostly focused since their impact on power system economics and management is considerably high.

7.2.1   Classification of Wind Forecasting

When specifying wind speed forecasting, for better generation of power and operations of power systems, it focuses on the following classification based on the prediction of wind velocity and they can be categorized based on the reference [9–11] as follows:

1. Immediate short duration forecasting
2. Short duration forecasting
3. Long duration forecasting

Immediate short duration forecasting is the prediction in the range from 10 seconds to 8 hours and is mainly used in wind prediction control for power management. Short-term forecasting is predicted before in the range from 8 hours to 168 hours. This type of prediction is more helpful in planning the strategies and taking decision of system commitments for the researchers in wind speed forecasting. Long-term forecasting ranges for more than a week and is used for the purpose of maintenance and study of wind farms. Usually, during this time scheduling, commitment, load balancing, and control are being carried out. For optimum grid operations, Immediate and short-term wind speed forecasting methods are however very challenging and critical.

7.2.2   Wind Forecasting Methods

The wind forecasting schemes are categorized based upon analyzing ancient time series of wind and using the predicting values from the numerical weather forecast. The data obtained from monitoring the weather conditions are insufficient to analyze the data for predictions. For better forecasting, numerical weather prediction models are employed [12]. Statistical models serves to maintain the plant output as expected production of wind energy with a necessary feedback system for improving output. Generally, wind forecasting models have been categorized into three methods as follows: (i) physical methods, (ii) statistical and computational methods, and (iii) hybrid method.

7.2.2.1 Physical Method

In this method, the variation in temperature, pressure and surface toughness are taken as inputs in weather forecasting data under numerical weather prediction. Generally, the speed of wind is measured from the meteorological service is being moved in the wind plant for the conversion of wind power. Wind farms are situated far away; these metrological forecast data inputs are enhanced to the level up to turbine hub height by constituting many sub data enhancing models between the site and the power grid. In each models, processing of all the physical data with suitable mathematical calculation is very important when developing this method to realize and improve the numerical weather predictions. The hub height and wind speed at the wind farm helps to convert the speed in to power with the availability of theoretical power curves supplied by the manufacturers of wind turbine and it is found very less utilized when compare to empirically delivered power curve [13]. The derived transfer function used in the model should predict the wind power at any moment without errors.

7.2.2.2 Statistical Method

Metrological data alone is not enough for forecasting, but huge amount of historical data is required for the analysis for the prediction by developing a relation as model with wind energy measurements. The drawback of physical method is that it is not disintegrated effectively by selecting correct metrological values in designing a model for forecasting wind power and also these values are updated very often for the estimation. Mostly, statistical methods can be employed with linear and non-linear models and they found very easy to use and cost effective. Since the values obtained from past history is taken for the prediction turned to be disadvantage for this method as the time for forecasting increases [14]. Time series approaches and deep learning (DL) techniques usually employed for these short time predictions as sub classifications. In time series approaches, auto-regressive moving average (ARMA) models contributing at the top in predicting wind speed. Also, the contribution of neural networks is very much developed nowadays to relate the input and output data once the training of the network for past data is done.

In all the statistical methods, model parameters are tuned based on the error between the predicted wind data and actual wind data. The use of learning networks are to relate the input and output with non-statistical approach during training to enhance the performance of the system even without the expertise knowledge. However, the efficiency of all these statistical approaches is based duration of the prediction time and will be best compare to direct predictions.

7.2.2.3   Hybrid Method

Combination of both physical and statistical methods referred for short and medium forecasting are called as hybrid method where weather forecasts and time series analysis are exclusively focused. The advantages of each above mentioned methods are effectively utilized in this hybrid method to obtain maximum performance of the system in forecasting studies. Though individual approaches have their own limitations, more chances for strengthening the information when combining two methods together and integrating information obtained from both approaches to perform with better accuracy in prediction are expected.

Wind power forecasting involves many hybrid models to predict power of wind. The following are the varieties of combinations [15, 16]:

- Mixture of physical and statistical approaches;
- Mixture of models for short term and medium term;
- Mixture alternative statistical models; and
- Mixture of alternative models of artificial intelligence (AI).

7.2.3   Prediction Frameworks

The wind prediction framework in general includes the following components as shown in Figure 7.6 [17].

7.2.3.1   Pre-Processing of Data

The wind data collected from using anemometers from the wind farm, wind vanes, and other sensors contains not only the wind data but also includes noises, missing data, and other anomalies due to inevitable reasons. For accurate forecasting, these irregularities have to be removed using appropriate

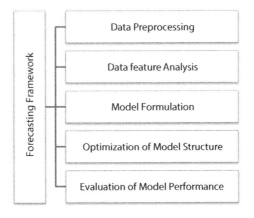

Figure 7.6 General forecasting framework.

processing algorithm which is the main task of data processing. The most common problem is the noise in the wind data which is removed using ideal designed filters which are categorized into time domain filtering, frequency domain filtering, and time-frequency domain filtering [17].

7.2.3.2   Data Feature Analysis

Selecting the features from the non-linear multi learning input is a challenge and of fundamental importance [17]. Some commonly used methods for feature analysis are correlation analysis, computational efficiency, network learning efficiency, and sample dimensionality.

7.2.3.3   Model Formulation

In order to extract the features from the input data, suitable learning models are designed and these models are broadly classified into two categories, namely, deterministic and probabilistic models. The DL models are of great benefit in extracting the data features with higher accuracy when compared to traditional methods. The various forecasting models based on DL include LSTM-based approach, SELM approach, convolutional neural network (CNN) approaches, and hybrid NN approaches [17].

7.2.3.4   Optimization of Model Structure

Optimization of model structure quandary is challenging where DL is involved because the polynomial time algorithm unfit the optimization of convex type when deep layer neural network is involved [17]. A consummate reliable optimization is not possible and the reason behind it is the optimization quandary is generally non-deterministic polynomial. The gradient descent optimization method is virtually best suited for DL model optimization.

7.2.3.5   Performance Evaluation of Model

Experiments are conducted on the model where the irrelevant variables are removed in order to improve the model's ability to predict accurate results [17]. The model order is calculated appropriately and frequency characteristics of wind are also considered for final modeling. The sampling frequency, average wind speed, wind direction, temperature, humidity, and air pressure are few variables considered for the evaluation purpose of the wind model.

7.2.3.6   Techniques Based on Methods of Forecasting

Some models used for the forecast of power of wind may not be applicable in complex prediction situation due to its computational cost. AI methods have been employed to improve the forecasting and conversion of wind power [18]. With the availability of these techniques, considerable scope has been created for optimizing the power in the renewable energy systems. The development of AI techniques addresses all the complexity in the generation of wind energy by providing optimal solutions for extracting the energy [19]. Artificial neural networks (ANNs), evolutionary computation, fuzzy logic, and probabilistic methods are the main sectors of AI methods [20, 21].

Based on literature, techniques are employed in the statistical approach or combination of both physical and statistical approach such as ANN, support vector machine (SVM), Fuzzy, and ANFIS handling huge amount of data used by the model which cannot give precise computation to compromise the operator. Therefore, to solve this issue, many techniques have been developed recently on DL to provide solutions for the complex and large scale data processing.

Deep belief networks, restricted Boltzmann machines (RBMs), CNN, RNN (recurrent neural networks) or LSTM (long short-term memory networks), stacked auto-encoder, and deep reinforcement learning are some few known DL methods [22]. Recent developments of DL algorithms employed at different fields of renewable energy to provide high accuracy in forecasting wind power.

7.3   Current Forecasting and Prediction Methods

There are several forecasting method proposed in the literature. The two fundamental methods are [23]:

1. Physical method
2. Statistical method

Physical method makes utilization of the physical characteristics of the region where the puissance plants are located. Physical approaches utilize Numerical Weather Prognostication (NWP) data, i.e., meteorological data such as temperature of atmosphere, pressure, coarseness in surface, and obstacles, for speed of wind prognostication [24, 25]. The speed of wind and its direction from the pertinent NWP level is maintained to the turbine's hub height. This includes a few steps, primarily finding the best-performing NWP level. The results of NWP model can be estimated for the geographical point of the wind farm or for a grid of circumventing points. In the first case, the models could be characterized as "advanced power curve models" [26], secondly, as a "statistical downscaling" model. The main disadvantage of this method is that it requires good quality on-line or off-line quantified data.

The statistical makes use of the historical data for prediction. The statistical approach includes several statistical linear and nonlinear models. The main demerit with this method is the prediction error and prediction time proportional to each other. Statistical methods are further categorized as seen in Figure 7.7 [27].

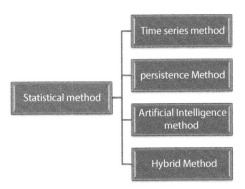

Figure 7.7 Classification of statistical methods.

7.3.1   Time Series Method (TSM)

The forecastings are generally classified as follows [28–30]:

a.   Very Short-Term Forecasting (VSTF): few seconds to 30 minutes ahead.
b.   Short-Term Forecasting (STF): 30 minutes to several hours ahead.
c.   Medium-Term Forecasting (MTF): several hours to 1 week ahead.
d.   Long-Term Forecasting (LTF): from 1 week to 1 year or more.

Figure 7.8 gives the classification of this method.

Stationary time series are those that are assumed to be stationary, i.e., they randomly develop themselves around a constant mean in time, reflecting stable equilibrium. In stationary models, the processes are assumed to be in equilibrium. In non-stationary time, the time series in not stationary, i.e., their mean will vary with time or variance or both. The non-stationary series can be deterministic or random in nature.

7.3.2   Persistence Method (PM)

In this method, it is assumed that the future value of the wind speed or power depends on the present value [31]. If $v(t)$ is the present value and $v(t + k)$ is the future value, then

$$v(t + k) = v(t) \quad k = 1, 2, 3, 4, \ldots \ldots \qquad (7.4)$$

$$P(t + k) = P(t) \quad k = 1, 2, 3, 4, \ldots \ldots$$

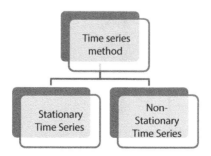

Figure 7.8 Classification of time series method.

where v(t) = wind speed and P(t) = power.

PM is the simplest and most economical method. The efficiency of prediction using PM is accurate for VSTF and STF.

7.3.3   Artificial Intelligence Method

It is the most commonly used method for short-term forecasting. ANN is the most widely used AI tool, which can be used for many applications including data classification and forecasting [32–35]. The most important components of any neural network are as follows:

- The transfer function which describes the neuron of different layers.
- The training algorithm used.
- The connected weights evaluated by the training process.

Among the various neural networks available, the following are the networks predominantly used for data classification.

- Feed-forward neural network (FFNN)
- Radial basis function neural network (RBFNN)
- Recurrent neural network
- Ridgelet neural network
- Adoptive linear element neural network

Figure 7.9 shows the network architecture of FFNN which, by changeable parameters, determines the overall input-output behavior of the system. The vectors x = $[x_1, x_2, x_3, ..., x_n]^T$ forms the input, and w the weight

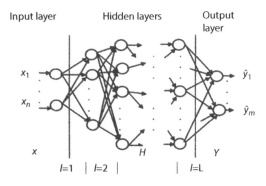

Figure 7.9 Multilayer feed-forward network.

matrix and $y = [y_1, y_2, y_3, \ldots, y_n]^T$ forms the output vector of the NN. FFNN contains one input layer with n neurons, single and multiple hidden layers and single output layer with m neurons. The output of the jth node o_j in l layer with k neurons can be computed using Equation (7.5)

$$o_j = f\left(\sum_{i=j}^{k} w_{ji}v_i + b_j\right) = f(w_j^T V + b_j) \qquad (7.5)$$

where
  b_j: bias of the jth neuron
  w_{ji}: weights
  v_i: inputs
  f: activation function
  $j = 1, 2, \ldots, k$

The most admired activation function is sigmoid function, due to its similarity in property of biological neurons behaviorally. The sigmoid function is defined as in Equation (7.6)

$$o_j = \frac{1}{1 + e^{-(w_j^T V + b_j)}} \qquad (7.6)$$

The FFNNs are most preferred because of their modularity. The input output mapping may be linear or nonlinear based on the activation function used in defining a neuron. FFNNs are generally trained using back propagation algorithm.

Different parameters like mean, standard deviation, and RMS are extracted from the raw data and are given as input for the ANN for prediction purpose.

7.3.4 Wavelet Neural Network

The work of Mallet (1989) and Daubechies (1990) made wavelets a very puissant implement for signal processing. Mallet introduced the concept of multiresolution analysis (MRA) cognate to multi-rate filters, while Daubechies cognate wavelets to sub-band decomposition. WT sanctions the utilization of shorter regions where high-frequency information is available and longtime intervals where low-frequency information are precisely available [36]. This property of variable window technique makes wavelet a very alluring implement for feature magnetization. WT compares

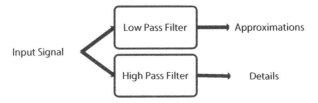

Figure 7.10 One-level decomposition.

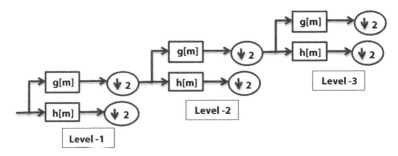

Figure 7.11 Wavelet tree decomposition with three detailed levels.

many stretched and shifted wavelets to the pristine pulse. The WT of a signal evolving in time is based on scale (or frequency) and time.

The scale and shift of wavelets determines the dilation and translation of mother wavelet in time/space axis. The "details" and "approximate" coefficients result as a part of wavelet decomposition as seen in Figure 7.10.

The "approximation" signal containing information about low frequency component can further be decomposed into new sets up to n levels. The high frequency component are reflected in the "details" signal. The n level decomposition eliminates the high frequency components. Selection of the wavelet order determines the burden computationally is directly related to the number of levels. Figure 7.11 gives a wavelet decomposition tree of three levels.

These wavelet coefficients are used as inputs for ANN for forecasting problems and hence referred to as wavelet neural network. The accuracy of prediction is better with ANN compared with time series method.

7.3.5   Adaptive Neuro-Fuzzy Inference System (ANFIS)

ANFIS, a network structure, consists of a number of points joined through directional links [37]. Each joint depicts a process unit, and the connection between joints designates the causal relationship among the connected joints. The cognition rule designates how the attributes (of the joints) updated to diminish prescribed error measure. By merging the positive features of neural network and fuzzy, a simple fault detection technique is developed.

The vital steps of the neuro-fuzzy modeling techniques are as follows:

- The input physical variables fuzzification.
- Computation of the degree of contentment for the available linguistic terms.
- Conjunction of the fuzzy inferred parameters and the premise.
- Output defuzzification.

ANFIS employs two methods for updating parameters of the membership function. These are as follows:

- For all parameters use of backpropagation (BP) (a technique of steepest descent).
- A hybrid method inclusive of BP for the attributes associated with the input membership and least squares estimation for the attributes associated with the output membership functions.

Here, ANFIS uses sub-clustering to generate fuzzy inference system (FIS) model for the input dataset and then uses BP algorithm to train the parameters of a Sugeno-type FIS. Till the number customized of epochs between the desired and the generated output is achieved, the training continues.

The fuzzy logic accounts for the imprecision and dubiousness of the system being modeled, and a sense of adaptability is given by neural network. Utilizing this hybrid process, first, a preliminary the input variables along with its fuzzy model is derived with the avail of rules bring out from the input-output data of the system which is being modeled. Secondly, the neural network is utilized to fine tune the rules of the preliminary fuzzy model to engender the final ANFIS model of the system.

ANFIS has an edge over the other techniques of soft computing as it exhibits features of both neural network and fuzzy.

7.3.6 ANFIS Architecture

Figure 7.12 gives the architecture of ANFIS network. The network consists of five layers. For the Sugeno model, the rule set is framed based on if-then

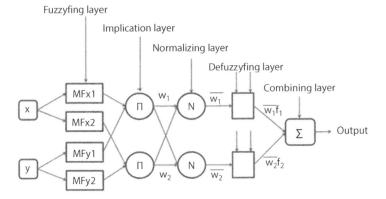

Figure 7.12 Architecture of ANFIS network.

fuzzy rules. In the ANFIS architecture, nodes of a layer will have similar function.

Layer 1 (Fuzzifying Layer): In this layer, the nodes are adaptive (vary based on parameters) along with a node function. Two inputs "x" and "y" to the node and one output "z" are there. The input values are scaled and mapped to the domain of variables known as linguistic variables. These variables are determined based on knowledge (intuition) and facts (inference). This layer is a two-step process:

- Assign linguistic variables.
- Assign numerical value to each label.

The linguistic labels which are defined in terms of quantity (small or large) are associated with suitable membership functions. These functions are dependent on parameters called premise parameters exhibiting membership functions for a fuzzy set of various forms.

Layer 2 (Implication Layer): Each joint is a fixed joint which denotes that it is independent of parameters and this layer output is called firing strength of a rule and it is evaluated as a product of incoming signals. In fuzzy clustering (FC), each rule is a joint in ANFIS rules layer using dot product (fuzzy AND) to enumerate the rule matching factor ωi which is weighted by the firing strength of the rule ωi.

Layer 3 (Normalization Layer): Each joint is a fixed joint and it measures the ratio of the firing strength rules to sum of all firing strength rules. Hence, this layers' output is called normalized firing strength. Each ω_i is scaled into $\overline{\omega}_i$ by calculating the ratio of the firing strength of the respective rule to the sum of the firing strength of all the rules.

Layer 4 (Defuzzifying Layer): In this, the joints are adaptive as the output is the product of normalized firing strength and the rules. The rules of this layer contain a set of parameters called the consequent attributes.

Layer 5 (Output Layer): Here, one joint and it is a fixed node which access the overall output as the summation of all incoming signals.

7.3.7   Support Vector Machine (SVM)

SVM is a supervised, non-probabilistic, and binary linear classifier and a regression implement [38, 39]. It can be applied in areas of stock price predict, advertisement recommendation systems and in image and verbalization apperception. The dataset separation is channelized in the form of a hyperplane (includes margin) and support vectors. The hyperplane functions to relegate the data into identical categories by maximizing the length of margin to match the desired output. The term support vector refers to a data points set that are adjoining to the hyperplane as shown in Figure 7.13. The margin fluctuates according to the type of dataset which reigns in the separable class or non-separable class. The margin is called as soft margin with reverence to non-separable data, which implicatively insinuates that a hyperplane dissevers several, but not all data points [40].

To classify the non-separable data, a different technique based on the kernel theory is utilized. The simplicity of the hyperplanes is maintained as it implicates variant mathematical approaches. SVM Kernels are applied to map inseparable data into feature space where they are separable linearly as indicated in Figure 7.14. The value of dot product of functions X and o is returned by the Kernel function, where ϕ maps inseparable data into linear

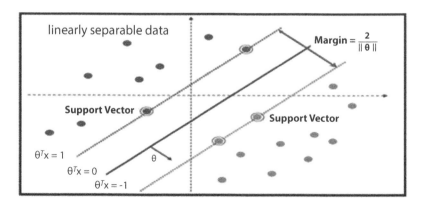

Figure 7.13 Hyperplane SVM architecture.

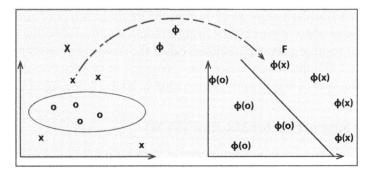

Figure 7.14 Architecture of Kernel-type SVM.

space as the classification becomes simple. The relationship between K and ϕ is displayed in Equation (7.7):

$$K(X, O) = \phi(X) \bullet \phi(o) \tag{7.7}$$

7.3.8   Ensemble Forecasting

A system using large number of samples for the prediction of wind power forecasting and ensemble forecasting strategy is developed with different models [41, 42]. The results obtained are evaluated by testing the distribution across all ensemble "members" of the forecast variables as shown in Figure 7.15. It is always found difficult to evaluate the data obtained due to uncertainty of wind characteristics effectively to maintain good power system conditions. Though many models have been developed for predicting wind power, the system instability and sensitivity in adapting to initial parameters and training the models will become difficult when single machine learning algorithm is used and the convergence rate is also found low. SVM model and the combination of SVR with RBF techniques used to predict the wind speed and direction to improve the performance further. To overcome these challenges, DL-based ensemble method will be suitable by reducing the errors in the models due to data noise and improper specification. Increased accuracy and provided probabilistic uncertainty will help in the preparation of future conditions, which is an added advantage.

7.4   Deep Learning–Based Wind Forecasting

In general, wind speed prediction can be divided into two broad categories [43–47].

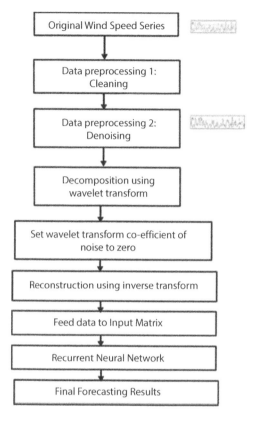

Figure 7.15 Flowchart depicting data pre-processing.

- Physical forecasting approach
- Statistical approach

The physical model-based approach relies on the equations provided by the aerodynamic models and enables forecasting over extended periods of time. The statistical model heavily relies on measured historical data and is accurate in short-term wind forecasting. The predicted speeds are as good as the authenticity of the data fed to the statistical model.

Statistical methods can be further categorized as solo predictions and ensemble model–based predictions (includes pre-processing and forecasting techniques). Ensemble techniques are preferred as they help to improve the accuracy of prediction as they highlight the best features of the models involved.

Although traditional statistical techniques have proven effective, the accuracy has not been good for time series–based data due to lack of deep feature extraction capability [48]. In order to solve this issue DL techniques have been employed for the past few years. In the recent past upgraded forms of RNNs such as LSTMs have been used in wind speed forecasting [49].

Data pre-processing is also a very important aspect in machine learning, especially required in wind speed forecasting as input data is unpredictable and noisy.

The data pre-processing steps are illustrated in Figure 7.15. In this study, a Wavelet Soft Threshold Denoising (WSTD) approach is used to pre-process the obtained data [47]. The WSTD provides a means to mitigate noise in the raw time series data. The chief advantage of this technique is that it can be used to denoise multiple datasets; WSTD along with a RNN can help in adaptive learning and extract important features from the raw wind speed data.

Following steps are followed once the raw data is collected.

1. All the data is collected and combined together. Then the data is cleaned and also normalized.
2. The WSTD technique is utilized to remove excess information from the collected raw time series data, denoising is done here.
3. The raw data once cleaned and denoised is fed to a RNN which is used for wind speed forecasting

7.4.1   Reducing Dimensionality

There is a need to reduce the dimensions of the input data to decrease computational complexness and to cut down on the forecasting error [50]. Feature selection is one of the means to achieve dimensionality reduction. Feature selection can be achieved by the following techniques.

a. **Correlation:** In literature a Grey Correlation Analysis (GCA) approach was used to find beneficial varying information in the time series data [51]. This approach used a ranking-based method. The analysis showed the data collected between every 10 minutes were an important symbol in feature selection.

b. **Clustering:** This feature selection technique has garnered attention in the past few years. Original raw time series data have been segregated into training samples. By using a Density-Based Spatial Clustering of Applications with

Noise (DBSCAN) technique outliers within the data were identified

c. **Based on Information:** A probabilistic approach of Conditional Mutual Information (CMI) is used.

7.4.2   Deep Learning Techniques and Their Architectures

There are four major network architectures used in DL. Figure 7.16 shows the four main architects along with their different varieties popularly used.

7.4.3   Unsupervised Pre-Trained Networks

In DL the main difficulty is to train a model for many layers in Deep networks of adaptive parameters. In DL, the main function is an extremely non-convex function of the attributes. Because of which many local minima in the parameter space of the model are created and all of these minima doesn't provide comparable errors. The optimisation of stochastic gradient descent (SGD) can be better handled by unsupervised pre-trained networks (UPNs) as it starts a discriminative neural net from unsupervised trained networks. The architecture is shown in Figure 7.17 with RBM layers.

This network uses three different architectures, and they are as follows:

a. Auto encoders
b. Deep Belief Networks
c. Generative Adversarial Networks

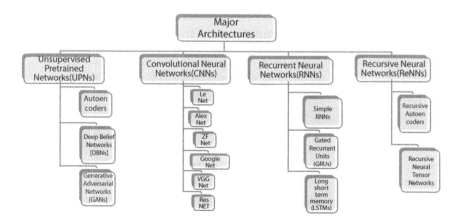

Figure 7.16 Different network architectures used in deep learning.

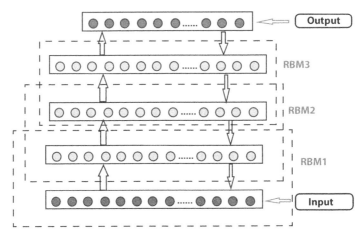

Figure 7.17 Unsupervised pre-trained network architecture.

7.4.4   Convolutional Neural Networks

CNN architecture basically has three layers, input layer, convolutional layer, and output layer. In convolutional layer, mainly feature extraction takes place through convolution, pooling, and activation. Figure 7.18 shows architecture of deep CNNs.

7.4.5   Recurrent Neural Networks

The architecture of RNN is shown in Figure 7.19.

7.4.6   Analysis of Support Vector Machine and Decision Tree Analysis (With Computation Time)

Performance of SVM has proven to be quite impressive for wind speed prediction [52]. A basic network structure of an SVM is shown in Figure 7.20. This technique has been applied for various applications such as image detection, natural language processing, and fault diagnosis. SVM can be used for either classification or regression problems.

SVM is one of the most used machine learning techniques which is especially useful in modeling non-linear relationships among input and output variables. It is based on kernel functions which maps the lower dimensional dataset into higher dimensions. In higher dimensions, unlike linear classifiers, it uses hyperplanes to classify different sets of data and the data points closest to the boundary are called support vectors. Similarly, in

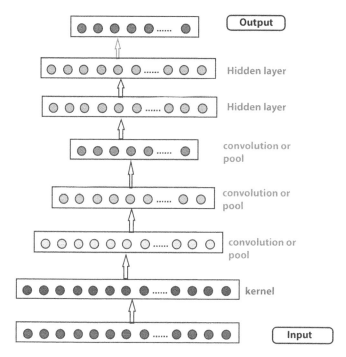

Figure 7.18 Deep CNN architecture.

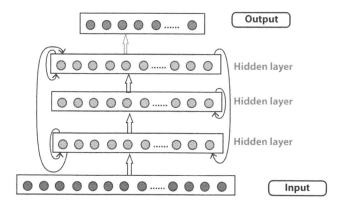

Figure 7.19 RNN architecture.

case of regression, the same hyperplane is used to best-fit the data in a non-linear fashion. There are multiple kernel functions and cost functions available, among which the best ones for the given dataset are determined by visually examining the data and performing cross-validation, respectively.

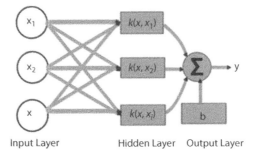

Input Layer   Hidden Layer   Output Layer

Figure 7.20 Support vector machine network structure.

7.4.7   Tree-Based Techniques

A decision tree is a technique which is built based on splitting the input data into two partitions using a technique termed as binary recursive partitioning. This is a repetitive method that repeatedly splitting each partition into tinier groups as the techniques moves down each branch. The structure of the tree is determined by the concept of information gain where each branch split is governed by picking the most important variable which helps in obtaining output closest to actual data.

Each node reaches a predefined set of nodes and thus becomes a terminal joint. Once the tree structure is fixed the test data is parsed through each node of the tree and gets partitioned based on its values.

In the literature, an ANN along with a least-squares SVM (LS-SVM) was used to improve wind power prediction. Raw data from a farm in Italy

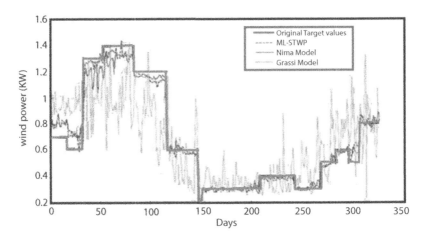

Figure 7.21 Prediction comparisons between various models.

was logged for 5 years; the resolution of the measurements was 10 minutes. LS-SVM proved to improve accuracy [53, 54].

Hybrid models built on SVM have also yielded promising results; they have been especially useful in predicting wind power for short durations. In this analysis, the performance of various models was compared and is summarized in Figure 7.21.

7.5   Case Study

Ministry of New and Renewable Energy (MNRE) under the Ministry of Power in India looks after all matters related to renewable energy which includes development and deployment of renewable energy across India. Since wind energy resource is intermittent and site specific, an extensive wind resource assessment is required which is achieved using around 800 wind monitoring stations across the country. The recent assessment indicates that the country have a wind energy potential of about 302 GW at 100 m above ground level. The country stands at fourth place in the world in terms of installed capacity of wind energy which is about 35.6GW (upto March 2019) [55]. Therefore, there is an urgent need for reliable wind energy forecasting techniques like DL techniques which was discussed in the earlier section. In order to prove the effectiveness and reliability of DL algorithm for wind energy forecasting, a simple case study is presented along with relevant data.

For the case study purpose, the mountain region in Himachal Pradesh is considered where wind energy potential is enough according to [56]. In [56], a DL algorithm based on ANNs is presented for forecasting the wind speed. The 10-minute averaged measured time series data of climatic variables like temperature, solar radiation, wind speed, and air pressure of Himachal Pradesh is measured during the year 2012 is used for creating the ANN model. The daily wind data averaged in 10-minute interval during that year is shown in Figure 7.22.

The wind speed forecasting accuracy is determined by a parameter called the mean absolute error, which is calculated using Equation (7.8) given by

$$\text{Mean Absolute Error} = \left(\frac{1}{n} \sum_{i=1}^{n} \frac{\left| WS_{i(ANN)} - WS_{i(measured)} \right|}{WS_{i(measured)}} \right) \times 100 \quad (7.8)$$

where n is the total number of input and output variables

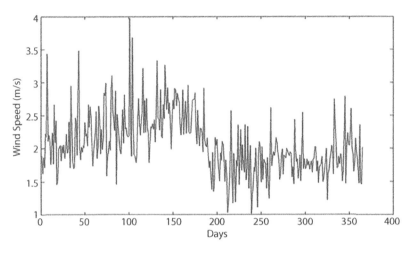

Figure 7.22 Daily variation of averaged wind speed.

$WS_{imeasured}$ is the measured wind speed on any i^{th} day
WS_{iANN} is the predicted wind speed on any i^{th} day

The accuracy of the ANN is decided based on the value of the mean absolute error as follows:

- When error is <10% means the high prediction.
- When 10% < Error < 20% means the prediction is good.
- When 20% < Error < 50% means the prediction is reasonable.
- When error is >50% means the prediction is inaccurate.

The author of [56] has used Artificial Network Fitting tool called as the ntool for forecasting the daily wind speed. The tool consists of two layer feed-forward neural network. The neurons are trained using Levenberge-Marquardt (LM) algorithm [56, 57]. The hidden layer neurons are decided by Equation (7.9) given by

$$H_n = \frac{I_n + O_n}{2} + \sqrt{S_n} \qquad (7.9)$$

where H_n and S_n are number of hidden layer neurons and data samples used for the ANN model, and I_n and O_n denote the number of input and output parameters as shown in Figure 7.23. For training, the ANN model 315 data points of average daily wind speed are used.

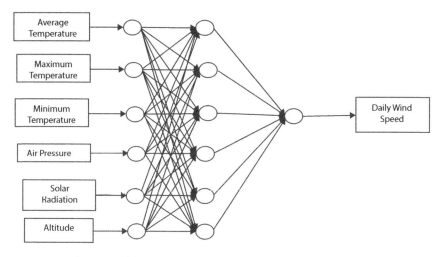

Figure 7.23 Structure of the proposed ANN model.

The mean absolute error calculated as per Equation (7.1) is found to be 4.55% which indicates that the proposed ANN model predicts the wind speed with high accuracy as shown in Figure 7.24. Thus, the DL algorithm is well suited for forecasting the wind speed with high accuracy. The wind speed prediction accuracy was evaluated by means of direct comparison between the predicted wind speed and measured wind speed for a given time duration.

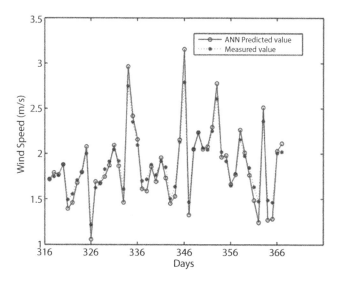

Figure 7.24 Comparison between the measured and predicted wind speed.

References

1. Future of Wind, in: *Deployment, investment, technology, grid integration and socio-economic aspects*, International Renewable Energy Agency, Abu Dhabi, October 2019.
2. https://gwec.net/publications/global-wind-energy-outlook/
3. Yaramasu, V. and Wu, B., *Model Predictive Control of Wind Energy Conversion Systems*, First Edition, The Institute of Electrical and Electronics Engineers, Inc. Published by John Wiley & Sons, Inc., India, 2017.
4. Salameh, Z., *Renewable Energy System Design*, Academic Press, USA, 2014.
5. Kavasseri, R. and Seetharaman, K., Day-ahead wind speed forecasting using f-ARIMA models. *Renewable Energy*, 34, 5, 1388–1393, 2009.
6. Wang, J. and Xiong, S., A hybrid forecasting model based on outlier detection and fuzzy time series – a case study on Hainan wind farm of China. *Energy*, 76, 526–41, 2014.
7. Su, Z., Wang, J., Lu, H., Zhao, G., A new hybrid model optimized by an intelligent optimization algorithm for wind speed forecasting. *Energy Convers. Manage.*, 85, 443–52, 2014.
8. Nazir, M.S., Alturise, F., Alshmrany, S., Nazir, H.M.J., Bilal, M., Abdalla, A.N., Sanjeevikumar, P., Ali, Z.M., Wind Generation Forecasting Methods and Proliferation of Artificial Neural Network: A Review of Five Years Research Trend. *Sustainability*, 12, 3778, 2020.
9. Foley, A., Leahy, P., Marvuglia, A., McKeogh, E., Current methods and advances in forecasting of wind power generation. *Renewable Energy*, 37, 1, 1–8, 2012.
10. Dongmei, Z., Yuchen, Z., Xu, Z., Research on wind power forecasting in wind farms, in: *Proceedings of the 2011 IEEE Power Engineering and Automation Conference (PEAM)*, Wuhan, China, 8–9 September 2011.
11. Zhao, X., Wang, S., Li, T., Review of evaluation criteria and main methods of wind power forecasting. *Energy Proc.*, 12, 761–769, 2011.
12. Lynch, P., *The emergence of numerical weather prediction:Richardson's dream*, Cambridge University Press, Cambridge, 2006.
13. Hayati, M. and Mohebi, Z., Application of artificial neural networks for temperature forecasting. *Int. J. Electr. Comput. Eng.*, 1, 4, 5, 2007.
14. Manwell, J.F., McGowan, J.G., Rogers, A.L., *Wind Energy Explained: Theory, Design and Application*, JohnWiley & Sons, Hoboken, NJ, USA, 2010.
15. Lei, M., Shiyan, L., Chuanwen, J., Hongling, L., Yan, Z., A review on the forecasting of wind speed and generated power. *Renewable Sustainable Energy Rev.*, 13, 915–920, 2009.
16. Wu, Y.-K. and Hong, J.-S., A literature review of wind forecasting technology in the world, in: *Proceedings of the 2007 IEEE Lausanne Power Tech*, Lausanne, Switzerland, 1–5 July 2007.

17. Deng, X., Shao, H., Hu, C., Jiang, D., Jiang, Y., Wind Power Forecasting Methods Based on Deep Learning: A survey. *Comp. Model. Eng. Sci.*, 122, 1, 273–301, 2020.

18. Wu, Y.-K. and Hong, J.-S., A literature review of wind forecasting technology in the world, in: *Proceedings of the 2007 IEEE Lausanne Power Tech*, Lausanne, Switzerland, 1–5 July 2007.

19. Soman, S.S., Zareipour, H., Malik, O., Mandal, P., A review of wind power and wind speed forecasting methods with different time horizons, in: *Proceedings of the 2010 North American Power Symposium (NAPS)*, Arlington, TX, USA, 26–28 September 2010.

20. Morettin, P.A. and Toloi, C., *Análise de Séries Temporais*, E. Blucher (Ed.), Blucher, São Paulo, Brazil, 2006.

21. Foley, A.M., Leahy, P.G., Marvuglia, A., McKeogh, E.J., Current methods and advances in forecasting of wind power generation. *Renewable Energy*, 37, 1–8, 2012.

22. Shamshirband, S., Rabczuk, T., Chau, K.-W., Survey of Deep Learning Techniques: Application in Wind and Solar Energy Resources. *IEEE*, 7, 164650–164666, 2019.

23. Zhao, X., Wang, S., Li, T., Review of Evaluation Criteria and Main Methods of Wind Power Forecasting. *Energy Proc.*, 12, 761–769, 2011.

24. Ramirez-Rosado, I.J., Alfredo Fernandez-Jimenez, L., Monteiro, C., Sousa, J., Bessa, R., Comparison of two short term wind power forecasting systems. *Renewable Energy*, 34, 1848–1854, 2009.

25. Grell, G.A., Dudhia, J., Stauffer, D.R., A description of the fifth-generation Penn State/NCAR mesoscale model (MM5). NCAR Technical Note-398, National Center for Atmospheric Research, Boulder, Colorado, 1995, Available from: <http://www.mmm.ucar.edu/mm5/documents/mm5-desc-doc.html>.

26. Wang, L.-j., Liao, X.-z., Gao, Y., Gao, S., Summarization of modeling and prediction of wind power generation. *Power Syst. Prot. Control*, 37, 13, 118–121, Jul. 2009.

27. Lei, M., Shiyan, L., Chuanwen, J., Hongling, L., Yan, Z., A review on the forecasting of wind speed and generated power. *Renewable Sustainable Energy Rev.*, 13, 915–920, May 2009.

28. Wang, X.C., Guo, P., Huang, X.B., A Review of Wind Power Forecasting Models. *Energy Proc.*, 12, 770–778, 2011.

29. Zhao, D.M., Zhu, Y.C., Zhang, X., Research on Wind Power Forecasting in Wind Farms. *Proceedings of the 2011 IEEE Power Engineering and Automation Conference*, Wuhan, 8-9 September 2011, pp. 175–178, 2011.

30. Zhao, X., Wang, S.X., Li, T., Review of Evaluation Criteria and Main Methods of Wind Power Forecasting. *Energy Proc.*, 12, 761–769, 2011.

31. Wu, Y.K. and Hon, J.S., A Literature Review of Wind Forecasting Technology in the World. *Proceedings of the IEEE Conference on Power Tech*, Lausanne, 1-5 July 2007, pp. 504–509, 2007.

32. Wu, Y.K., Lee, C.Y., Tsai, S.H., Yu, S.N., Actual Experience on the Short-Term Wind Power Forecasting at Penghu-From an Island Perspective. *Proceedings of the 2010 International Conference on Power System Technology*, Hangzhou, 24-28 October 2010, pp. 1–8, 2010.

33. Sfetsos, A., A Novel Approach for the Forecasting of Mean Hourly Wind Speed Time Series. *Renewable Energy*, 27, 163–174, 2002.

34. Chang, W.Y., Application of Back Propagation Neural Network for Wind Power Generation Forecasting. *Int. J. Digit. Content Technol. its Appl.*, 7, 502–509, 2013.

35. Chang, W.Y., Wind Energy Conversion System Power Forecasting Using Radial Basis Function Neural Network. *Appl. Mech. Mater.*, 284–287, 1067–1071, 2013.

36. Li, L.L., Li, J.H., He, P.J., Wang, C.S., The Use of Wavelet Theory and ARMA Model in Wind Speed Prediction. *Proceedings of the 1st International Conference on Electric Power Equipment-Switching Technology*, Xi'an, 23-27 October 2011, pp. 395–398, 2011.

37. Yang, Z.L., Liu, Y.Q., Li, C.R., Interpolation of Missing Wind Data Based on ANFIS. *Renewable Energy*, 36, 993–998, 2011.

38. Zeng, J.W. and Qiao, W., Support Vector Machine-Based Short-Term Wind Power Forecasting. *Proceedings of the IEEE/PES Power Systems Conference and Exposition*, Phoenix, 20-23 March 2011, pp. 1–8, 2011.

39. Zhou, J.Y., Shi, J., Li, G., Fine Tuning Support Vector Machines for Short-Term Wind Speed Forecasting. *Energy Convers. Manage.*, 52, 1990–1998, 2011.

40. Liu, D., Niu, D.X., Wang, H., Fan, L.L., Short-term wind speed forecasting using wavelet transform and support vector machines optimized by genetic algorithm, *Renewable Energy*, 62, 592–597, 2014.

41. Wang, H.-z., Li, G.-q., Wang, G.-b., Peng, J.-c., Jiang, H., Liu, Y.-t., Deep Learning Based ensemble approach for probabilistic wind power forecasting. *Appl. Energy*, 188, 56–70, 2017.

42. Tang, Z., Zhao, G., Wang, G., Ouyang, T., Hybrid Ensemble Framework for Short term Wind Speed Forecasting. *IEEE Access*, 8, 45271–45291, 2020.

43. Giebel, G., Badger, J., Landberg, L., Haa, N., Nielsen, T., Madsen, H. *et al.*, *Wind power prediction ensembles*. Report 1527, Risø National Laboratory, Denmark, 2005.

44. Lang, S.J. and McKeogh, E.J., Forecasting wind generation, uncertainty and reserve requirement on the Irish power system using an ensemble prediction system. *Wind Eng.*, 33, 5, 433–48, 2009.

45. Lang, S., Möhrlen, J., Jørgensen, J., O'Gallachóir, B.P., McKeogh, E., Application of a multi-scheme ensemble prediction system for wind power forecasting in Ireland and comparison with validation results from Denmark and Germany. *Proceedings of the European wind energy conference, EWEC2006*, Athens, Greece, 2006.

46. Costello, R., McCoy, D., O'Donnell, P., Dutton, A.G., Kariniotakis, G.N., Potential benefits of wind forecasting and the application of more-Care in Ireland. *Proceedings of the 3rd MED power conference 2002*, Athens, Greece, 2002.

47. Peng, Z., Peng, S., Fu, L., Lu, B., Tang, J., Wang, K., Li, W., A novel deep learning ensemble model with data denoising for short-term wind speed forecasting. *Energy Convers. Manage.*, 207, 112524, 2020.

48. Wang, H.-Z., Li, G.-Q., Wang, G.-B., Peng, J.-C., Jiang, H., Liu, Y.-T., Deep learning based ensemble approach for probabilistic wind power forecasting. *Appl. Energy*, 188, 56–70, 2017.

49. Liu, H., Mi, X.-W., Li, Y.-F., Wind speed forecasting method based on deep learning strategy using empirical wavelet transform, long short term memory neural network and Elman neural network. *Energy Convers. Manage.*, 156, 498–514, 2018.

50. Liu, H. and Chen, C., Data processing strategies in wind energy forecasting models and applications: A comprehensive review. *Appl. Energy*, 249, 392–408, 2019.

51. Jiang, P., Wang, Y., Wang, J.Z., Short-term wind speed forecasting using a hybrid model. *Energy*, 119, 561–77, 2017.

52. Zendehboudi, A., Baseer, M.A., Saidur, R., Application of support vector machine models for forecasting solar and wind energy resources: A review. *J. Cleaner Prod.*, 199, 272–285, 2018.

53. Giorgi, M.G.D., Campilongo, S., Ficarella, A., Congedo, P.M., Comparison between wind power prediction models based on wavelet decomposition with least-squares support vector machine (LS-SVM) and artificial neural network (ANN). *Energies*, 7, 5251e5272, 2014.

54. Najeebullah, Zameer, A., Khan, A., Javed, S.G., Machine Learning based short term wind power prediction using a hybrid learning model. *Comput. Electr. Eng.*, 45, 122–133, 2015.

55. https://mnre.gov.in/wind/current-status/

56. Ramasamy, P., Chandel, S.S., Yadav, A.K., Wind speed prediction in the mountainous region of India using an artificial neural network model. *Renewable Energy*, 80, 338–347, 2015.

57. Khosravi, A., Machado, L., Nunes, R.O., Time-series prediction of wind speed using machine learning algorithms: A case study Osorio wind farm, Brazil. *Appl. Energy*, 224, 550–556, 2018.

8

Deep Feature Selection for Wind Forecasting-II

S. Oswalt Manoj[1]*, J.P. Ananth[2], Balan Dhanka[3] and Maharaja Kamatchi[4]

[1]Department of Computer Science and Business System, Sri Krishna College of Engineering and Technology, Coimbatore, India
[2]Department of Computer Science and Engineering, Sri Krishna College of Engineering and Technology, Coimbatore, India
[3]University of Rajasthan, Rajasthan, India
[4]Engineering Department, University of Technology and Applied Sciences, Al Mussanah, Oman

Abstract

In recent years, large production of energy from renewable sources is significantly getting boosted in every part of the world. Due to the expeditious development of the penetration of the power related to wind into the present day power grid, the forecasting of wind speed turns into an expanding noteworthy assignment in power generation process. Accordingly, the scope of the chapter is to determine the forecasting of the wind speed in short term by incorporating the adaptive ensembles of Deep Neural Network, and the work is compared with the machine learning algorithms like Gated Recurrent Unit (GRU), Long Short-Term Memory Neural Network (LSTM), and Bidirectional Long Short-Term Memory Neural Network (Bi-LSTM). Various existing approaches for the forecasting of wind speed like physical and statistical models, along with artificial intelligence models is used by numerous researchers. The dataset has been received from various authenticated sources like Windmills in Jaipur, globalwindatlas.info and data.gov. in. It comprises of the parameters like time, dew point, wind speed, humidity, temperature (air), pressure, and month. This data can be used to determine the wind speed and the air density. Parameters like wind speed, blade swept area, and air density will be used to decide on the output power. The swept area is relied upon the design and the speed of the wind and air density has been predicted from the input data provided. Various parameters like the mean absolute error (MAE) and

*Corresponding author: oswaltmanojibm@gmail.com

Ajay Kumar Vyas, S. Balamurugan, Kamal Kant Hiran and Harsh S. Dhiman (eds.) *Artificial Intelligence for Renewable Energy Systems*, (181–200) © 2022 Scrivener Publishing LLC

the root mean square error (RMSE) have been computed. Also, the mean square error (MSE) has been computed for the given algorithms, and the performance of the Bi-LSTM is comparatively good considering MSE, RMSE, and MAE.

Keywords: Deep learning, forecasting, wind speed, LSTM, deep neural network

8.1   Introduction

Energy crisis has hit the world and wind energy which is considered to be the renewable source is predictable as one of the feasible answer in order to see the energy crisis and it has attracted worldwide attention. The power from wind is produced throughout by the wind turbines by means of the flow of air. This is a noteworthy feature of the resources related to renewable energy because of the accessibility of wind turbines which is having even megawatt size, available facilities for management along with the subsidies by government, and low cost of maintenance. One of the most gifted renewable energy technologies has been normally considered. Wind speed is one among the major factors in the production of wind power. The operating cost can be increased based on the repeated and the variant characteristics of the wind speed, and also, the power system's reliability could be challenged. The wind farms are to be protected and the scheduling of the power system also has to be improved. This can happen only by the accurate wind speed forecasting. The speed of wind is considered to be one of the difficult meteorological parameters to be predicted. The speed of wind is stochastic in nature and many complex factors can be may affect the same. Similarly, forecasting the speed of wind accurately is also a serious concern. During the recent years, abundant models related to wind speed have been established, and it can also be sorted into many varied categories conferring to varied principles.

The models that have been used for the prediction of wind speed are often categorized into three groups based on the time horizon prediction. These are as follows: the long-term future prediction models, the short-term future prediction models, and the medium-term prediction models. The future prediction models for the long-term prediction are utilized in the approximation capacity, and possibly, in selecting the location for the wind farm, the prediction models related to medium term are utilized specifically for the maintenance and operation of the wind farm and therefore the the future prediction models related to the short term are utilized in the optimal control of wind turbine, load decision, operational security, and also in the real-time operation of grid. It is also used to optimally control the wind turbine. On comparing all the three prediction models, the short term-wind speed prediction model requires less computation as compared with the medium- and long-term wind speed prediction models. So, most of the focus is on the short-term wind speed forecasting models. However, the standard uniqueness related to the models toward prediction of the wind speed play a vital role here. The prediction models related to wind speed are often branded into five categories of models, namely physical, conventional statistical, artificial intelligence (AI)–based, spatial correlation, and hybrid models along with the event of forecasting the wind speed. The models which are considered as hybrid has the ability to provide improved accuracy in prediction. The single models give least performance when it is compared with the hybrid models.

The precise and consistent methodology for forecasting wind generation supports the grid dispatching process, and it enhances the standard of the energy based on electricity. Current wind generation prediction methods are often categorized as physical, statistical, and combined physical statistical. A physical prediction model for wind generation considers the phenomena related to weather or the weather processes. The modeling can be done with the suitable laws related to physics which includes the momentum conservation and therefore the conservation of energy. The prediction of wind generation round the wind farm also requests the control of successive momentum of the positive state and it is attained by inspecting the atmospheric state which incorporates the neighboring air pressure, roughness, and temperature along with the obstacles. Based on the changes in the atmosphere, the numerical prediction of weather is done. Real-time environmental data is required because the physical prediction model is used for forecasting the wind generation. The data transmission network and the knowledge acquisition is in high demand always.

There is a complexity in the physical wind generation building process. The model is extremely subtle as far as the instruction is presented, and it is based on the standards. These standards of the physical data can be acquired as an alternate to the physical models. An equivalent weather might not induce an equivalent weather change. The weather changes can be treated as a random process at most of the time [11]. Similarly, the phenomena related to weather or the relevant process can be contingent in nature. This can be assumed by the statistical prediction models. The likelihood of existence of a precise sort of weather is really questionable because the equivalent weather might not encourage an equivalent weather change. The variety of independent variables can be fused by other statistical models like Kalman filtering and neural networks. The behaviors due to the physical interpretations can be easily understood by the researchers.

There is a connection between the wind generation and the wind prediction. This is because of the modeling method, and therefore, the historical data is established. When considering the accurate forecasting, the statistical methods of the wind prediction does not consider the particular physical data and due to this the statistical methods could not correlate variety of things. There is a serious drawback when considering the delay in time for the generation of the wind characteristic analysis.

Over the years, machine learning techniques are extensively used for the prediction of wind speed. A number of the recent examples including the applications of artificial neural networks are also used in the prediction of wind speed. The extensively used statistical models include moving average models, autoregressive models, autoregressive moving average models, and also the autoregressive integrated moving average. The wind generation prediction models associate multiple forecasting methods against the utilization of one forecasting model with the confidence that will improve the accuracy of wind generation forecasting. Soft computing method is shown as a joint power production model. The increasing number of wind turbines in various locations is an important factor. Higher degree of accuracy in forecasting the wind power is really an important matter of concern. This is better compared with the physical and the statistical model. There comes a fast improvement in the knowledge induced in the prediction of wind based on the factors including humidity, the wind direction, wind speed, temperature, and the wind generation. The sampling variance is taken in real time.

In general, there can be two major issues while using the wind forecasting model. One is on the selection of the proper features that is important for the prediction of wind. Second issue is on the extraction of data from the information set. This data can be obtained from the wind turbines. Varied data samples can be used to obtain many features that will be useful in the wind forecasting. In this regard, the temperature and wind direction can be considered as one of the parameter along with the wind speed. All the extracted features may not have the equivalent contribution in getting the forecasting accuracy. The accuracy in selecting the best features is also an important factor. After that the model must be perfectly ready to retrieve proper information from the samples. One of the applications for the information extract is using the neural networks concept.

8.1.1 Contributions of the Work

In this chapter, we have included four important algorithms for the wind prediction. These are long short-term memory neural network (LSTM), gated recurrent unit (GRU), and bidirectional long short-term memory neural network (Bi-LSTM). The dataset has been trained and tested with all the four algorithms, and the performance has been evaluated. LSTM networks are a distinct kind of RNN which is proficient in learning long-term dependencies. So, we have used it in our work.

8.2   Literature Review

When considering the wind speed prediction, genetic programming, fuzzy logic [2, 7], ANN [3], as well as deep learning algorithms along with machine learning algorithms are applied, and the results were discussed. In this section, we will discuss about some of the techniques used.

Salcedo-sans *et al.* [20] recommended a hybrid model that supported a model related to Mesoscale along with the neural network for the prediction of wind which is short term in nature at some accurate values. Li and Shi [13] linked three ANNs for forecasting the wind speed just like the back propagation, adaptive linear element, and radial basis function. Cadenas and Rivera [4] proposed a forecasting method toward predicting the speed of wind especially for the regions of Mexico which is constructed on ARIMA-ANN. Hui and team [9] projected a statistical predicting process that is based on improved time series along with wavelet. This is used to forecast the speed and power based on wind. Guo *et al.* [8] established an EMD-based FFN model to enhance the accuracy of the methods that predicted monthly and daily mean wind speeds. Shi *et al.* [19] projected a method with cumulative weighting coefficients for the prediction.

Liu *et al.* [14, 15] suggested a completely unique method that supported The ARIMA model along with the EMD model to find short-term wind. Wang *et al.* [10] established strong shared model adopting BLM, ARIMA, LSSVM, and SVM. The researchers demonstrated the shared estimating technology are able to do improved estimation performance when compared with the single models. This approach could not find the nonlinear association of single models compared with more progressive estimation support methods. This can be introduced to reinforce the predicting performance instead of simple machine learning algorithms.

Cadenas *et al.* [4] suggested a prediction model based on ARIMA and NARX. On the opposite hand, AI models, soft computing technologies, and artificial neural networks like multi-layer perceptron, back propagation, Bayesian neural networks, and radial basis function neural networks along with the extreme learning method are applied in the forecasting of wind process.

Chang *et al.* [5] delivered an enhanced neural network–based approach with the feedback error to forecast short-term power and speed of wind. Genetical algorithm–based SVM [18] that is associated with the state space along with Kalman filter for the prediction of wind speed was employed by some authors. Most preferably, the investigation of using single or hybrid models selection is used to soften the problem. The foreseen results are combined to offer the ultimate prediction based on the weights. Ambach *et al.* [6] joined the threshold seasonal autoregressive conditional heteroscedastic model and the time-varying threshold autoregressive model for forecasting wind speed. Quershi *et al.* [1] used the DBN, deep encoders, and the learning methods for wind forecasting.

Feng and team [16] recognized a knowledge driven framework. This claimed many of the approaches like Granger casualty test, principal component analysis, autocorrelation, and partial autocorrelation. Chen and team [9] foreseen the technique by adopting some encoders and claimed that their model is efficient. Yu *et al.* [17] considered a LSTM-based model. This model could be the perfect fit to study the future dependency. In current ages, the use of statistic modeling stimulated the research attention of many individuals.

8.3   Long Short-Term Memory Networks

The LSTM networks which are usually called as LSTMs are a distinct type of RNN, and it is capable of learning long-term dependencies. They work extremely well when performing on large sort of problems. The LSTMs are clearly considered to evade the problem of long-term dependency. Memorizing data for long periods of time is almost their default conduct. All the recurrent neural networks (RNNs) have the shape of a sequence of repeating modules of neural network. In typical RNNs, this repeating module will have a really simple structure like tanh layer. Whereas within the LSTM, they even have the chain like structure but the repeating module features a different structure. Rather than having the only neural network layer, there are four layers interacting during a very special way. The key to LSTM is the cell state.

In Figure 8.1 [21], we have the line which carries the entire vector, specifically from the output of one node and to the inputs of other nodes. The circles which is colored in pink characterize pointwise processes like vector addition and the boxes that are colored in yellow are learned layers of neural network. The joining lines represents the concatenation process, while

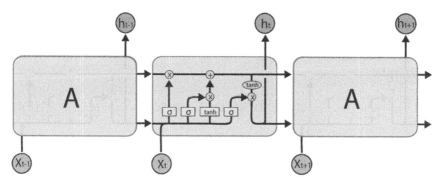

Figure 8.1 LSTM with four interacting layers.

the line that is been forked represents the content is copied and the copies are moving to dissimilar positions. The horizontal line represents the cell state. It is a sort of a conveyer belt that runs straight down the whole chain, with just some minor linear communications. It is very easy for the data to only flow along it unchanged. LSTM does not have the power to feature or remove the data to the cell state carefully that is regulated by the structure called gates. The LSTM weights can be found by the operation gates. The operation gates can be Forget, Input, and Output gates.

$$ftgt = \sigma \ (wtf \ [\ hft - 1, xtf \ ] + btf) \qquad (8.1)$$

This is considered as the sigmoid layer. It is taking the output at $t - 1$. The current input at the time t is also considered. After that it is combined into a tensor. The linear transformation along with a sigmoid is applied. Due to the sigmoid, the output of the gate lies between 0 and 1. The predicted value is then multiplied with the internal state. Because of this reason the state is named as forget gate. If ftgt = 0, then the previous internal state is entirely elapsed; whereas if ftgt = 1, then it can be agreed as not altered.

$$itgt = \sigma \ (wti \ [\ hft - 1, xtt \ ] + bti) \qquad (8.2)$$

The input state takes the previous output composed with the new input and passes them through another sigmoid layer. This gate returns a value between 0 and 1. The value of the input gate is then multiplied with the output of the candidate layer.

$$ctgt = tanh \ (wti \ [\ hft - 1, xtt \ ] + bti) \qquad (8.3)$$

Next, the layer applies hyperbolic tangent in association with the input and preceding output. This returns the candidate vector. The candidate vector is then added to the interior state, which is updated along with the given rule:

$$ctgt = fti \,^*ctgt - 1 + ift^*ctgt \qquad (8.4)$$

The previous gate is then multiplied by the forget gate, and also it is added to the fraction of the new candidate that is allowed by the output gate.

$$otgt = \sigma \,(wto \,[\, hft - 1, xft \,] + bto) \qquad (8.5)$$

The gate controls what proportion of the interior state is accepted to the output and it works in a comparable means to the next gates. Figure 8.2 shows the loss incurred by the LSTM testing and training set. Here, we have used 30 epochs.

Let us have a look into Figure 8.2. As from the curve, we could see that the training loss is decreasing as the epochs are increasing, and after some time, they became constant which means our loss function is converged properly. In this process, the wind data has been taken and then the dataset is preprocessed. Then, the selective parameters like temperature, humidity, pressure, and wind speed are taken for processing and predicting the wind

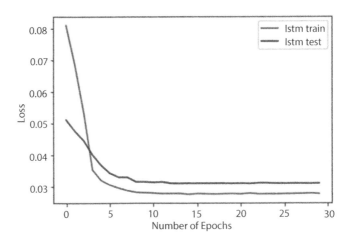

Figure 8.2 No. of epochs vs. loss.

speed. Then, the input features are normalized. Now, we need to create the time series dataset looking back one time step. Then, 70% of data is utilized as the training data and 30% of data is utilized for testing purpose. We need to split them into inputs as well as output and then the input is reshaped to be 3D (samples, time steps, and features). The optimizer used for the process is Adam optimizer. We have used 44,071 total parameters for this process. The loss is calculated in each epoch.

Figure 8.3 shows the plotting amid the predicted test value and the real test value. The x axis consists of the time period and the y axis consists of the wind speed. Figure 8.4 shows the visualization over the full data.

Figure 8.5 is the plot over the small part of the data. Similarly, the plot over the very small part of the data is given in Figure 8.6.

In Figure 8.6, we can see that the actual and predicted pattern in the curve is almost similar which means that the algorithm is showing good results with less error.

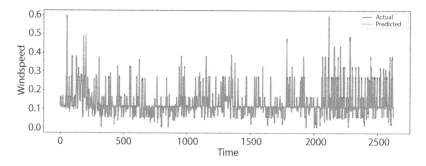

Figure 8.3 Actual and predicted test value.

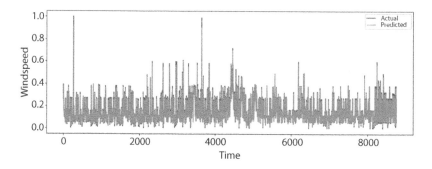

Figure 8.4 Visualization over full data.

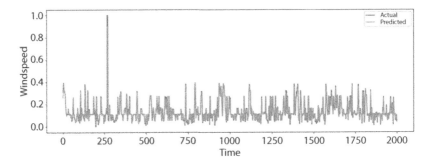

Figure 8.5 Plot over small part of the data.

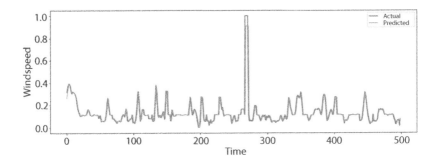

Figure 8.6 Plot over very small part of the data.

8.4   Gated Recurrent Unit

In general, RNNs have the problem of short-term memory. The RRNs suffer from vanishing gradient problem during the back propagation process. The gradients are the values which are used to apprise the neural network weights. The gradient shrinks during the vanishing gradient problem and the back propagation process is done by the time. When the gradient value becomes tremendously minor, it does not contribute much in learning.

$$nw = w - lr * g \qquad (8.6)$$

nw stands for new weight, w stands for weight, lr stands for learning rate, and g stands for gradient. In RNN, the layers which get minor update break learning. These can be the previous layers. Due to the non-learning activity, it has the tendency to forget what are often perceived in longer sequences. Because of this, it has got a STM. GRU is one among the answer to STM and it is the interior mechanism called gates. These gates can regulate the flow of the data. The role of the gates here is that it can study the data within the sequence. This is the vital information used to decide whether to stay back or throw away. Due to this property, it is the potential of passing applicable evidence down the sequences with a long chain value. This is often helpful especially in doing certain predictions.

Figure 8.7 [22] shows the update gate and the reset gate. The forget gate and the update gate seems to be the same. The update gate acts almost like that of the input gate and forget gate of an LSTM. It decides on what information to throw away and what new information are often added. The reset gate is another gate and it is used to decide on what proportion past information has got to be forgotten. The GRUs are faster to train when compared with the LSTM. This is due to the fewer number of weights and parameters to update during training. In this process, the wind data has been taken and then the dataset is preprocessed. Then, the selective parameters like temperature, humidity, pressure, and wind speed are taken for processing and predicting the wind speed [12].

Then, the input features are normalized. Now, we need to create the time series dataset looking back one time step. Then, 70% of data is utilized as the training data and 30% of data is utilized for testing purpose. We need to split them into inputs as well as output and then the input is reshaped to be 3D (samples, time steps, and features). The optimizer used for the process is Adam optimizer. We have used 33,466 total parameters for this process. The loss is calculated in each epoch.

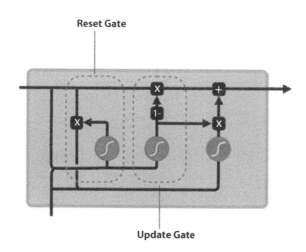

Figure 8.7 GRU.

Figure 8.8 shows the loss during each epoch. As from the curve, we could see that the training loss is decreasing as the epochs are increasing, and after some time, they became constant which means our loss function is converged properly. In the entire dataset, the number of epochs is a hyper parameter which describes the degree to which the learning algorithm will work through. So, one epoch is that each sample in the training dataset has got a chance to apprise the interior model parameters. The epoch is the combination of one or more than one batches.

Figure 8.9 shows the plotting among the foreseen test value and the actual test value. The x axis consists of the time period and the y axis consists of the wind speed. Figure 8.10 shows the visualization over the full data.

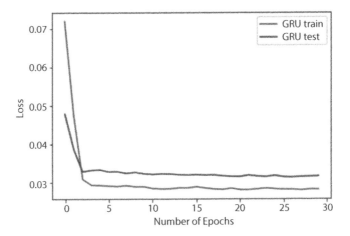

Figure 8.8 Number of epochs vs. loss.

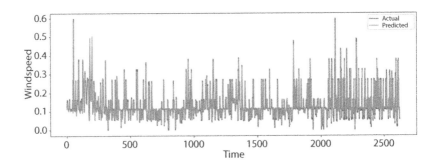

Figure 8.9 Plot of actual and predicted test value.

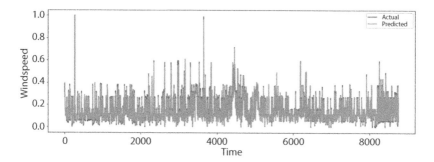

Figure 8.10 Visualization over full data.

The overall small part of the data for the actual and foreseen speed of the wind is shown in Figure 8.11.

Figure 8.12 shows the plot over the very small part of the data.

In Figure 8.12, we can see that the actual and predicted pattern in the curve is almost similar which means that the algorithm is showing good results with less error.

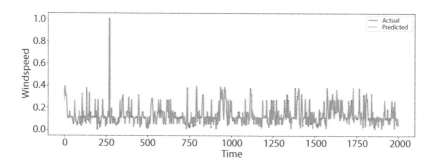

Figure 8.11 Plot over the small part of the data.

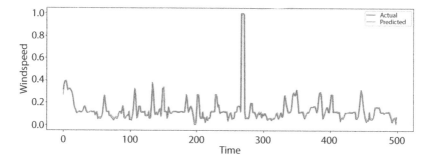

Figure 8.12 Plot over very small part of data.

8.5   Bidirectional Long Short-Term Memory Networks

The bidirectional RNNs puts two autonomous RNNs together. This structure permits the networks to possess both backward and forward information about the sequence at each time step. Using bidirectional will run the input in two ways: one from past to future and one from the future to past, and this varies the method from unidirectional is that within the LSTM that runs backward, and therefore, the information is preserved from the future and using the two hidden states has combined the information from both past and future are often preserved. The Bi-LSTM is shown in Figure 8.13 [23].

In this process, the wind data has been taken and then the dataset is preprocessed. Then, the selective parameters like temperature, humidity, pressure, and wind speed are taken for processing and predicting the wind speed. Then, the input features are normalized. Now, we need to create the time series dataset looking back one time step. Then, 70% of data is utilized as the training data and 30% of data is utilized for testing purpose. We need to split them into inputs as well as output and then the input is reshaped to be 3D (samples, time steps, and features). The optimizer used for the process is Adam optimizer. We have used 44,071 total parameters for this process. The loss is calculated in each epoch.

Figure 8.14 shows the loss during each epoch. As from the curve, we could see that the training loss is decreasing as the epochs are increasing, and after some time, they became constant which means our loss function is converged properly. Figure 8.15 shows the plotting among the forecast test value and the real test value. The x axis consists of the time period and the y axis consists of the wind speed. Figure 8.16 shows the visualization over the full data.

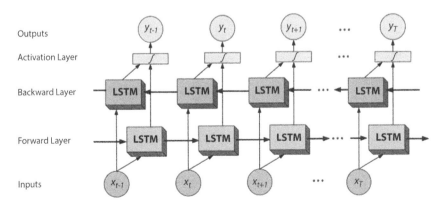

Figure 8.13 Bidirectional LSTM.

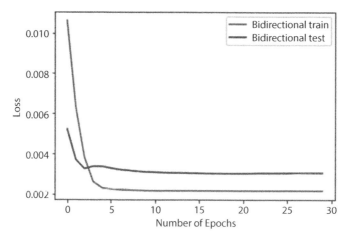

Figure 8.14 No. of epoch vs. loss.

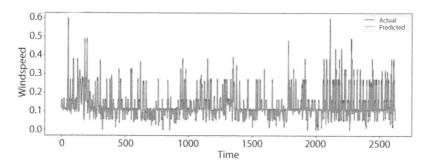

Figure 8.15 Actual and predicted test value.

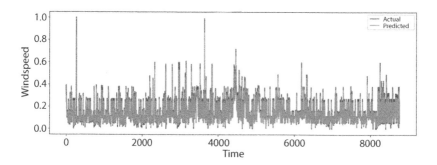

Figure 8.16 Visualization over full data.

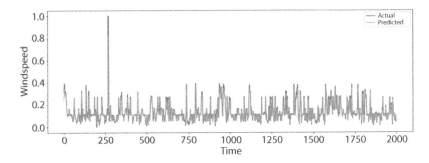

Figure 8.17 Plot over small part of the data.

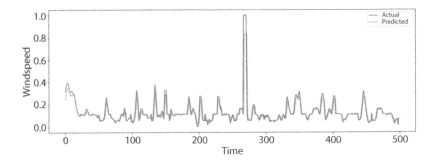

Figure 8.18 Plot over very small part of the data.

Figure 8.17 shows the plot over the small part of the data, and the plot over the very small part of data is shown in Figure 8.18.

In Figure 8.18, we can see that the actual and predicted pattern in the curve is almost similar which means that the algorithm is showing good results with less error.

8.6   Results and Discussion

The root mean square error (RMSE) is a strange key performance index, and it is also a very helpful parameter. It is well defined as the square root of the average squared error. RMSE can be considered as the square root of mean square error (MSE).

$$\text{RMSE} = \sqrt{\frac{1}{N} \sum_{i=1}^{n} (Yi - \widehat{Yi})^2} \tag{8.7}$$

Table 8.1 Comparison of the methodologies with the parameters.

Methodology	MSE	R-Squared	RMSE	MAE
LSTM	0.003223	0.444921	0.056776	0.031272
GRU	0.003238	0.442399	0.056905	0.031254
Bi-LSTM	0.003027	0.478620	0.055026	0.031164

Table 8.1 comprises of the MSE, R-Squared, RMSE and MAE of the methodologies like LSTM, GRU and Bidirectional LSTM. The mean absolute error (MAE) characterizes the average of the absolute variance between the real and forecast values in the dataset. It measures the average of the residuals in the dataset.

$$\text{MAE} = \frac{1}{N} \sum_{i=1}^{N} |f(i) - h(i)| \tag{8.8}$$

MSE signifies the average of the squared difference between the original and the foreseen values in the dataset. It measures the variance of the residuals.

$$\text{MSE} = \frac{1}{N} \sum_{i=1}^{n} (Yti - \widehat{Yti})^2 \tag{8.9}$$

N can be considered as the number of data points, Yti is the observed values, and $\widehat{Yti}$ is the predicted values. The smaller the MSE, the closer we are to find the line of best fit. Initially, the difference between the Y and $\widehat{Yti}$ for each available observation is taken, and then, the difference value is squared, and then, the sum squared values is found, and finally, it is divided by the total number of observations.

8.7 Conclusion and Future Work

In this chapter, the deep learning methodologies like LSTM, GRU, and Bi-LSTM are used for extracting the chief trend content of the wind speed data. In comparing the performance of the algorithms, we can conclude the following results. Bi-LSTM is considered to be the good feature extractor, and it is followed by LSTM, GRU, and CNNLSTM. The coefficient of determination (R²), MSE, MAE, and RMSE has been computed for the given algorithms and the performance of the Bi-LSTM is comparatively good considering MSE, RMSE, and MAE.

In future, the quantity of the data related to wind speed would be considered. We will try to gather more data and thereby build more sensible replicas. New techniques based on deep learning can be deployed for getting better results. Automatic learning prediction models can also be used thereby learning the parameters which is consistent with the data.

References

1. Qureshi, A.S., Khan, A., Zameer, A., Usman, A., Wind power prediction using deep neural network based meta regression and transfer learning. *Appl. Soft Comput.*, 58, 742–755, 2017.
2. Barbounis, T.G. and Theocharis, J.B., A locally recurrent fuzzy neural network with application to the wind speed prediction using spatial correlation. *Neurocomputing*, 70, 7–9, 1525–1542, 2007.
3. Bilgili, M. and Sahin, B., Comparative analysis of regression and artificial neural network models for wind speed prediction. *Meteorol. Atmos. Phys.*, 109, 1, 61–72, 2010.
4. Cadenas, E. and Rivera, W., Wind speed forecasting in three different regions of Mexico, using a hybrid ARIMA–ANN model. *Renewable Energy*, 35, 12, 2732–2738, 2010.
5. Chang, G.W., Lu, H.J., Chang, Y.R., Lee, Y.D., An improved neural network-based approach for short-term wind speed and power forecast. *Renewable Energy*, 105, 301–311, 2017.
6. Ambach, D. and Schmid, W., A new high-dimensional time series approach for wind speed, wind direction and air pressure forecasting. *Energy*, 135, 833–850, 2017.
7. Damousis, I.G., Alexiadis, M.C., Theocharis, J.B., Dokopoulos, P.S., A fuzzy model for wind speed prediction and power generation in wind parks using spatial correlation. *IEEE Trans. Energy Convers.*, 19, 2, 352–361, 2004.
8. Guo, Z., Zhao, W., Lu, H., Wang, J., Multi-step forecasting for wind speed using a modified EMD-based artificial neural network model. *Renewable Energy*, 37, 1, 241–249, 2012.
9. Liu, H., Chen, C., Tian, H.Q., Li, Y.F., A hybrid model for wind speed prediction using empirical mode decomposition and artificial neural networks. *Renewable Energy*, 48, 545–556, 2012.
10. Wang, J., Hu, J., Ma, K., Zhang, Y., A self-adaptive hybrid approach for wind speed forecasting. *Renewable Energy*, 78, 374–385, 2015.
11. JP, A., MapReduce and Optimized Deep Network for Rainfall Prediction in Agriculture. *Comput. J.*, 63, 6, 900–912, 2020.

12. Kavasseri, R.G. and Seetharaman, K., Day-ahead wind speed forecasting using f-ARIMA models. *Renewable Energy*, *34*, 5, 1388–1393, 2009.
13. Li, G. and Shi, J., On comparing three artificial neural networks for wind speed forecasting. *Appl. Energy*, *87*, 7, 2313–2320, 2010.
14. Liu, H., Tian, H.Q., Chen, C., Li, Y.F., A hybrid statistical method to predict wind speed and wind power. *Renewable Energy*, *35*, 8, 1857–1861, 2010.
15. Liu, H., Tian, H.Q., Li, Y.F., An EMD-recursive ARIMA method to predict wind speed for railway strong wind warning system. *J. Wind Eng. Ind. Aerodyn.*, *141*, 27–38, 2015.
16. Cai, H., Jia, X., Feng, J., Yang, Q., Hsu, Y.M., Chen, Y., Lee, J., A combined filtering strategy for short term and long term wind speed prediction with improved accuracy. *Renewable Energy*, *136*, 1082–1090, 2019.
17. Yu, R., Gao, J., Yu, M., Lu, W., Xu, T., Zhao, M., Zhang, Z., LSTM-EFG for wind power forecasting based on sequential correlation features. *Future Gener. Comput. Syst.*, *93*, 33–42, 2019.
18. Cristin, R., Ananth, J.P., Raj, V.C., Illumination-based texture descriptor and fruitfly support vector neural network for image forgery detection in face images. *IET Image Proc.*, *12*, 8, 1439–1449, 2018.
19. Shi, J., Ding, Z., Lee, W.J., Yang, Y., Liu, Y., Zhang, M., Hybrid forecasting model for very-short term wind power forecasting based on grey relational analysis and wind speed distribution features. *IEEE Trans. Smart Grid*, *5*, 1, 521–526, 2013.
20. Salcedo-Sanz, S., Perez-Bellido, A.M., Ortiz-García, E.G., Portilla-Figueras, A., Prieto, L., Paredes, D., Hybridizing the fifth generation mesoscale model with artificial neural networks for short-term wind speed prediction. *Renewable Energy*, *34*, 6, 1451–1457, 2009.
21. https://colah.github.io/posts/2015-08-Understanding-LSTMs/
22. https://towardsdatascience.com/illustrated-guide-to-lstms-and-gru-s-a-step-by-step-explanation-44e9eb85bf21
23. https://www.i2tutorials.com/deep-dive-into-bidirectional-lstm/

9

Data Falsification Detection in AMI: A Secure Perspective Analysis

Vineeth V.V.[1]* and S. Sophia[2]

[1]Department of Electrical and Electronics, Sri Krishna College of Engineering and Technology, Coimbatore, India
[2]Department of Electronics and Communication, Sri Krishna College of Engineering and Technology, Coimbatore, India

Abstract

Advanced metering infrastructure (AMI) being a crucial component of smart grid environment has enormous attractive characteristics and relatively low cost of installation. AMI makes communication in two-way possible between the smart metering infrastructure and utility centers which facilitates functionalities like automated reading of meter data and power distribution monitor and control. Nevertheless, the implementation of AMIs poses several challenges and threats which can, in turn, deteriorate its benefits. This paper gives an overview of various attack scenarios associated with AMI with major focus on data falsification attacks. In data falsification attacks, attackers aim to inject malicious codes or false data to tamper legitimate data. A detailed analysis of the various detection schemes that are available to effectively detect such attacks is also given on the paper.

Keywords: Advanced metering infrastructure, smart meter, false data injection, detection

9.1 Introduction

The numerous enhancements and improved innovative potential of smart grid environment create grid architecture complex and expose the grid to a variety of attacks. Advanced metering infrastructure (AMI) acts as a basic

*Corresponding author: vineethvv@skcet.ac.in

Ajay Kumar Vyas, S. Balamurugan, Kamal Kant Hiran and Harsh S. Dhiman (eds.) *Artificial Intelligence for Renewable Energy Systems*, (201–210) © 2022 Scrivener Publishing LLC

element of the smart grid, as it answerable for gathering, estimating, investigating vitality use information, and transmitting this information to the information concentrator and afterward to a focal framework in the utility side [1]. However, they may experience diversity of threats, together with both physical and cyberattacks. Malicious attackers or software may attempt to obliterate meter reading. Recognizing attacks toward smart meters is a crucial test for building a security system. Smart grid primarily has four segments including supervisory control and data acquisition (SCADA), AMI, communication protocols, and standards and plug-in hybrid vehicle (PHEV). Smart meter being a part of AMI gives exact estimation with robotize remote perusing intensity utilization. Certain smart meters can likewise combine with home machines of smart nature in order to control them so as to work effectively utilizing power. Each of the capacities accomplished using communication in two-way manner using sensors. Smart meters carry out mainly two different functions on communication. The primary function is to transfer gathered information to the service organization in order to get orders for operation. Subsequent function is trading of information to hardware so as to maintain the home energy management system (HEMS). In addition, there exist other correspondence methods that are generally utilized on smart meters for transmitting information to service organization. The methods are power line carrier (PLC) and radio frequency (RF). Because of smart meter information assortment along with correspondence capacities, this might turn into an objective by malicious attackers wishing to make profit by taking or controlling smart meter information [2]. The protection for these attacks can be made by securing all interchanges among smart meters and utility organizations. In addition, smart meters must be introduced at secure areas so they cannot be handily messed with genuinely.

For smart meter protection, three major techniques may be observed: first one being intrusion detection system (IDS), second one is remote attestation technologies, and third method is smart meter software modeling. Detecting false data injection (FDI) attacks are given main focus here. Remaining part of paper is ordered as follows. Section 9.2 provides an outline of AMI. In Section 9.3, there is a close look at the AMI attack scenario. In Section 9.4, data falsification attacks in AMI are discussed, and Section 9.5 gives an analysis of data falsification detection methods. Section 9.6 concludes paper.

9.2 Advanced Metering Infrastructure

AMI deployment combines three main functionally intense components including smart meters, communications network, and data organization system which facilitate bidirectional communication among customers and utility companies [3]. System as a whole enables numerous vital functionalities which otherwise would not have been possible or that needed manual effort. Such functions include the capability of automatic and remote power usage measurement, service connection and disconnection, tamper detection, outage identification and isolation, and voltage monitoring. AMI, in addition, enables utility centers to provide novel time-based programs and incentive schemes to support customer community to decrease power demand peaks and handle power consumption charges. This is done by collaborating with customer technologies like programmable communicating thermostats and in-home displays, web portals, etc.

The main component of AMI is smart meters that are deployed at the customer's site and are used to collect power collection data at specified intervals. Such data can be made use of for several major tasks like on demand response, load management, and automatic billing. Communication networks enable the smart meters to convey precise, consistent, and huge data streams in a well-timed manner. These network systems join end systems and smart meters so as to handle data communicating among information systems and smart meters in AMI [4]. The end system performs functions

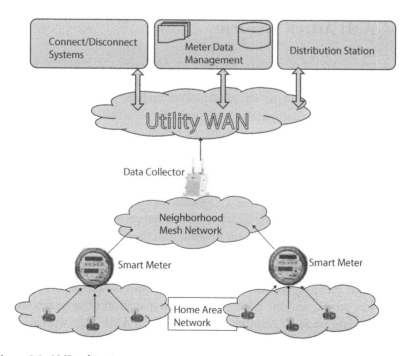

Figure 9.1 AMI architecture.

like transmission and reception of data, propagating operational instructions to meters along with storing time-based load information of meters in order of supporting billing customers. Without deployment of smart meters and communications management systems which connects them, most of demand-reducing and cost saving impacts and benefits from AMI would not be benefited. The data management system in AMI serves the data acquisition and organization function along with real-time monitoring and report generation. This component usually validates and cleans data before its processing and also deals with long-term storage and management of data. Figure 9.1 shows AMI architecture.

Various devices for control along with sensors are deployed in smart meter for the correct identification of different devices and parameters in order to permit transmit instruction signals and data. Enormous number smart meters are deployed to correspond with utility centers by way of AMI network. The two-way networks are either mesh, hierarchical, or hybrid. Intermittent collection, storage, and propagation of voluminous data packets are done via the communication network. Each element of the AMI executes its own purpose and together attains the overall functionality of the infrastructure.

9.3   AMI Attack Scenario

The wireless nature of communication in AMI and the inherent properties of its implementation create suitable attack surface for attackers. The main features of AMI that attract attackers include the provision to have access to lots of low computation equipments, sensitive end user information access, visibility of cases like energy outage, and knowledge of energy consumption–related financial information. As a result, attackers find it easy to perform malicious activity on communication system and may intend to steal end user information, disconnect certain regions, etc. [5].

Distributed Denial of Service (DDoS) can be considered as a major attack type of AMI. In this case, the attack is performed on the data collection unit of AMI which affects the communication functionality of communication network. Usually, attackers consider smart meters as their entry point and would perform malicious actions like physical tampering and malware installation, forming coordination among compromised meter to target for further attack, and the generation and propagation of large amount of malicious data packets. Another type of attack in AMI deals with stealing customer information. Here, the attacker performs eavesdropping on network traffic of smart meters to get customer information and learn their behavior. Steps like physical access of meter by way of methods like brute force attack to get decryption key, intercepting of messages, and decryption and content collection from messages are done as part of this attack. Another type of attack is the sending of remote commands like disconnect. Here, attacker tries to use remote messages to smart meters to disconnect many of the end users [6]. The attacker would carry out steps like exploit network vulnerability or physically tamper device like data communication unit to install malware, collect data from meters including IP addresses, and may send remote disconnect commands to meters.

Several types of attack categories have been identified on AMI. These include Denial of Service (DoS), spoofing, eavesdropping, physical attack, and communication attacks. DoS attacks include collision in packet propagation, packet flooding, jamming, routing table alteration, packet drop, node destruction, and resource deterioration. Spoofing attacks include impersonation of regular or master nodes, man-in-the-middle attack and wormhole problem. Attacks in AMI can also be categorized as physical attacks and cyberattacks based on the location of its occurrence. Physical attacks include physically destroying meter components, disconnecting meters, reversing the meters, and the likes. Cyberattacks involve network exploitation, injection of malicious code or data, eavesdropping of network communication and data, and flooding of network bandwidth so as to make it unavailable to legitimate users.

9.4   Data Falsification Attacks

Among the different types of attack scenarios for AMI as discussed in the previous section, a characteristic attack in real time is the tampering of legitimate information of a smart meter infrastructure by way of injecting malicious code of data or falsified data for monetary benefits. This type of attack can be either a cyberattack or a physical attack (by way of physically tampering the components). The problem is usually done using consequent steps. In the start, attacker weakens network capacity so as to disconnect the network to consume physical memory information. The second step is to inject malicious data to meters and executing illegal modification of legal data in physical memory [7]. Data falsification could be categorized as deductive, additive, and camouflage mode of attack. These three attack modes are associated with electricity theft where in attackers aim at stealing electricity power. In deductive mode strategy, customers of compromised meters reduce meter reading of consumed power, whereas in additive mode, a load altering would be launched in order to increase power consumption reading to affect both end users and utilities. In camouflage method, entire margin of deductive mode is balanced using additive mode, in which a set of end users will have lesser power bills at the expense of others, and the overall mean aggregate energy consumption of a microgrid remains unaffected.

9.5   Data Falsification Detection

Detection of data falsification attacks is a major concern so as to implement security measures to mitigate the same. Several data falsification detection mechanisms are found in the literature and they could be generally classified as state estimator detection, classification-based detection, and consensus detection. Classification-based schemes make use of total and detailed profiling of each meter to detect attacks. It makes use of ideas like neural network and support vector machines for detection [8]. These systems are computationally very expensive and arc impractical in real scenarios of AMI which are enormously large with millions of meters. State-based detection requires additional hardware components to be deployed at various areas of AMI for detection. This makes it complex and expensive. Consensus-based approach uses parametric techniques, nonparametric techniques, and mean aggregate outlier analysis for detecting data falsification. The detection is done by comparing predicted and observed consensus, that is, if the variation among two is bigger than particular predefined value, then falsification is confirmed. The difficulty with this technique is that the mean energy consumption data vary readily and have innate unstable nature of consumption and thus create major barriers for comparison.

Several detection schemes have been proposed for detecting FDI in smart grid environment. Though such schemes cannot be as such used in AMI scenario, many of the schemes designed for AMI resemble certain characteristic feature of smart grid schemes. Many algorithms are identified for detection in grid scenario like generalized likelihood ratio test and geometrically designed residual filter [9]. Authors in [10] and [11] introduced cumulative sum test–based detection method (CUSUM) to detect FDIA. Machine learning approaches was also been proposed to identify such attacks [12, 13]. To identify vulnerable nodes, relationship of physical parameters of system can be used [14]. In [15], a detection scheme is proposed where the entire system categorized as subsystems by means of partition algorithm and extended distributed state estimation is carried out. In [16], investigation of two main properties of smart grid that reflect its property is used. A parameter that indicates voltage fluctuation and another one is quantitative node voltage stability index. A higher value of the second parameter indicates a higher risk aspect. Cluster algorithm is used to group the nodes and detect suspicious ones. State forecasting detection is done to find sensitive measurements and several attack vectors are built for further results.

A model for smart meter threat is proposed in [17] for AMI network. Colored Petri net model is exploited in the paper to build the threat model. The detection mechanism is based on spying domain, secret data for meters and event log and the system is found to work even if the underlying software changes [18]. Paper discusses a real-time and light weight method uses a two-tier detection scheme for AMI. The primary tier examines if Harmonic to Arithmetic Mean Ratio in cumulative daily energy consuming data outside an ordinary value or not. Confirming discrepancies is identified in first tier are definitely attacks, tier 2 observes total residuals value among proposed value and safe range for some days. If the residual value is beyond a standard limit, then FDI is confirmed. The data omission aspect is not dealt with in the paper which could be implemented with a slight modification in second tier. Principal component–based data falsification detection is identified in [19]. A parameter called Mahalanobis distance is calculated between test data and historical data, and if its value is found to be outside an already fixed standard value, then test data is confirmed to be falsified. The scheme is found to have high detection ratio. An efficient hidden Markov model–based FDI detection and HMM based-method to detect false data injection attacks in AMI is discussed in this chapter [20, 21]. The method quickly and accurately detects attack by building a global state vector and training it using available meter data. The storage space problem is lessened using a fast Viterbi algorithm, and it also improves data decoding that is done using the vector.

9.6   Conclusion

Various attack scenarios of AMI are identified in the paper with prime focus given on data falsification attacks. Several detection schemes are available in literature that can effectively detect such FDI of AMI and concise analysis in those approaches is given in the paper. Though numerous attack detection schemes are available for smart grid, they cannot be as such implemented for AMI because of its unique characteristics. Detection of data falsification attacks in AMI is of a major concern based on which efficient security schemes have to be implemented considering its computational potential and limited memory.

References

1. Khattak, A.M., Khanji, S.I.R., Khan, W.A., Smart Meter Security: vulnerabilities, threat impacts, and countermeasures. *2019 Springer.*
2. Mehra, T., Dehalwar, V., Kolhe, M., Data Communication Security of Advanced Metering Infrastructure in Smart Grid. *2013 5th International Conference on Computational Intelligence and Communication Networks.*
3. Depuru, S.S.S.R., Wang, L., Devabhaktuni, V., Gugi, N., Smart meters for power grid: Challenges, issues, advantages and status. *Power Systems Conference and Exposition (PSCE)*, pp. 1–7, 2011.
4. Parvez, I., Sarwat, A.I., Wei, L., Sundararajan, A., Securing Metering Infrastructure of Smart Grid: A Machine Learning and Localization Based Key Management Approach. *Energies*, 9, 691, 2016.
5. Bhattacharjee, S., Thakur, A., Silvestri, S., Das, S.K., Statistical Security Incident Forensics against Data Falsification in Smart Grid Advanced Metering Infrastructure. *2017 ACM.*
6. Grochocki, D., Huh, J.H., Berthier, R., Bobba, R., Sanders, W.H., AMI Threats, Intrusion Detection Requirements and Deployment Recommendations. *2012 IEEE Third International Conference on Smart Grid Communications (SmartGridComm).*
7. Sgouras, K.I., Kyriakidis, A.N., Labridis, D.P., Short-term risk assessment of botnet attacks on advanced metering infrastructure. *IET Cyber-Phys. Syst.: Theor. Appl.*, 2, 3, 143–151, 2017.
8. Lo, C.-H. and Ansari, N., CONSUMER: A Novel Hybrid Intrusion Detection System for Distribution Networks in Smart Grid. *2013 IEEE*, vol. 1, no. 1, June 2013.
9. Oozeer, M.I., and Haykin, S., Cognitive Risk Control for Mitigating Cyber-Attack in Smart Grid. *IEEE Access*, 7, 125806–125826, 2019.
10. Pasqualetti, F., Dörfler, F., Bullo, F., Cyber-physical attacks in power networks: Models, fundamental limitations and monitor design, in: *Proc. Decision Control Eur. Control Conf.*, pp. 2195–2201, 2011.
11. Kosut, O., Jia, L., Thomas, R.J., Tong, L., Malicious data attacks on the smart grid. *IEEE Trans. Smart Grid*, 2, 4, 645–658, Oct. 2011.
12. Li, S., Yilmaz, Y., Wang, X., Quickest detection of false data injection attack in wide-area smart grids. *IEEE Trans. Smart Grid*, 6, 6, 2725–2735, Dec. 2014.
13. Liu, L., Esmalifalak, M., Ding, Q., Emesih, V.A., Han, Z., Detecting false data injection attacks on power grid by sparse optimization. *IEEE Trans. Smart Grid*, 5, 2, 612–621, Mar. 2014.
14. Xiao, Y., Chen, H.H., Du, X., Guizani, M., Stream-based cipher feedback mode in wireless error channel. *IEEE Trans. Wireless Commun.*, 8, 2, 662–666, Feb. 2009.
15. Anwar, A., Mahmood, A.N., Tari, Z., Identification of vulnerable node, clusters against false data injection attack in an AMI based smart grid. *Inf. Syst.*, 53, 201–212, Oct. 2015.

16. Cramer, M., Goergens, P., Schnettler, A., Bad data detection and handling in distribution grid state estimation using artificial neural networks, in: *Proc. IEEE Eindhoven PowerTech*, Jun. 2015, pp. 1–6.

17. Xu, R., Wang, R., Guan, Z., Wu, L., Wu, J., Du, X., Achieving efficient detection against false data injection attacks in smart grid, special section on security analytics and intelligence for cyber physical systems. *IEEE Access*, 5, 13787–13798, 2017.

18. Liu, X., Zhu, P., Zhang, Chen, K., A collaborative intrusion detection mechanism against false data injection attack in advanced metering infrastructure. *IEEE Trans. Smart Grid*, 6, 5, 2435–2443, 2015.

19. Bhattacharjee, S. and Das, S.K., Detection and Forensics against Stealthy Data Falsification in Smart Metering Infrastructure. *2018 IEEE*.

20. Singh, S.K., Bose, R., Joshi, A., Energy Theft Detection in Advanced Metering Infrastructure. *2018 IEEE*.

21. Li, B., Lu, R., Xiao, G., HMM-Based Fast Detection of False Data Injections in Advanced Metering Infrastructure, vol. 6, pp. 1–6, Dec. 2017.

10

Forecasting of Electricity Consumption for G20 Members Using Various Machine Learning Techniques

Jaymin Suhagiya[1], Deep Raval[1]*, Siddhi Vinayak Pandey[2], Jeet Patel[2], Ayushi Gupta[3] and Akshay Srivastava[3]

[1]Department of Information and Communication Technology, Adani Institute of Infrastructure Engineering, Ahmedabad, Gujarat, India
[2]Department of Electrical Engineering, Adani Institute of Infrastructure Engineering, Ahmedabad, Gujarat, India
[3]Department of Electronics and Communication Engineering, Pranveer Singh Institute of Technology, Kanpur, Uttar Pradesh, India

Abstract

Forecasting the actual amount of electricity consumption with respect to demand of the load hasa always been a challenging task for each electricity generating station. In this manuscript, electricity consumption forecasting has been performed for G20 members. Recurrent Neural Networks, Linear Regression, Support Vector Regression, and Bayesian Ridge Regression have been used for forecasting, while sliding window approach has been used for the generation of the dataset. During experimentation, we have achieved Mean Absolute Error of 16.0714 TWh, R^2 score of 0.9995, and Root Mean Squared Error of 31.3758 TWh with LSTM-based model trained on dataset created with window size of 6. Furthermore, predictions of electricity consumption have also been included till 2025.

Keywords: Electricity consumption, forecasting, machine learning, LSTM, GRU

10.1 Introduction

Electric consumption is the form of energy consumption that uses electric energy. On other words, electric consumption is the actual energy demand

---

*Corresponding author: deepraval.ict17@gmail.com

Ajay Kumar Vyas, S. Balamurugan, Kamal Kant Hiran and Harsh S. Dhiman (eds.) *Artificial Intelligence for Renewable Energy Systems*, (211–228) © 2022 Scrivener Publishing LLC

made on existing electricity supply. Various factors like weather, economic growth, and population affect the electricity consumption.

10.1.1   Why Electricity Consumption Forecasting Is Required?

Electricity consumption rate is reaching its peak and still being developmented using renewable and clean electricity resources is not globally practiced [1]. So, electricity demand management has become very important in the past few decades, and for same, people need to know how much electricity is consumed by any country in a particular time slot. Henceforth, electricity consumption forecasting is required to attain a balance in resources and electricity consumption [1]. Also, an unequivocal forecast helps various managers of electricity sector in various ways like setting up the future budgets and electricity consumption targets [2]. It also plays an important role in power industries as it helps to plan and make decisions on operation and working.

As the use of electricity is increasing day by day, the electricity consumption forecasting becomes important due to many reasons. One of the major reasons is that non-renewable sources are decreasing drastically, while the efficiency of renewable energy source is not a quite reliable in nature. Electricity consumption forecasting also helps during the power system expansion which starts from the future electricity consumption anticipations. If future increase of the load is needed, then cost and capacity of new power plant can be estimated. Electricity consumption forecasting can also be used for safety purpose. In industrial sector, the load consumed is peak load most of the time, but there is always a limit for a particular industry above which they cannot draw the power from the grid or else they are charged very heavy for the carelessness.

10.1.2   History and Advancement in Forecasting of Electricity Consumption

In 1880s, the power companies simply used Layman method for predicting the use of electricity in future. They predicted the future consumption by manually forecasting the future usage using charts, tables, and graphs [3]. Some factors of past methods like heating/cooling degree days, temperature-humidity index, and wind-chill factor are inherited by today's consumption forecasting models.

In 1940s, when air conditioners were invented, the demand of electricity got tremendously affected by weather change and climate change.

In winters, electricity usage got down, but in summers, it raised. After the discovery of air conditioners, there came electric heaters for winters. So, prediction and estimation of electricity consumption became very hectic by using the traditional method.

Presently, in this period of booming increment in innovation, demand of electricity has come to at apex [4, 5], so industrialists require a few progressed strategies for electricity consumption forecasting. There are created strategies like short-term, medium-term, and long-term electricity consumption forecasting [6, 7]. The long-term electricity consumption forecasting covers horizons of 1 to 10 years [8] and, in some cases, for various decades [9]. It confers month to month figure for top and valley in loads for different dissemination frameworks [10]. On the other hand, short-term load forecasting covers the variations from half an hour to few weeks [11].

10.1.3   Recurrent Neural Networks

Traditional feed forward neural networks cannot process the data of arbitrary length as their fundamental unit neuron does not support it. A recurrent cell is cell in which the output for the current timestep t (o_t) depends on the previous hidden state (h_{t-1}) of the cell. This makes recurrent cell suitable for the sequence-based tasks such as Speech Recognition, Natural Language Processing, and Forecasting, as now it can process input of any arbitrary length by iteratively updating its own hidden state which preserves some information from previous states. A neural networks containing recurrent cells instead of traditional neurons is known as Recurrent Neural Network (RNN). RNNs are mainly distinguished based on type of the cells used and their architecture. Figure 10.1 shows the basic RNN unrolled over t timesteps, where x_t is input and h_t is hidden state of the cell at timestep t.

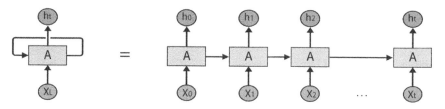

Figure 10.1 Traditional RNN unrolled over t timesteps [12].

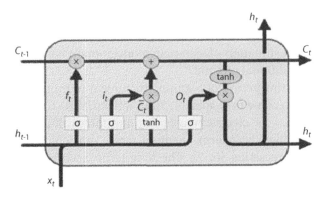

Figure 10.2 LSTM cell [16].

10.1.3.1 Long Short-Term Memory

Long Short-Term Memory (LSTM) was introduced by Hochreiter *et al.* [13] as a solution for the unstable (Vanishing/Expoding) gradients problem faced in traditional RNN. LSTM contains the additional "gates" which controls the flow of information in and out of the cell. Since the introduction of LSTM, there has been significant research aimed at improving it such as [14] and [15]. Although many variants of LSTM cell exist such as LSTM with a forget gate, LSTM without a forget gate and LSTM with a peep-hole connection, etc., the term LSTM generally refers to the LSTM with a forget gate. Figure 10.2 shows the internal structure of the LSTM cell. LSTM cell gets three inputs: previous cell state (C_{t-1}), previous hidden state (h_{t-1}), and current input (x_t) and gives three outputs: current cell state (C_t), current hidden state (h_t), and current output (o_t). LSTM cell contains three gates: forget gate (f), input gate (i), and output gate (o). Forget gate determines what information will be discarded from the previous state; this is controlled by the value of f_t. Input gate determines which new information will be added to the cell state, and output gate determines the output based on the current cell state.

10.1.3.2 Gated Recurrent Unit

With LSTM being better and more sophisticated compared to traditional RNN, it also has the down side as it is computationally heavy. To address the same problem, Gated Recurrent Unit (GRU) was proposed by Cho *et al.* [17]. GRU contains only two gates, namely, a reset gate (r) and an update gate (z) which are the key factors in reducing and simplifying computation. Update gate combines the functionality of two gates of LSTM (forget gate and input gate) into one. Figure 10.3 shows the internal structure of

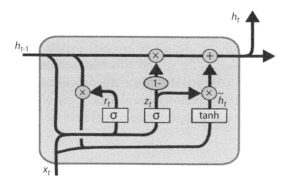

Figure 10.3 GRU cell [12].

typical GRU cell. GRU cell gets two inputs: previous hidden state (h_{t-1}) and current input (x_t) and gives only two outputs: current hidden state (h_t) and current output (o_t). GRU does not have the dedicated cell state as compared to LSTM's cell state (C_t). Compared to LSTM, GRU struggles in the areas like context-free language and the cross-language translations [18, 19]. LSTM and GRU both are really solid candidates as a recurrent cell both of them perform similarly on many tasks.

10.1.3.3   Convolutional LSTM

To get the benefit of LSTM on spatiotemporal data, convolutional LSTM (ConvLSTM) was introduced leveraging power of both CNN (Convolutional Neural Network) and LSTM [20]. Figure 10.4 shows the

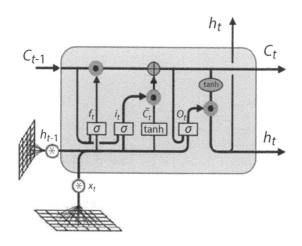

Figure 10.4 ConvLSTM cell.

structure of typical ConvLSTM cell. Internal structure of the cell is similar to LSTM cell as ConvLSTM uses LSTM internally. As ConvLSTM uses convolutional operator (*) instead of normal matrix multiplication (as used in LSTM). It preserves the spatial information from the data which is very helpful multidimensional data (like videos and audio). Even though ConvLSTM specializes in spatiotemporal data, it can also be also used on 1D data sequences by using appropriate kernel size.

10.1.3.4   Bidirectional Recurrent Neural Networks

Traditional RNN can only use the prior context to make predictions. Aimed at solving the same problem, Bidirectional RNN (BRNN) was proposed by Schuster *et al.* [21] which is simultaneously trained on the both time directions while using separate hidden layers for each time direction. Graves *et al.* [22] proposed the combination of both BRNN and LSTM, namely, Bidirectional LSTM. Training is similar to a regular RNN as two layers do not interact with each other directly their outputs are only concatenated. Figure 10.5 shows the demonstration of a typical BRNN.

10.1.4   Other Regression Techniques

Linear Regression is one of the most simple regression techniques. Linear Regression typically try to generalize the function of type $f(x) = \text{m} \cdot x + b$ on given data, where x is an input, m is a slope, and b is a bias. Optimization techniques (such as Gradient Descent) are used to get the optimal values of m and b such that error function (like MSE and MAE) is minimum.

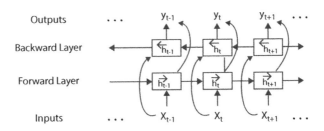

Figure 10.5 Bidirectional RNN.

Linear regression can be further extended for multiple inputs, more formally for n inputs: $f(x_1, x_2,\ldots, x_n) = m_1 \cdot x_1 + m_2 \cdot x_2 + \ldots + m_n \cdot x_n + b$.

Support Vector Regression (SVR) creates a system in which data is trained from series of examples in accordance to successfully predict the output. It is a type of supervised learning. A SVR model is formed by using kernels sparse matrix and solutions, Vapnik-Chervonenkis control model, and support vectors [23]. In SVR, symmetrical loss function is used for training the datasets. Binary classification problems can be solved using SVR models by formulating them as convex optimization problems [23].

Bayesian Ridge Regression is a regression model with parameter estimation method where parameter is estimated by multiplying posterior distribution with prior distribution. In linear regression model using OLS estimation method, the error as well as variables are normally distributed. The Bayesian approach can be done by using MCMC (Markov Chain Monte Carlo) algorithm [24]. To estimate the efficiency of linear model by Bayesian regression, Theil's Coefficient is used, which is a statistical technique that predicts the efficiency by calculating the difference between original value and the predicted value.

10.2   Dataset Preparation

The dataset utilized in this paper is prepared by Enerdata organization [25]. The dataset originally contains yearly electricity domestic consumption (in TWh) for 61 entities (including countries, continents, and unions) for the years 1990 to 2019. This paper focuses on G20 members, which includes Argentina, Australia, Brazil, Canada, China, France, Germany, India, Indonesia, Italy, Japan, South Korea, Mexico, Russia, Saudi Arabia, South Africa, Turkey, United Kingdom, United States, and European Union. Among all G20 members, 19 are the countries and one is the European Union.

The raw dataset is the time-series dataset as it gives us the electricty consumption data on regular interval (i.e., year). To tackle the forecasting of the future years as a supervised learning problem, we created the new dataset from the original one using sliding window approach. In each sample, N timesteps are given and the model should the $(N + 1)^{th}$ timestep, where N is the window size. In other words, previous N years will be input to the model and $(N + 1)^{th}$ year will be the label. For example, in the case of window size 4, previous 4 years' electricity consumption is given and next year is there as a label. This way model can learn trend from previous timesteps and make appropriate prediction for the next timestep. This approach can

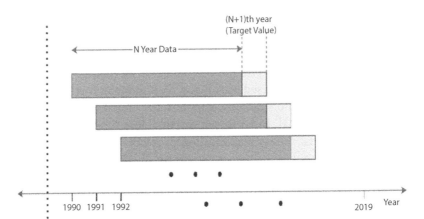

Figure 10.6 Demonstration of the sliding window approach.

Table 10.1 Training and test size for generated dataset from each window size.

Window size	Training samples	Testing samples
3	460	80
4	440	80
5	420	80
6	400	80
7	380	80

give us the large amount of training data compared to raw training data at the cost of data repetition. Figure 10.6 shows the demonstration of sliding window on the time-series data. Window sizes 1 and 2 will not be enough for learning trend, and on the other hand, window sizes greater than 7 would just make dataset much smaller. Hence, we created five seprate datasets with window sizes 3–7 keeping the data of the years 2016–2019 for testing purpose. Table 10.1 shows the number of training and testing samples in all datasets created using different window sizes.

10.3   Results and Discussions

All the experiments have been performed in Python using TensorFlow and ScikitLearn libraries. Computational specifications of machine utilized during experimentation are Ryzen 5 4600H, NVIDEA GTX 1650 4GB, and 8 GB DDR4 Ram.

Table 10.2 Performance of all trained models.

Cell type	Window size	R^2 score	MAE	RMSE
LSTM	3	0.998749625	21.44645568	52.01252557
	4	0.999258582	19.49052397	40.05153819
	5	0.999271694	20.73799729	39.69580909
	6	0.999544997	16.07145371	31.37582087
	7	0.999216397	19.84262385	41.17519839
GRU	3	0.999352065	19.44009694	37.44153438
	4	0.99943614	18.98304995	34.9279822
	5	0.999360785	19.37603302	37.18873189
	6	0.999435172	18.08372996	34.95793729
	7	0.999324213	19.17705701	38.23779332
Biodirectional LSTM	3	0.998901652	20.68070089	48.74811593
	4	0.998855535	20.34128753	49.76098863
	5	0.999180335	19.30442693	42.11201091
	6	0.999426774	17.55318267	35.21685526
	7	0.999206407	20.02302547	41.43683245
ConvLSTM	3	0.999091009	19.33748763	44.34734645
	4	0.999277166	19.27017771	39.54640382
	5	0.999234165	19.86183365	40.70571966
	6	0.99948358	17.51624149	33.42638218
	7	0.999426936	18.16709740	35.21189519
Support Vector Regression	3	0.999397458	18.54912241	36.10615607
	4	0.999470774	18.75444142	33.83827126
	5	0.999218605	22.26829334	41.11714657
	6	0.999059587	24.65530079	45.10731731
	7	0.998177736	28.27401743	62.79041968

(Continued)

Table 10.2 Performance of all trained models. (*Continued*)

Cell type	Window size	R^2 score	MAE	RMSE
Linear Regression	3	0.999493775	18.78475962	33.09475573
	4	0.999239879	21.56018059	40.55356501
	5	0.999243397	22.45643728	40.45961526
	6	0.999091294	24.85775704	44.34036331
	7	0.998655929	26.14611200	53.92607458
Bayesian Ridge Regression	3	0.999506349	18.69629528	32.68115425
	4	0.999253988	21.22020898	40.17541841
	5	0.999124103	22.34981485	43.53255683
	6	0.999025962	24.57856065	45.90665126
	7	0.998969954	24.72536657	47.20803097

We experimented with LSTM, GRU, Bidirectional LSTM, ConvLSTM, Linear Regression, SVR, and Bayesian Ridge Regression. Models based on LSTM, GRU, and Bidirectional LSTM have two recurrent layers stacked followed by a dense layer. Each recurrent layer has 36 units, while the last layer has only 1 unit. First two layers have *ReLU* as an activation function, while the last has linear activation function which simply gives the activation values without applying any additional computation. ConvLSTM-based model has similar architecture except; it has 64 filters in first two layers followed by the flatten layer which flattens the previous layer's output, so it can be fed to the last dense layer. All of the recurrent models were trained for the maximum of 200 epochs with *Adam* [26] as an optimizer (having the slow learning rate of $1e^{-3}$) and *huber* (which is less sensitive to outliers compared to Mean Squared Error) as the objective function. Grid search was used (to search for the best parameters) in Linear Regression, SVR, and Bayesian Ridge Regression. SVR was performed with the *linear* kernel. All of the models were trained on four different datasets. Table 10.2 performance of all the models on test data in terms of R^2 score, Mean Absolute Error (in TWh), and Root Mean Squared Error (in TWh).

Seeing the test error rates, it can be concluded that we get the best performance for *window size* = 6 while using the LSTM-based model. Ignoring the best model, these are not far away in terms of the test error rates.

However, performance of Linear Regression, SVR, and Bayesian Ridge Regression is slightly worse than that of recurrent models. Furthermore, in our experiments, we have found regression techniques tend to over estimate the values of future by large margin because of the same reason, we have used only recurrent models for forecasting. Figure 10.7 shows the actual predictions of the different recurrent models (trained with *window size* = 6) for the all G20 members. Before the vertical line, all model's performance can be compared to the ground truth at particular timestep (i.e.. year). After the vertical line, up to the year 2025, all models try to predict next values independently of each other. Years where previous true values are not available, model is self-fed its own predicted values. Although this carries the error forward, we can get a rough estimate of the next values models that would actually predict if they were given true values. Table 10.3 analyzes predictions further by comparing the demand in 2019 with the predicted demand in 2025.

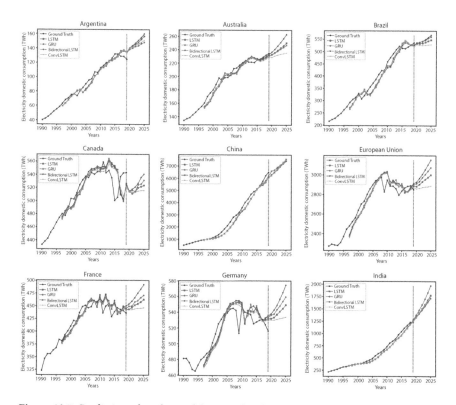

Figure 10.7 Predictions done by models trained with window size = 6.   (*Continued*)

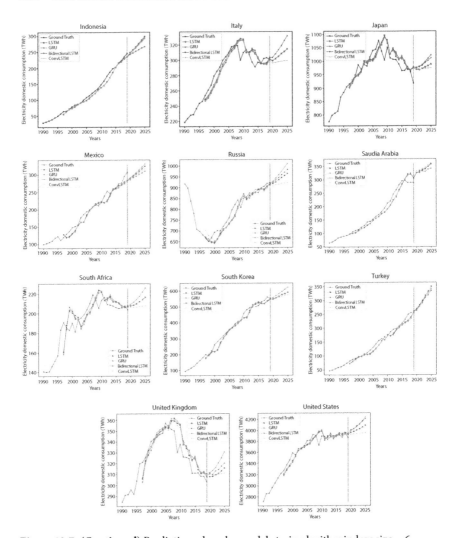

Figure 10.7 (Continued) Predictions done by models trained with window size = 6.

Table 10.3 Statistical analysis of the prediction done by LSTM model (*widow size* = 6).

Member	2019 (TWh)	2025 (TWh)	Absolute difference (TWh)	Percentage difference (%)	Individual mean absolute error (TWh)
Argentina	124.802	156.596	31.794	25.476	6.53
Australia	234.977	250.202	15.225	6.4792	0.734
Brazil	536.047	547.57	11.523	2.1496	8.882
Canada	542.986	523.695	–19.291	–3.553	15.257
China	6510.22	7570.87	1060.6	16.292	80.19
France	436.556	462.671	26.135	5.9866	5.707
Germany	516.801	549.677	32.876	6.3614	5.423
India	1230.35	1774.14	543.79	44.198	29.926
Indonesia	245.308	298.302	52.994	21.603	2.648
Italy	300.614	314.38	13.766	4.5793	3.997
Japan	918.219	987.93	69.712	7.592	18.98
South Korea	553.414	589.763	36.348	6.568	11.722

(Continued)

Table 10.3 Statistical analysis of the prediction done by LSTM model (*widow size* = 6). (*Continued*)

Member	2019 (TWh)	2025 (TWh)	Absolute difference (TWh)	Percentage difference (%)	Individual mean absolute error (TWh)
Mexico	307.31	323.838	16.528	5.3784	5.24
Russia	922.277	964.14	41.863	4.5391	6.084
Saudi Arabia	288.784	353.749	68.965	23.881	19.638
South Africa	203.651	216.293	12.642	6.2078	1.85
Turkey	254.486	349.566	95.08	37.362	8.678
United Kingdom	302.716	315.553	12.837	4.2407	2.432
United States	3865.06	4085.8	220.74	5.7111	53.528
European	2850.4	2999.73	149.33	5.2389	33.976
Total	21144.98	23638.49	2493.51	11.81 (*Average*)	16.0715 (*Average*)

10.4   Conclusion

Forecasting electricity consumption for G20 members has been performed using various machine learning techniques. The best recurrent model was able to achieve MAE of 16.0714 TWh, R^2 score of 0.9995, and RMSE of 31.3758 TWh, while the best regression techinque achieved MAE of 18.549 TWh, R^2 score of 0.9994, and RMSE of 36.106 TWh. As RNNs are better at handling longer sequences, they perform well with window size of 6, while other regression techniques perform well on window size of 3. Taking into consideration forecasting done by recurrent models, it can be concluded that total electricity demand of all G20 countries (excluding European Union) combined can increase anywhere from 1,957.35 TWh to 2,549.67 TWh in upcoming 5 years. Furthermore, countries like Argentina, India, Indonesia, Saudi Arabia, and Turkey can see rapid increase in electricity demand, while India being at top with 44.198%.

Acknowledgement

The authors would like to thank Enerdata Organization for allowing us to use the Domestic Energy Consumption Data prepared by them and cooperating with us in the completion of this chapter.

References

1. Ghalehkhondabi, I., Ardjmand, E., Weckman, G.R., Young, W.A., An overview of energy demand forecasting methods published in 2005–2015. *Energy Syst.*, 8, 2, 411–447, 2017.

2. Amber, K.P., Aslam, M.W., Hussain, S.K., Electricity consumption forecasting models for administration buildings of the uk higher education sector. *Energy Build.*, 90, 127–136, 2015.

3. Hong, T., Gui, M., Baran, M.E., Willis, H.L., Modeling and forecasting hourly electric load by multiple linear regression with interactions, in: *IEEE PES General Meeting*, pp. 1–8, 2010.

4. Wang, Z., Li, J., Zhu, S., Zhao, J., Deng, S., Shengyuan, Z., Yin, H., Li, H., Qi, Y., Gan, Z., A review of load forecasting of the distributed energy system. *IOP Conference Series: Earth and Environmental Science*, 03 2019, vol. 237, p. 042019.

5. Alagbe, V., Popoola, S.I., Atayero, A.A., Adebisi, B., Abolade, R.O., Misra, S., Artificial intelligence techniques for electrical load forecasting in smart

and connected communities, in: *International Conference on Computational Science and Its Applications*, Springer, pp. 219–230, 2019.

6. Scott, D., Simpson, T., Dervilis, N., Rogers, T., Worden, K., Machine learning for energy load forecasting. *J. Phys.: Conf. Ser.*, 1106, 012005, 10 2018.

7. Xiao, L., Shao, W., Liang, T., Wang, C., A combined model based on multiple seasonal patterns and modified firefly algorithm for electrical load forecasting. *Appl. Energy*, 167, 135–153, 2016.

8. Baliyan, A., Gaurav, K., Mishra, S.K., A review of short term load forecasting using artificial neural network models. *Proc. Comput. Sci.*, 48, 121–125, 2015.

9. Esteves, G.R.T., Bastos, B.Q., Cyrino, F.L., Calili, R.F., Souza, R.C., Long term electricity forecast: a systematic review. *Proc. Comput. Sci.*, 55, 549–558, 2015.

10. Daneshi, H., Shahidehpour, M., Choobbari, A.L., Long-term load forecasting in electricity market, in: *2008 IEEE International Conference on Electro/Information Technology*, IEEE, pp. 395–400, 2008.

11. Jacob, M., Neves, C., Greetham, D.V., *Short Term Load Forecasting*, pp. 15–37, Springer International Publishing, Cham, 2020.

12. Understanding lstm networks, colah's blog. https://colah.github.io/posts/2015-08-Understanding-LSTMs/, United States, 2020, [Online; accessed 01-October-2020].

13. Hochreiter, S. and Schmidhuber, J., Long short-term memory. *Neural Comput.*, 9, 1735–80, 12 1997.

14. Gers, F.A. and Schmidhuber, J., Recurrent nets that time and count, in: *Proceedings of the IEEE-INNS-ENNS International Joint Conference on Neural Networks. IJCNN 2000. Neural Computing: New Challenges and Perspectives for the New Millennium*, vol. 3, IEEE, pp. 189–194, 2000.

15. Gers, F., *Long short-term memory in recurrent neural networks*, Doctoral dissertation, Verlag nicht ermittelbar, 2001.

16. Varsamopoulos, S., Bertels, K., Almudever, C.G., Comparing neural network based decoders for the surface code. *IEEE Trans. Comput.*, 69, 2, 300–311, 2019.

17. Cho, K., Van Merriënboer, B., Gulcehre, C., Bahdanau, D., Bougares, F., Schwenk, H., Bengio, Y., Learning phrase representations using rnn encoder-decoder for statistical machine translation, computation and language: machine learning. *arXiv preprint arXiv:1406.1078*, 1–15, 2014.

18. Weiss, G., Goldberg, Y., Yahav, E., On the practical computational power of finite precision rnns for language recognition, 1–9, 2018. https://arxiv.org/abs/1805.04908

19. Britz, D., Le, Q., Pryzant, R., Effective domain mixing for neural machine translation. In *Proceedings of the Second Conference on Machine Translation*, pp. 118–126, 2017.

20. Xingjian, S., Chen, Z., Wang, H., Yeung, D.-Y., Wong, W.-K., Woo, W.-c., Convolutional lstm network: A machine learning approach for precipitation

nowcasting, in: *Advances in neural information processing systems*, pp. 802–810, 2015.

21. Schuster, M. and Paliwal, K.K., Bidirectional recurrent neural networks. *IEEE Trans. Signal Process.*, 45, 11, 2673–2681, 1997.

22. Graves, A. and Schmidhuber, J., Framewise phoneme classification with bidirectional lstm and other neural network architectures. *Neural Networks*, 18, 5–6, 602–610, 2005.

23. Awad, M. and Khanna, R., *Support Vector Regression*, pp. 67–80, Apress, Berkeley, CA, 2015.

24. Permai, S.D. and Tanty, H., Linear regression model using bayesian approach for energy performance of residential building. *Proc. Comput. Sci.*, 135, 671–677, 2018, The 3rd International Conference on Computer Science and Computational Intelligence (ICCSCI 2018): Empowering Smart Technology in Digital Era for a Better Life.

25. World Power consumption, Electricity consumption, Enerdata, https://yearbook.enerdata.net/electricity/electricity-domestic-consumption-data.html, Grenole - France, 2020, [Online; accessed 01-October-2020].

26. Kingma, D.P. and Ba, J., A method for stochastic optimization. *Anon. International Conference on Learning Representations*, SanDiago ICLR, pp. 22–31, 2015.

11

Use of Artificial Intelligence (AI) in the Optimization of Production of Biodiesel Energy

Manvinder Singh Pahwa[1], Manish Dadhich[2*], Jaskaran Singh Saini[1]
and Dinesh Kumar Saini[3]

[1]Department of Business Administration, Manipal University Jaipur (MUJ),
Jaipur, India
[2]Sir Padampat Singhania University, Udaipur, India
[3]Department of Computer and Communication Engineering,
Manipal University Jaipur (MUJ), Jaipur, India

Abstract

In the present chaotic scenario, the entire world is integrally dependent on the effective ways of using non-renewable energy sources and its appropriate management system. The conventional methods of energy creation have a mammoth side effect on the environmental deterioration, global climate changes, and distraction of natural resources. The paper deals with the ways and means available for India to harness biodiesel energy. It also dwells into the significant issues inhibiting India in the realm of biofuels in general. The objective is to highlight the measures taken for achieving the 40% renewable energy target under the Paris Agreement. The researchers have further proposed a novel model that can be utilized for optimizing the use of ICT in the extraction, marketing, and management of biodiesel energy. Green and clean fuel is not a luxury anymore; instead, it will make India more self-reliant in a real sense, paving the way for a sustainable Atmanirbhar Bharat.

Keywords: Sustainable energy, AI, biofuels, ICT, RES, process automation

---

Corresponding author: manish.dadhich@spsu.ac.in

Ajay Kumar Vyas, S. Balamurugan, Kamal Kant Hiran and Harsh S. Dhiman (eds.) Artificial Intelligence for Renewable Energy Systems, (229–238) © 2022 Scrivener Publishing LLC

11.1   Introduction

Energy is a vital component for economic growth as much as the promotion and advancement of essential services, *viz.*, health, industry, education, communication, and social well-being [17, 18]. Energy protection and environmental sustainability have been some of the most critical economic issues of the last few decades. Energy consumption needs to be augmented as the energy demand at the global level is projected to be double by 2030. To prevent the rise of 2 degrees in global temperature, meeting the target of the Paris Agreement [1], we must leave 88% of global coal reserve, 52% of the gas reserve, and 35% of oil reserve unburn [2, 6]. The time has arrived to explore renewable energy source (RES) ways and means to meet our energy demands. The sense of urgency in RES has rightly prompted the Indian Government to set the Intended Nationally Determined Contributions (INDC) to achieve 40% of energy demand through RES by 2030. All the more, the lifetime of oil reserves and fossil fuels is very limited and may only last for the next 50 years or so (considering the current fossil fuel demands).

The energy produced from biodiesel is a promising source of RES. First of all, it is a biodegradable, non-toxic, and eco-friendly fuel alternative. Secondly, it is readily available at affordable prices. Thirdly, it can utilize waste as raw material to produce energy. The price of Biodiesel directly depends upon the input cost of the raw material used for the extraction. Biofuels are classified into four generations.

Biodiesel is preferably produced from first and second generations of biofuels. First-generation biofuels pose a risk to food security as many food crops may be diverted for fuel consumption. As a matter of fact, 95% of biodiesel is produced from edible plants worldwide [3]. Second-generation biodiesel is the preferred one, as it utilizes waste materials or by-products for making biodiesel. Hence, the choice of crops for making biodiesel are many; some are oil palm, beauty leaf tree, Pongamia, castor, bran, coconut, moringa, soybean, rapeseed, jojoba, sunflower, Jatropha, neem, cotton, rice, etc.

11.2   Indian Perspective of Renewable Biofuels

Biodiesel can be considered as a viable fuel alternative to combat desertification and afforestation in India. According to the Desertification and Land Degradation Atlas of India prepared by ISRO, approx. 25% of the area is under desertification [4]. Here, desertification signifies regions that are classified as arid, semi-arid, and sub-humid. Jatropha Curcas, a suitable crop suited to arid and semi-arid conditions, is a viable alternative to explore biodiesel in India. The chemical characteristics (flash point, calorific value, ignition temperature, etc.) of biodiesel produced from Jatropha are comparable to petro-diesel. It will increase the farm income of farmers from the Rajasthan, Gujarat, and Central India region; instead, it will attract more FDI.

ISRO has become a pioneer space agency globally in terms of the cost effectiveness of launching space missions. Artificial Intelligence (AI) has helped ISRO, in collaboration Department of Land Records (Ministry of Rural Development), to come out with Wasteland Atlas of India [3]. As per the atlas, 16.96% of India's Total Geographical Area (TGA) is classified as wasteland. Such AI interventions help in identifying suitable areas where second-generation biofuel can be grown (Figure 11.1). Moreover, AI also helps in process automation, wherein farmers involved in producing biofuels can be integrated on a single platform. AI facilitates capturing the real-time data from Indigenous Indian Satellites (RESOURCESAT-2, RISAT-2B) and relays directly to the farmers. This may help in crop selection and do surveillance by using GIS (Geographic Information System) mapping.

The Minimum Support Price (MSP) regime was introduced to relieve the ailing price mechanism in the Indian agriculture sector. But with time, MSP silently got transformed into an unofficially Maximum Support Price. It promoted a practice of crop monoculture among Indian farmers and completely distorted the forces of market economics in the pricing of agri-commodities [25]. Biodiesel is a strong incentive for Indian farmers

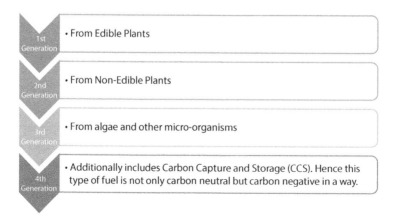

Figure 11.1 Classification of biofuels.

to diversify their crops and adopt a multi-crop approach. Because mono-culture has not only distorted economics but also provided an avenue for farmers to exploit natural resources. A declining water level, especially in Northern India, is attributed to rice and other water-intensive crops. The agriculture sector employs 50% of farmers and contributes 20% to Indian GDP [5]. It indicates that there is an acute problem of hidden unem-ployment. The need is to push Indian farmers into more productive and meaningful employment opportunities in the near future. But such a push should be done with extreme caution so that the food security of coming generations is not compromised. Second-generation biodiesel can pro-vide an impetus to government's flagship resolve, i.e., to Double Farmers Income by 2022.

11.3 Opportunities

During the winter season, the stubble burning of Kharif is the primary cause of concern. New farm bills also try to impose a penalty on the farm-ers for burning the crop residue in the open. But here is a blessing in dis-guise. IOCL and HPCL set up refineries in Haryana and Punjab to generate second-generation biofuel ethanol. It will make the environment more liv-able and utilize, hitherto, a waste (stubble) to produce fuel, providing better income support to farmers. National Biofuel Policy 2018 (Government of India, 2018) mandates 5% blending biodiesel with diesel which would be further increased to 10% by 2022 and 30% by 2030. It will make India more self-reliant in a real sense, paving the way to our Prime Minister (PM) vision of Atmanirbhar Bharat [7]. India has successfully tested first biofuel flight from Dehradun to New Delhi in 2018 [8]. It used biofuel obtained from the Jatropha plant in the ratio of 25:75, i.e., 25% of biofuel with 75% of Aviation Turbine Fuel (ATF). The use of biofuels in commercial flights will reduce emissions from the Airline Sector (total CO_2 from the Airline Sector is 12%) and make air tickets more affordable [9].

India has more than 7,500 km of coastline. The marines and fisheries sector is on the agenda of the government for its promotion and invest-ment. The GoI (Government of India) has recently created a special dedi-cated Ministry of Fisheries, Animal Husbandry, and Dairying. This sector has tremendous potential to generate export income, leading the agricul-ture sector from the front. The waste generated from fisheries can be used to make fish oil methyl ester, a biodiesel, having comparable properties to conventional diesel [10, 24]. The need is to invest in marine infrastructure to enable the farmers to explore new AI-enabled fish-catching methods.

The Information, Communication, and Technology (ICT) intervention will help the government track the shipments in real time and have surveillance over the marine waste generated via satellite imagery. Biodiesel production from the fisheries sector can be linked to already running schemes such as Pradhan Mantri Matsya Sampada Yojna (PMMSY), which aims to bring sustainable Blue Revolution, Fisheries, and Aquaculture Infrastructure Development Fund (FIDF). International collaboration on biofuels is already in the pipeline under the program Mission Innovation (MI). The program participates in 24 partner countries and the European Commission (EC) addressing the eight broad challenges, of which sustainable biofuel is one of the challenges [11, 23].

India's refining capacity of crude oil is one of the best in the world. Jamnagar refinery in Gujarat is the world's largest refinery. We need to use our refining capacity to our advantage by blending biodiesel with petrodiesel to decrease the import dependency in the future. Indian Strategic Petroleum Reserves Limited (ISPRL) is a company established to maintain the buffer stock of oil in case of any contingency. But keeping reserves such come at a considerable cost to the exchequer and requires regular maintenance to avoid any environmental hazards. Biodiesel has relatively high flash point temperature at 105°C (temperature above which fuel vaporizes and ignites), making biodiesel safe for storage (conventional diesel has a flash point temperature of 68°C).

11.4   Relevance of Biodiesel in India Context

The emissions from clean fuels must comply with international standards to ensure the minimal release of toxic gases in the air upon combustion. Blending fuel with biodiesel results in the reduction of carbon monoxide, toxic hydrocarbons, and particulate matter emissions to a large extent. Biodiesel is considered one of the safest fuel alternatives due to the absence of lead in its emission. The experiment conducted by [12] shows that emission further decreases as engine speed (internal combustion engine was used for the experiment) increases. The only exception is nitrogen oxide (NO_x) emissions, which increase during combustion. Another point of caution is the engine running of biodiesel may experience a relative (around 20%) decrease in output power [10]. Hence, the switch to biodiesel on a mass scale needs to be done with prior due diligence.

While considering biodiesel as an alternative to conventional fossil fuel, the cost becomes an essential component. According to [13], 75% of the cost of biodiesel depends upon the price of the crops used in the extraction.

Only 1.5% of transportation fuel is biodiesel. But 40% of the biodiesel is sourced from emerging and developing nations [18]. Moreover, the developed countries under the World Trade Organization (WTO)'s Agreement on Agriculture (AoA) [14] tend to divert their vast portions of subsidies toward food crops. Further, especially in the USA, the wheat crop is sown on a mass scale only to produce biofuels. If the developing nations divert their food crops for producing fuels, then this may lead to a situation of food crises in the country. India is ranked 94th position in the Global Hunger Index 2020 [15], thus clearly highlighting the urgent need to address food poverty. Digitalization of land records is required to monitor and identify the areas and crops selected for making biofuels. AI may come to the rescue to prevent the diversion of fertile lands for sowing the feedstock required for biofuel. National Biofuel Policy explicitly underscores the use of the only second and third-generation crops for biofuels. It also prohibits the export of biofuels and permits only domestic consumption (Government of India, 2018).

11.5   Proposed Model

Every moment globally has been changing at a breakneck pace due to human endeavor. The researchers propose a novel model for the extraction, marketing, and management of biodiesel in India (as shown in Figure 11.2). As already discussed earlier, there are different alternatives

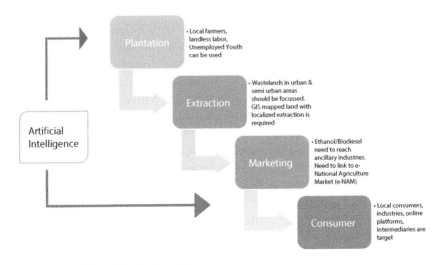

Figure 11.2 AI-based biodiesel model.

available for the extraction of biodiesel in India. Jatropha Carcus is best suitable as per Indian conditions, as it can germinate in areas hitherto that was a wasteland. Biodiesel extraction in India is in the nascent stage. GoI is currently emphasizing the blending of conventional fuel with biofuels. Several industries widely use ethanol which is produced in the industrial process, as input material. We can have more green and cleaner ethanol by utilizing the waste materials. As of now, the need is to focus on the extraction of ethanol from second-generation biomaterials [15]. With time the blending of biodiesel in regular fuel will gradually increase, we may shift our focus toward the production of biodiesel in the future.

Our model integrates the different stages of the plantation, extraction, marketing, and consumers via AI. The role of AI is to provide the inputs at each stage in real time and create a feedback loop. In the plantation stage, identification of different geographic areas, crops (feedstock), laborers, or farmers is made. We also propose to launch a new scheme as Urban Employment Guarantee Scheme (UEGS) to address the issue of urban unemployment based on biodiesel production. Such a plan should not be limited to farmers but also include laborers, unemployed youth, and budding entrepreneurs. Government can deploy different models for implementing the program; for instance, government can provide the subsidy for the biofuel crops upfront and later, giving farmers the option to sell the feedstock to the government or in the open market. The UEGS needs to be a Demand-Driven Scheme [23]. The GIS mapping will determine the total crop area under plantation, and estimation of biofuel production per area is done in advance. Blockchain technology can help mitigate the issue of ghost account, which were created in the MGNREGA (Mahatma Gandhi National Rural Employment Guarantee Act). It will also ensure the accountability of personnel involved in the implementation of the scheme. An accountable method will benefit society by creating meaningful infrastructure, rather than focusing merely on outlays and ignoring the outcomes.

The next stage is the extraction of biofuels. Under this stage, government and private industries will be allowed to purchase the feedstock from the farmers directly. We propose to procure the feedstock in a decentralized manner if the feedstock is used for making the ethanol. Use a centralized procurement methodology if the procurement is done for producing the biodiesel. There is an urgent need for the Fuel Price Regulator in the country to regulate the production and management of alternate forms of fuels. Proper storage and distribution of biodiesel are necessary to avoid any hazard in the mass movement or storage of the fuel. Ethanol has multiple uses in many industries, including the manufacturing of liquor. At this stage, we recommend choosing a wasteland area for the extraction of biodiesel.

The marketing of the produced biofuels is the next vital stage to ensure adequate remuneration to the farmers. The government has already launched an e-NAM (National Agriculture Market) platform for integrating different consumers and producers under one roof. As biodiesel or ethanol are hazardous materials, we strongly recommend regulatory supervision by the government under this stage. AI is the perfect tool to eliminate intermediaries and provide a level playing field to all the players involved at different locations. The ethanol dispatched via various online platforms such as Flipkart and Amazon needs to mark the consignment using blockchain technology. It will ensure that each delivery is time-stamped and can be traced by the regulator in the future if the need arises [21].

Most consumers of biodiesel or ethanol might be intermediaries using it in the next stage of the production cycle to produce the final product. We recommend centralized planning and a decentralized approach for the distribution of the product to consumers. AI is the key to ensuring that different consumers have a legitimate certification (issued by the government) to purchase biodiesel/ethanol [22]. Digitalization of services has already created an enabling platform where consumers can get clearances from the government in a faceless manner. The current study fills in the gaps by examining in-depth research publications from various journals and conferences on optimizing production in the AI era and making future industry preparation easier.

11.6   Conclusion

In this chapter, we discussed AI is at the core, and it integrates all the stages by creating a feedback mechanism. Biodiesel is the future of the oil industry worldwide. The need is to invest in the infrastructure that can sustain the green technologies while establishing synchronization with the conventional technologies. The prospect of biofuels in the waste-to-energy realm is the key to meeting future energy demands. However, we need to traverse the path toward cleaner technologies sagaciously. The shift to biofuels cannot (and should not) happen overnight. The conventional technologies that have, hitherto, served as a backbone to our growth story also need to be preserved. Our objective should be to reform and transform the current technologies so that they can be leveraged to our benefit in the future, rather than outrightly rejecting them. Indian power generation capacity is currently 377 GW [16–19], inhabiting 1.3 billion people.

In contrast, China's reported power generation capacity is around a whopping 2,000 GW occupying 1.4 billion people. It shows a gross wedge that needs to be addressed in the coming decades or years. Biofuel optimized with the AI is a perfect match to fill the energy gap and make India a Vishwaguru envisaged by our PM.

India's prowess in the services sector is paving the way for implementing AI in almost every sector. The catchphrase Internet of Things (IoT) transforms the utility of conventional objects toward a new era of connectedness. The services sector is well supported by the Indian indigenous space agency ISRO to devise novel, cost-effective, and innovative programs in line with the motto of Atmanirbhar Bharat [7–20]. The depleting oil reserves and the process of climate change is a real thing. A switch to biofuels for meeting our energy demands does not remain a luxury anymore. An era of sheer economic growth has come to an end, and now, any growth needs a prefixed Sustainable with it. Biofuels as technology are still work in progress, but it has many positive externalities cutting across multiple sectors. Harnessing energy from biofuels is a silver bullet in green energy and utilizing waste as a fuel.

References

1. United Nation, Paris Agreement, vol. 1, no. 21, pp. 1–32, 2015.
2. Steffen, W., *Unburnable carbon: Why we need to leave fossil fuel in the ground.* vol. 1, no. 1, pp. 1–44, Climate Council of Australia Limited, 2015.
3. El Boulifi, N., Bouaid, A., Martinez, M., Aracil, process optimization for biodiesel production from corn oil and its oxidative stability. *Int. J. Chem. Eng.,* 2010, 518070, 2010.
4. Hiran, K.K., Doshi, R., Fagbola, T., Mahrishi, M., *Cloud Computing: Master Cloud Computing Concepts, Architecture and Applications with Real-world Examples and Case Studies,* BPP publication, New Delhi, 2019.
5. Dadhich, M., An Analysis of Volatility of Macro Economic Variables on Gold Price. *Pacific Bus. Rev. Int.,* 9, 12, 21–25, 2017.
6. Ministry of Petroleum & Natural Gas, National Biofuel Policy 2018, vol. 1, no. 1, pp. 1–7, Press Information Bureau, 2018.
7. Ministry of Finance, Atmanirbhar Bharat Abhiyan, vol. 1, no. 1, pp. 1–27, Press Information Bureau, 2020.
8. Manish, D. and Naresh, K., An Analysis of Factors Affecting to Entrepreneur Development in Rajasthan. *Int. J. Manage. IT Eng.,* 5, 12, 41–48, 2015.
9. Sharma, N. and Dadhich, M., Predictive Business Analytics: The Way Ahead. *J. Commer. Manage. Thought,* 5, 4, 652, 2014.
10. Kumar, M.S., Prabhahar, M., Sendilvelan, S., Singh, S., Venkatesh, R., Bhaskar, K., Combustion, performance and emission analysis of a diesel engine fueled

with methyl esters of Jatropha and fish oil with exhaust gas recirculation. *Energy Proc.*, 160, 2018, 404–411, 2019.

11. Ministry of Science & Technology, Mission Innovation, vol. 1, no. 1, p. 1, Press Information Bureau, 2019.

12. Bhuiya, M., Rasul, M., Khan, M., Ashwath, N., Performance and emission characteristics of a compression ignition (CI) engine operated with beauty leaf biodiesel. *Energy Proc.*, 160, 2018, 641–647, 2019.

13. Anwar, M., Rasul, M.G., Ashwath, N., Rahman, M.M., Optimization of second-generation biodiesel production from Australian native stone fruit oil using response surface method. *Energies*, 11, 10, 2566, 2018.

14. Dadhich, M., Impact of Demonetization on Indian Economy. *Int. J. Res. Soc. Sci.*, 7, 8, 208–215, 2017.

15. von Grebmer, K. *et al.*, Global hunger index 2020, vol. 1, no. 1, pp. 1–80, Chatham House, 2020, [Online]. Available: https://www.globalhungerindex.org/pdf/en/2020.pdf.

16. M. of Power, Power Sector at a Glance ALL INDIA | Government of India | Ministry of Power, 2021. https://powermin.gov.in/en/content/power-sector-glance-all-india (accessed Mar. 10, 2021).

17. Dadhich, M., Hiran, K.K., Rao, S.S., Teaching–Learning Perception Toward Blended E-learning Portals During Pandemic Lockdown, in: *Soft Computing: Theories and Applications*, pp. 119–129, Springer, Singapore, 2021.

18. Hiran, K.K. and Doshi, R., An artificial neural network approach for brain tumor detection using digital image segmentation. *Brain*, 2, 5, 227–231, 2013.

19. Tyagi, S.K.S., Mukherjee, A., Pokhrel, S.R., Hiran, K.K., An intelligent and optimal resource allocation approach in sensor networks for smart Agri-IoT. *IEEE Sens. J.*, 21, 16, 17439–17446, 2021.

20. ISRO, Desertification and Land Degradation Atlas of India, Space Applications Centre, ISRO, Ahmedabad, 2016.

21. Air Transport Action Group, Aviation Beyond Borders, p. 96, Atag, Dehradun, India, 2020.

22. WTO, The WTO agreement series, 2002. https://www.wto.org/english/res_e/booksp_e/who_wto_e.pdf.

23. Ministry of Finance, Economic Survey, 2021, India, https://www.indiabudget.gov.in/economicsurvey/doc/echapter.pdf

24. Hiran, K.K., Investigating Factors Influencing the Adoption of IT Cloud Computing Platforms in Higher Education: Case of Sub-Saharan Africa with IT Professionals. *Int. J. Hum. Cap. Inf. Technol. Prof. (IJHCITP)*, 12, 3, 21–36, 2021.

25. Times, T.E., SpiceJet operates India's first biofuel-powered flight from Dehradun to Delhi, The Economic Times, 2018.

Index

Also of Interest

Check out these published and forthcoming titles in the "Artificial Intelligence and Soft Computing for Industrial Transformation" series from Scrivener Publishing

Advances in Artificial Intelligence and Computational Methods for Transportation Safety
Edited by Naga Pasupuleti, Naveen Chilamkurti, B. Balamurugan, T. Poongodi
Forthcoming 2022. ISBN 978-1-119-76170-9

The New Advanced Society
Artificial Intelligence and Industrial Internet of Things Paradigm
Edited by Sandeep Kumar Panda, Ramesh Kumar Mohapatra, Subhrakanta Panda and S. Balamurugan
Forthcoming 2022. ISBN 978-1-119-82447-3

Digitization of Healthcare Data using Blockchain
Edited by T. Poongodi, D. Sumathi, B. Balamurugan and K. S. Savita
Forthcoming 2022. ISBN 978-1-119-79185-0

Tele-Healthcare
Applications of Artificial Intelligence and Soft Computing Techniques
Edited by R. Nidhya, Manish Kumar and S. Balamurugan
Forthcoming 2020. ISBN 978-1-119-84176-0

Impact of Artificial Intelligence on Organizational Transformation
Edited by S. Balamurugan, Sonal Pathak, Anupriya Jain, Sachin Gupta, Sachin Sharma and Sonia Duggal
Forthcoming 2022. ISBN 978-1-119-71017-2

Artificial Intelligence for Renewable Energy Systems
Edited by Ajay Kumar Vyas, S. Balamurugan, Kamal Kant Hiran, Harsh S. Dhiman
Forthcoming 2022. ISBN 978-1-119-76169-3

Artificial Intelligence Techniques for Wireless Communication and Networking
Edited by Kanthavel R., K. Ananthajothi, S. Balamurugan and R. Karthik Ganesh
Forthcoming 2022. ISBN 978-1-119-82127 4

Advanced Healthcare Systems
Empowering Physicians with IoT-Enabled Technologies
Edited by Rohit Tanwar, S. Balamurugan, R. K. Saini, Vishal Bharti and Premkumar Chithaluru
Forthcoming 2022. ISBN 978-1-119-76886-9

Smart Systems for Industrial Applications
Edited by C. Venkatesh, N. Rengarajan, P. Ponmurugan and S. Balamurugan
Published 2022. ISBN 978-1-119-76200-3

Intelligent Renewable Energy Systems
Edited by Neeraj Priyadarshi, Akash Kumar Bhoi, Sanjeevikumar Padmanabam,, S. Balamurugan, and Jens Bo Holm-Nielson
Published 2022. ISBN 978-1-119-78627-6

Human Technology Communication
Internet of Robotic Things and Ubiquitous Computing
Edited by R. Anandan, G. Suseendran, S. Balamurugan, Ashish Mishra and D. Balaganesh
Published 2021. ISBN 978-1-119-75059-8

Nature-Inspired Algorithms Applications
Edited by S. Balamurugan, Anupriya Jain, Sachin Sharma, Dinesh Goyal, Sonia Duggal and Seema Sharma
Published 2021. ISBN 978-1-119-68174-8

Computation in Bioinformatics
Multidisciplinary Applications
Edited by S. Balamurugan, Anand Krishnan, Dinesh Goyal, Balakumar Chandrasekaran and Boomi Pandi
Published 2021. ISBN 978-1-119-65471-1

Fuzzy Intelligent Systems
Methodologies, Techniques, and Applications
Edited by E. Chandrasekaran, R. Anandan, G. Suseendran, S. Balamurugan
and Hanaa Hachimi
Published 2021. ISBN 978-1-119-76045-0

Biomedical Data Mining for Information Retrieval
Methodologies, Techniques and Applications
Edited by Sujata Dash, Subhendu Kumar Pani, S. Balamurugan and
Ajith Abraham
Published 2021. ISBN 978-1-119-71124-7

Design and Analysis of Security Protocols for Communication
Edited by Dinesh Goyal, S. Balamurugan, Sheng-Lung Peng and
O.P. Verma
Published 2020. ISBN 978-1-119-55564-3

www.scrivenerpublishing.com

Printed and bound by CPI Group (UK) Ltd, Croydon, CR0 4YY

27/10/2024

14580129-0001